Pat Tung's Cooking School

A Complete Course in Chinese Cuisine

PAT TUNG

Drawings by Elaine Emmanuel

A FIRESIDE BOOK
Published by Simon & Schuster, Inc.
New York

A Fireside Book
Published by Simon & Schuster, Inc.
Simon & Schuster Building
Rockefeller Center
1230 Avenue of the Americas
New York, New York 10020
FIRESIDE and colophon are registered trademarks
of Simon & Schuster, Inc.
Manufactured in the United States of America
3 5 7 9 10 8 6 4 2
Library of Congress Cataloging in Publication Data
Tung, Pat.
Pat Tung's cooking school.
Includes index.
1. Cookery, Chinese. I. Title.
TX724.5.C5T85   1985   641.5951   84-20287
ISBN: 0-671-46040-4 Pbk.

To my parents, Mr. and Mrs. Chieh Hsu, who taught me to love and to share

To my husband, Ted, and our children, Candice and Roderick, who gave me inspiration, advice, and support

To my students, who encouraged me to write this book for all lovers of Chinese food

Acknowledgments

My heartfelt thanks to Meredith Emerson Brown for her painstaking effort in reviewing the first draft of the manuscript; to Julia Loxterman Ball, Cynthia Aletto Satterlee, and Ann Dawson Stokr for their willingness and enthusiasm in typing; and to Kendra Crossen for editing and shaping the final book.

Acknowledgments

Contents

4

Menu Planning for All Occasions   *135*

5

Casual Entertaining   *160*

1
Introduction to Chinese Food

An old Chinese proverb tells us, "Whatever satisfies hu.\ger is good food." Yet, through thousands of years, China has developed ways of preparing good food that satisfy not only the stomach but also the five senses. The sound of foods sizzling as they are tossed into hot oil; the appetizing sight of a dish made of many-colored ingredients, sliced with care, artfully arranged on a plate, and beautifully garnished; subtle fragrances and contrasting flavors; and a pleasing array of textures and shapes—these are the hallmarks of Chinese cuisine at its best. A sense of balance, proportion, and harmony is seen in the planning of a large feast as well as in the selection of ingredients for a single dish. Variety is limited only by the extent of the cook's imagination.

All these qualities are reflected in the recipes and menus in this book, which preserve authentic Chinese methods yet are tailored to American taste and convenience. When all is said and done, you will find that these nutritious meals do satisfy your hunger, too. Many of my students report that they have successfully converted their confirmed "meat-and-potatoes" husbands or families to Chinese gourmet cooking—with great benefit to everyone's health and waistline.

With its abundant use of fresh vegetables, soy products, and relatively fewer animal products than are used in American cooking, Chinese cuisine promotes sound nutrition without oversupplying calories or straining the budget. The joy of providing our family and friends with delicious food increases when we know that we are also doing our best to ensure their well-being. The Chinese have another saying, "All illness comes in through the mouth, and all trouble comes out of the mouth." We can do much to tackle the first half of this "mouth" problem by taking the time to follow the simple suggestions listed on pages 41-42, such as trimming fat from meats and skimming grease from soups and sauces. Making these little extra efforts is a practical way to show genuine love and concern for the people we feed. Reminders of health tips appear in numerous recipes in Chapter 3. See also the tips on avoiding excess oil absorption when deep-frying on page 40.

For American cooks, convenience and ease of preparation are often as important as the healthfulness and tastiness of a meal. My recipes have been carefully designed to make the most efficient use of your time. Many dishes can be prepared ahead of time and refrigerated overnight. Helpful hints on timing the preparation of dishes are given in Chapter 4, which gives menu suggestions ranging from dinners for one to feasts for forty, and in Chapter 5, which offers party ideas and recipes for casual entertaining. In Chapter 4 you will also learn about Chinese mealtime customs, although most of the menus are designed to satisfy American preferences.

As I have already mentioned, the attractive appearance of food is a vital element in the art of Chinese cuisine. Chapter 6, Beautifying Your Table, describes creative ideas for making garnishes that are both pretty and edible, for folding napkins into pagoda shapes for a festive look, and for decorating Chinese-style with cutouts that you can make yourself.

I feel it is important to share some of the fun (as well as the work) of cooking with children, and so Chapter 7 proposes ways that youngsters can enjoy taking part in food preparation.

Food is intimately associated with a nation's customs and traditions, especially when it comes to holidays. My students always say they enjoy learning about Chinese culture in my classes, so I have devoted Chapter 8 to a discussion of the major Chinese festivals and celebrations. Comments about the background of dishes or other interesting asides also appear elsewhere throughout the text.

Before proceeding to the next chapter, in which you will enter the kitchen, so to speak, for what is perhaps your first encounter with Chinese cooking, let us have an overview of the major culinary styles of China.

Regional Cuisines

China is a vast country that encompasses many different cooking methods and specialty ingredients. The four major cuisines are the Mandarin, Shanghai, Cantonese, and Sichuan (Szechuan).* Since the Cantonese were the first group of Chinese to emigrate to the United States, their style of cooking was the first to become widespread, and many Americans think of Cantonese dishes when they think of Chinese food. In recent years, however, "Mandarin food" has gained popularity in large American cities. Restaurants use the term "Mandarin" to mean any type of Chinese cooking other than Cantonese—such as Peking, Shanghai, Sichuan, and Hunan. Strictly speaking, however, "Mandarin" refers only to the food of the northern region.

MANDARIN OR PEKING (NORTHERN REGION)

Peking and Shandong (Shantung) are representative of the northern region of China. The main crops here are wheat and corn. Thus, flour products such as

*Throughout this book, words in Mandarin Chinese are spelled according to the Pinyin system, which is used in mainland China and widely accepted in the West. For the reader's convenience, old spellings are sometimes given in parentheses. Only in the case of very familiar names such as Peking (Beijing in the Pinyin spelling) and Canton (Guangzhou) are the old spellings retained. Cantonese words are not subject to the rules for Pinyin.

Mandarin pancakes, dumplings, noodles, and steamed rolls all originated here and then spread to other provinces. Peking cuisine was heavily influenced by the Mongolians and the Manchus who once ruled China. They raised sheep and goats, and so a famous Mandarin dish is Mongolia hot pot (or fire pot), which involves cooking (or "rinsing") paper-thin slices of lamb in boiling broth. Peking duck is another world-famous specialty. Garlic, ginger root, green onions, and wine are liberally used in Mandarin cooking. People in Shandong Province even eat green onions and garlic raw—an unthinkable act to someone from the southern provinces. In general, northern food is not very fancy or rich, and not many dishes are stir-fried. The food is salty, and star anise and peppercorns are common seasonings.

SHANGHAI (EASTERN SEACOAST)

The eastern seacoast includes the provinces of Jiangsu (Kiangsu) and Zhejiang (Chekiang), the cities of Shanghai, Nanjing (Nanking), Yangzhou (Yangchow), Suzhou (Soochow), and Hangzhou (Hangchow). These places lie in the richest and most fertile region of China. With the long growing season, two crops of rice can be raised. Fresh seafood, agricultural products, and livestock are all abundant. Each major city has its own specialty: Shanghai's seafood dishes are legendary; Nanjing's preserved duck is renowned; and Hangzhou is famous for its sweet-sour fish. In general, Shanghai cuisine is rich and elaborate, with many time-consuming, fancy dishes. More oil is used in cooking, and sugar is added for flavoring. Red-cooking originated in this region. Soybean products, pickled greens, and preserved foods are widely used. Complementary ingredients are added to make a meal fancier, not just to achieve variety in texture and color. Ginger, garlic, and green onions flavor many dishes but are not themselves eaten. The noodles, pastries, and dumplings of the north can be found in the eastern seacoast region, but the methods of cooking them are improvised and the ingredients varied so that they become unique specialties, such as tiny meat-filled rolls *(bao-zi)* steamed in a small bamboo steamer, spring rolls (called egg rolls in the U.S.), wontons, and pan-fried rolls.

CANTONESE (SOUTHEAST SEACOAST)

Guangdong Province lies in a subtropical area and enjoys an abundance of produce and seafood. Seasoning does not rely on soy sauce alone but makes use of oyster sauce and fermented black beans. Canton, the capital of the province, was formerly a major commercial center for the Western nations, which left their mark on Cantonese cuisine, so that tomatoes, ketchup, and thickened sauces appear in many recipes. The colorfulness of foods is greatly emphasized. Cantonese cooking is characterized by light flavoring, delicate seasoning, much use of sauces, resilient texture, and natural sweetness.

Dim Sum. In Cantonese, *dim* means "dot" and *sum* means "heart." These "dot-heart" morsels are enjoyed in small doses served with hot tea for brunch, at lunch, in midafternoon, or even as a midnight snack. Specialized *dim sum* restaurants often serve piping-hot items from a cart, and diners are asked to pick their favorites. The final bill is usually determined by the number of emptied plates on the table. A good number of Chinese restaurants in the U.S., especially in large cities, offer tea lunches on weekends, serving items ranging from succulent meat- or shrimp-filled dumplings to fancy sweet pastries. In a broad sense, *dim sum* consists of an array of tasty items ranging from savory snacks to dessertlike sweets. It includes various filled rolls, whether baked, pan-fried, deep-fried, or steamed; turnovers, *shao mai*, and dumplings; deep-fried spring rolls and shrimp toast; wontons and noodles; braised chicken or duck feet, chicken wings, spareribs, barbecued pork, and beef tripe; sweet rolls, cakes, and egg custard tarts.

Chow Mein. In Cantonese, *chow* means "stir-fry" and *mein* means "noodles." To Americans, chow mein is the deep-fried noodles that are served in Chinese restaurants or sold in cans in the supermarket. This is the American version of fried noodles; it is not used in China. Authentic Chinese fried noodles are either stir-fried (as in my recipe for Beef Chow Mein) or pan-fried until both sides are brown and crispy. The noodles are then topped with stir-fried meat and vegetables.

Sub Gum. In Cantonese, *sub* means "ten" or "miscellaneous" and *gum* means "precious items," so sub gum is a dish containing many precious ingredients. It may contain meat, poultry, fresh or dried seafood, and vegetables. A sub gum dish is named after its main ingredient, such as the chicken in chicken sub gum. Sub gum is considered the forefather of chop suey.

Chop Suey. This stir-fried dish features one type of meat with a variety of vegetables. It is not originally a Chinese dish but is rather an American version of Chinese food which will not be found on an authentic Chinese menu. I was puzzled at seeing signs advertising chop suey when I first arrived in Honolulu. Then I was told the origin of the dish, as follows.

It seems that many, many years ago in Honolulu, a ship arrived at Waikiki late in the evening. The hungry sailors could not find a place to eat, as the restaurants they approached were all closed. Finally they saw one restaurant with its lights still on, so they rushed in with the hope of being served. The owner told them he was just closing, but the sailors pleaded with him to serve them something—anything! The kind-hearted restaurateur went to the kitchen to check the food supply, then asked the men to wait. Soon after, he had a tasty meal ready for them.

After thoroughly cleaning their plates, the sailors asked the owner the name of the dish so that they could come back for more the next day. He frowned and scratched his head, searching for a name. Suddenly he said, "It is called chop suey!" In Cantonese, *chop* means "miscellaneous" or "mixing," and *suey* denotes "bits" or "pieces." Apparently, the restaurateur had used whatever leftover sliced or chopped ingredients he had on hand to create a delicious meal.

In restaurants in the United States, chop suey consists of a main meat ingredient—beef, pork, chicken, or shrimp—and various vegetables such as bean sprouts, bamboo shoots, bok choy, water chestnuts, celery, and onions. The cutting and slicing of ingredients is done ahead of time. When the order comes in, the chef gathers the various ingredients on a plate and stir-fries them, serving the dish in just a few minutes. My recipe for Beef Chop Suey appears in Chapter 3.

SICHUAN AND HUNAN (SOUTH-CENTRAL INLAND REGIONS)

These are the southwestern and south-central provinces of China. Hot, spicy dishes with strong flavoring are characteristic here. The dishes are known for their tartness, sweetness, and fragrance as well as their pungency. The most commonly used ingredients are dried and fresh chili peppers, hot pepper oil, chili powder, Sichuan peppercorns (whole, powdered, or cooked in very hot oil), bean sauce, hot bean sauce, sesame butter, and large amounts of green onions, ginger root, and garlic. These ingredients may be used alone or in various combinations to season a dish.

Please turn now to the next chapter for a closer look at the ingredients, tools, and methods of Chinese cooking.

2
The Basics of Chinese Cooking

Ingredients

In Chinese dishes, no matter what the regional origin, some or all of the following cetegories of ingredients are used:

main ingredients
complementary ingredients
fresh-flavored ingredients
seasoning and spices

Main ingredients are any meat, poultry, seafood, or vegetable that is the major part of dish, such as beef in Jade Beef, chicken in Chicken and Snow Pea Pods, or tofu in Spicy Tofu.

Complementary ingredients accompany the main ingredient and play a supporting role in the dish, adding color, texture, flavor, and interest to it. They are used sparingly, like the green pepper in Jade Beef; the snow pea pods, bamboo shoots, and water chestnuts in Chicken with Snow Pea Pods; or the ground meat in Spicy Tofu. Chinese dried mushrooms, cloud ear, wood ear, tiger lily buds, water chestnuts, and bamboo shoots are characteristic complementary ingredients. Any vegetable in a meat or poultry dish, or any meat in a predominantly vegetable of soup dish, is considered complementary.

Fresh-flavored ingredients are the "magic" in Chinese dishes. In this category are green onions, fresh ginger root, and garlic, which can be used separately or in combination to flavor the main and complementary ingredients. In such methods as boiling, steaming, stewing, and red-cooking, the fresh-flavored ingredients are cooked along with the other ingredients, then removed when the cooking is done. In stir-fried dishes, the fresh-flavored ingredients are first cooked briefly in the oil to impart flavor to it. (This technique may explain why food served in Chinese restaurants has a special subtle flavoring that diners often cannot identify.) They are then removed from the oil before the other ingredients are added. Removing these items from a dish will save your guests and family from the perhaps unpleasant surprise of biting into a spicy piece of ginger, garlic, or green onion.

Green onions can also be used as a garnish, as they are when chopped fine in Egg Drop Soup. They may be minced and combined with soy sauce, vinegar, or sesame oil for a dipping sauce. Garlic is used with soy sauce or sesame oil for chicken livers, or with chicken and meat dishes in which the flavoring should be subtle. Grated, minced, or sliced ginger root in vinegar is a tasty dipping sauce for steamed crabs. (Further information on green onions, garlic, and ginger appears later in this chapter.)

Seasonings and spices are the "soul" of a dish. They enhance the natural flavors of the food or add a special flavor of their own. This category includes soy sauce, salt and sugar, vinegar, sherry, oyster sauce, hoisin sauce, bean sauce, sesame oil, black and white pepper, hot chili pepper, Sichuan peppercorn, hot pepper oil, sha-cha sauce, star anise, five-spice powder, and other items.

MEAT

The recipes in this book make use of meats that are easily available and popular in the U.S. However, it is interesting to note the great variety of meats enjoyed in China.

Pork is the Chinese favorite. Tenderloin and loin are ideal for stir-frying and deep-frying. Shoulder butt, leg, and picnic shoulder are usually cooked as a whole piece by the long, slow method. The head, brains, ears, tongue, heart, liver, kidney, maw, lung, intestines, hocks, feet, tendons, and pork fat are all looked upon as great delicacies. The Chinese waste nothing!

Of the cured meats, the most popular are jin-hua ham and Chinese sausages. *Jin-hua ham* is a dark-reddish, well-seasoned ham that adds zest and aroma to many dishes. It is also used sparingly as a garnish. The closest in taste to it in the United States is Smithfield ham. *Chinese sausage* is made with pork or liver or both and has a slightly sweet flavor. The sausages may be steamed whole or cut into diagonal slices to be cooked with rice. They may also be cut up for use in fried rice or in poultry stuffing.

Beef is used widely in Chinese cooking. The tender cuts, such as flank steak, filet mignon, sirloin, top round, and eye of round, are favored for stir-frying. Shank, shin, chuck roast, and plate are suitable for stewing and braising. Tongue, liver, heart, kidney, beef tripe, oxtail, and tendon are all delicacies.

Lamb and mutton are not used as much as pork and beef, except by the Chinese Muslims. In northern China, lamb appears in the famous dish known as the fire-pot (I call my recipe for this dish Chinese Fondue). Lamb is considered to have a warming effect on the body. The shoulder and leg are suitable for stir-frying and for the fire-pot.

Small groups of Chinese eat meats such as rabbit, horse, mule, camel, venison, dog, snake, and monkey.

POULTRY AND EGGS

Chicken is used a great deal in China, just as it is in the United States. The boneless breast is ideal for stir-frying. Whole or in parts, chicken is also deep-fried and red-cooked.

Duck is usually served as a banquet dish. Peking duck is probably the best-know Chinese duck among Americans. The Chinese also use preserved ducks, which are salted, then flattened and stretched with wooden strips, and finally air-dried. The preserved flesh can then be steamed and enjoyed on special occasions.

Goose, pigeon, pheasant, quail, squab, turkey, and wild duck may also appear as delicacies on the Chinese table.

Chicken and duck eggs are commonly used in China; less common are quail, goose, and pigeon eggs. So-called *thousand-year eggs* are preserved in a coating of lime, ashes, and salt for about a hundred days. The egg white turns a dark grayish color, and the yolk becomes greenish-gray. These eggs are a delicacy in China and are often served sliced as part of a "cold plate," the first course in an elaborate dinner. Thousand-year eggs may also be eaten with congee (rice porridge) for breakfast. *Salted duck eggs* are another delicacy often served with congee. These eggs are pickled in brine for five to six weeks. Then they must be hard-boiled or steamed before eating.

SEAFOOD

Both saltwater and freshwater fish appear widely in Chinese cuisine, as well as the many varieties of shellfish. Also used are cuttlefish, eel, squid, octopus, jellyfish, turtle, and frog. Preserved and dried kinds of seafood include dried abalone, fish maw, scallops, sea cucumber (bêche-de-mer), shark fins, shrimp roe, and squid.

VEGETABLES

Vegetables can be divided into the following categories:

- *Bean and seed type:* bean sprouts, corn fava beans, green beans, green peas, snow pea pods, sword beans
- *Bulb and stem type:* bamboo shoots, celery, garlic, garlic greens, green onion, leek, shallot, water chestnut, yellow onion
- *Flower type:* broccoli, cauliflower, tiger lily buds
- *Fruit type:* bitter melon, cucumber, eggplant, green pepper, hairy (or fuzzy) melon, loofah, squash, tomato, winter melon, zucchini
- *Leafy type:* amaranth, bok choy, cabbage, Chinese cabbage (celery cabbage and napa cabbage), Chinese parsley (coriander leaves), chrysanthemum greens, Chinese lettuce, Chinese chard, Chinese chives, mustard greens, kale, spinach, watercress
- *Mushrooms and fungi:* Chinese dried mushrooms, cloud ears, fresh mushrooms, silver ears, straw mushrooms, wood ears
- *Root type:* beet, carrot, ginger root, icicle radish, kohlrabi, lobak, lotus root, potato, taro, turnip, yam
- *Seaweeds:* agar-agar, hairlike seaweed, kelp, laver

Baby Corn. These miniature ears of corn are harvested before pollination or just before the silk is formed. Baby corn is available canned in Oriental groceries as well as some supermarkets. Transfer any unused corn to a glass jar and cover with water. In the refrigerator it should keep one week.

Bamboo Shoots. The ivory-colored shoots of the bamboo plant are tender in spring, but the winter shoots have more flavor. Fresh bamboo shoots add flavor and texture to any dish, whether stir-fried or braised, simmered or steamed—and they contribute valuable roughage to the diet. Canned bamboo shoots packed in water are sold in Oriental groceries. Supermarkets carry sliced bamboo shoots, which are suitable for most recipes. Brine-covered bamboo shoots and ready-to-eat braised bamboo shoots (served as a side dish) are also available in Oriental groceries. Canned bamboo shoots will last for weeks, covered with cold water, in a jar in the refrigerator. Use them in Beef Chow Mein, Beef Shao Mai, Chicken with Snow Pea Pods, Crab Egg Fu Yung, Eight Precious Vegetables, Moo Goo Gai Pan, and Shanghai-Style Egg Rolls.

Bean Sprouts. The young sprouts of mung beans have a white stem and a pale yellowish-green head often covered by a grayish husk, which should be rinsed off before using the sprouts. Sprouts lend crunchy texture to many dishes. They are most suitable for salads and stir-fried dishes, as well as for egg roll fillings. You can buy them in Oriental groceries and in supermarkets. Canned bean sprouts are also available but tend to be soggy. Try growing your sprouts fresh at home (see Chapter 7). Use bean sprouts in Bean Sprouts and Leek, Bean Sprouts in Spicy Vinegar Sauce, Bean Sprout Salad, Beef Chop Suey, Cold-Style Noodles, Eight Precious Vegetables, Hunan Chicken, and Jiffy Egg Rolls.

Bok Choy. In Cantonese, *bok* means "white" and *choy* means "leafy." The Chinese call this vegetable "white leafy greens," for it has long white stalks widening into large, dark green leaves. Bok choy can be used in soups or stir-fried dishes, either alone or with meat, poultry, seafood, or other vegetables. Use bok choy in Beef Chop Suey and Beef Chow Mein.

Chinese Cabbage (Celery Cabbage and Napa Cabbage). Napa cabbage is a tightly packed, off-white or pale green stalk with wrinkled leaves. It is also known as Shandong cabbage. It has a delicate flavor and juicy stalks. Celery (or Tianjin) cabbage is another variety of Chinese cabbage. It is longer and resembles celery in shape, but has broad, flat leaves tightly packed in a light green stalk. Chinese cabbage may be used in salads, soups, and stir-fried dishes with or without meat, and in my recipe for Shanghai-Style Egg Rolls.

Chinese Dried Mushrooms. These dehydrated black-brown mushrooms are variously known as Chinese black mushrooms, black mushrooms, dried mushrooms, winter mushrooms, or fragrant mushrooms. They add a distinctive piquancy and a delicious flavor to soups, stir-fried dishes, meat, and vegetables. The mushrooms vary in size, appearance, thickness, and flavor according to variety and grade. The best-quality ones are large, meaty, and flavorful, and have a natural design on the caps. Dried mushrooms are mostly imported from China and Japan.

They must be soaked in warm water until soft before cooking. Store them dry in a glass container in the refrigerator. They can be kept up to a year. Use them in Beef Chow Mein, Beef Shao Mai, Eight Precious Vegetables, Paper-Wrapped Chicken, Snow Pea Pods with Mushrooms, and Stuffed Mushrooms.

Chinese Edible Fungi. Dried Chinese fungi are sold in Oriental groceries. Stored in a glass jar in a cupboard or pantry, they keep up to a few years. Use wood ears and cloud ears in recipes such as Eight Precious Vegetables, Mu Xu Pork, Sichuan Pork with Water Chestnuts, and Vegetarian's Garden.

Wood ears (also called tree ears) are small, crinkly black fungi. They must be soaked in warm water to return to their original ear shape. It is advisable to snip off the sandy tip by which the fungus was attached to the tree. Although wood ears are tasteless by themselves, they absorb the flavors of other ingredients. They also add texture and nutrients to stir-fried, steamed, or braised dishes and soups.

Cloud ears are larger than wood ears. Soaking in warm water will restore their cloud shape. After being cut into smaller pieces, they can be used interchangeably with wood ears.

Silver ears (or white wood ears or white fungi) are most often used as a dessert when cooked in water and sweetened with rock candy or sugar.

Chinese Parsley (Coriander, Cilantro). This aromatic dark green herb has flat, serrated leaves and willowy stems. The Chinese have nicknamed it "fragrant green" for its unique and dominant aroma. Some people love it, while others can't stand it! Coriander leaves can be used as a garnish as well as a seasoning.

Garlic. Peeled garlic cloves are used to flavor oil in stir-frying (in which case it is removed before adding the other ingredients) or to flavor the food itself. Crushed garlic is better for flavoring oil than whole cloves. To simultaneously crush garlic and remove the peel, whack the clove hard with the side of a cleaver (with cutting edge to your right). Thus crushed, garlic is easier to mince if it is to be used in a dipping sauce or other such dish. Garlic can be stored either in the refrigerator or in a cupboard.

Ginger Root. The knobby, fibrous root of the ginger plant is widely used in Oriental cooking. It has a refreshing smell and a sharp, spicy taste. Ginger brings out the flavor of seafood (and helps to diminish fishy odor) and enhances the taste of meat and poultry. When used to flavor oil before stir-frying, it lends a subtle flavor to dishes.

Ginger root should be fresh. It is sold by weight in the produce sections of many supermarkets and in Oriental groceries. Break off and buy a small amount at a time, as needed. For recipes that call for ginger, you will usually need a slice or two about one-eighth inch thick and about one inch in diameter. Before using the root, either wash the skin well or peel it off. I place it flat on a chopping board for peeling, which is easier than holding it in the hand to pare.

At room temperature, an uncut fresh ginger root lasts quite a while before it shrivels and dries. It will keep five days stored in a plastic container in the refrigerator.

I have heard some people say they put ginger root in the freezer for longer storage. However, a much better method is preservation in sherry. Choose a bunch of fresh, wrinkle-free roots. Wash the skin, cut the roots into chunks, and put them into a clean glass jar. Add sherry (cooking sherry is fine) to cover. This will keep up to six months in the refrigerator. Use a clean utensil to remove a piece from the jar. An unused portion may be returned to the jar, provided the knife and cutting board that came into contact with it are clean. As you use up the ginger, you can also use the sherry in cooking. When all the ginger is used up, wash out the jar and start a new supply.

Incidentally, ginger is a valuable part of traditional Chinese medical treatment, which makes use of natural herbal remedies. Since ginger root has a warming effect on the body, it is believed that drinking ginger-scallion liquid at the onset of a minor cold will clear up the infection. This liquid is made by adding six to eight slices of ginger root and two or three green onions, cut into sections, to 1½ cups water in a pot. Cover and bring to a boil. Perhaps the hotness of this home remedy—both in temperature and in taste—makes you "sweat out" the illness.

Green Onion (Scallion). Unless otherwise stated, both the white bulb and the green top are used. Cut off the tiny roots (they may be planted in your garden), discard wilted pieces, and rinse onions clean. Green onions are used in the following ways:

- To flavor oil before stir-frying meat and vegetables, cut green onions into six equal pieces. First cut in half. Place the halves side by side, then cut into thirds.
- To add flavor during long cooking, and for easy removal afterward, tie green onion into a loose knot.
- To sliver, cut into six equal sections. Cut the white bulb section in half lengthwise. Then stack the green sections and sliver them lengthwise. Or you may slice the green onion diagonally into 1¼- to 1½-inch slivers, starting from the green tip. A third alternative is to whack the green onion flat with the side of a cleaver, then cut into six sections and sliver lengthwise.
- To mince, first cut into pieces ⅛ to 1/16 inch long, then chop fine.
- To garnish soup or other dishes, cut green onion in half, place the two halves side by side, cut them in half again, place the four pieces side by side, and cut once more, into ⅛-inch pieces.
- To make Green Onion Brushes for garnishing Peking Duck, see page 115.

Refrigerated, green onions keep five to seven days. Large quantities may be wrapped in foil and refrigerated for up to three weeks. Wipe each onion dry first. You may use one large piece of foil for all the onions. Place one onion at the end of the foil, roll to cover it, then add another onion, and so on.

Lobak (Luobo, Chinese Radish, Daikon). The Cantonese name for this white, crisp root vegetable is lobak; daikon is the Japanese term. It looks like a giant icicle radish, two to four inches in diameter and about six to twelve inches long. After being peeled and sliced or shredded, it may be used in soups, salads, or stir-fried dishes. Large pieces are used in braised dishes with meat or in pickling. The cylinder-shaped lobak is often carved into various flower shapes for garnishing.

Lobak is available in Oriental groceries and some supermarkets, especially during the season of the Chinese New Year. I use lobak in Eight Precious Vegetables.

Snow Pea Pods. The snow pea is a flat, light green pod containing a few tender, immature peas. The pod is eaten whole, the strings having been removed. Crisp, tender, sweet, and delectable, snow pea pods are used often in stir-fried dishes. Try them in Chicken with Snow Pea Pods, Scallops Supreme, Snow Pea Pods with Mushrooms, Vegetarian's Garden, Oriental Cauliflower, and Beef Chow Mein.

Tiger Lily Buds. The brownish-gold dried bud of the tiger lily is long and thin like a needle, so the Chinese call it "golden needle." The buds have a mild, delicate flavor. They are used in stir-fried dishes or soups after being soaked in water. Stored in a glass jar in a cupboard or pantry, they will keep up to a few years. Dishes containing tiger lily buds include Eight Precious Vegetables and Mu Xu Pork.

Water Chestnut. The bulb of a water plant which grows in marshy soils, the water chestnut has a crunchy white flesh covered by thin dark-brown skin. The Chinese have nicknamed this vegetable "horseshoes" because of its shape. Fresh water chestnuts, which have a sweet, refreshing taste, can be purchased only from Oriental groceries. The canned water chestnuts sold in supermarkets are peeled and packed in water, either whole or sliced. Water chestnut is often added to stir-fried dishes for its crunch, or to meat fillings not only for its texture but also to loosen up the meat. It also can be used in salads after blanching, or as a substitute for fruits. Ground water-chestnut flour is used as a thickening agent. An unused portion of water chestnuts may be stored in a container of water in the refrigerator. Change the water often if you must keep it longer than a week. Dishes containing water chestnuts include Beef Chop Suey, Beef Chow Mein, Beef Shao Mai, Chicken Kow, Chicken with Snow Pea Pods, Chinese Taco, Crisp Wontons, Fried Shrimp Toast, Ham Fried Rice, Moo Goo Gai Pan, Oyster-Flavored Fried Rice, Pearl Balls, Sichuan Pork with Water Chestnuts, "Six Happiness" Beef Kabobs, Stuffed Mushrooms, and Wonton Soup.

BEANS AND BEAN PRODUCTS

Soybeans (which the Chinese call "yellow beans"), black beans, red beans, and mung beans are all used. Soybeans are the most popular and are high in protein. Soy products include tofu (see below), soy milk, soy sprouts, soy oil, and soy sauce (see page 28). Mung bean products include bean sprouts (see page 21) and a kind of noodle called bean threads (see page 27). Various bean sauces and pastes are used as seasonings (see pages 30-31).

Red Bean Paste. Red beans are cooked, hulled, and mashed into a thick paste, then sweetened with sugar. Red bean paste is used in fillings for cakes, pastries, and rolls. After opening the can, transfer the paste to a glass jar and refrigerate. It will keep for several months. Use it in Sweet Bean Rolls, Suzhou Cakes, and Sweet Wontons.

Tofu (Bean Curd). Tofu, which has long been a favorite food among the Chinese and Japanese, is a pure soybean product made by adding a solidifier such as calcium sulfate to boiling-hot soy milk. When the mixture has gelled, it is drained and the excess water is pressed out. The result is high in protein (7.8 grams of protein in 3½ ounces of tofu) yet low in calories (only 147 calories in a pound). Tofu is very inexpensive in China, so everyone can afford it. Therefore, it is considered a poor man's meat and a rich man's vegetable, not to mention that it is a vegetarian's delight. Its bland taste combines well with the more flavorful ingredients in a dish.

Several varieties of tofu are sold in Oriental food stores in the United States. The most common ones are soft tofu, which is tender and easy to break; "old" or firm tofu, which has less water content; dried tofu, which has no water content and looks like a form of smoked cheese; and fried bean curd, which is dried tofu deep-fried.

The soft and firm varieties of tofu are also available in health-food stores and in some supermarkets. The tofu is usually packed in water in plastic containers with see-through tops. Refrigerate tofu after purchase. If bubbles are present in the package, open it and change the water immediately. Changing the water two or three times a week and refrigerating the tofu will keep it fresh. If it tastes sour or has a yellowish-brown coating, it is spoiled and should not be used.

Most people prefer soft tofu, which is similar in consistency to custard; it is smooth to the palate and rather fragile. Firm or "old" tofu is harder in texture and drier to the taste. A slang expression in Chinese—"to eat someone's tofu"—subtly refers to flirting or excessive flattery. Apparently, the smooth-talking flatterer is having a good time, as if he were enjoying some smooth, soft tofu. To accept his compliments with ease, one might say, "Oh, don't eat my tofu." An older person might say, "Don't eat my old tofu," which implies: "I am no longer young and fragile—the old tofu is not so tasty anymore!"

FRUITS AND NUTS

Fruits (both fresh and dried) and nuts eaten in China include almonds, apples, apricots, bananas, black dates, crab apples, cherries, coconut, cashews, longan (dragon's eye fruit), dried chestnut, gingko nuts, grapes, kumquats, lotus seeds, litchi fruit, loquat, mangoes, muskmelon, melon seeds, oranges, peaches, pears, persimmons, pineapple, plums, pomelos, peanuts, pine nuts, red dates (jujubes), star fruit, tangerines, walnuts, and watermelon.

RICE

The importance of rice in the Chinese diet is reflected by several colloquial expressions. A husband—traditionally considered the "bread winner" in Western culture—is jokingly referred to among Chinese as his wife's "long-term rice ticket." The loss of a job may be spoken of symbolically as the breaking of one's rice bowl. And a common greeting to a friend, indicating concern for his well-being, translates as "Have you eaten cooked rice?"

So important is rice to the Chinese, in fact, that all other dishes in a meal are regarded as serving to help "send the rice down." By contrast, Americans usually consider rice as taking second place to their portion of meat—or, at best, as being of the same importance, since it is a member of the "starch" group. Americans sometimes say that they feel hungry an hour after consuming a Chinese meal—and yet Orientals in the United States often have the exact same complaint about American meals, because there is simply not enough rice to satisfy them!

Thus, the consumption of rice is the main purpose of lunch and dinner in China. (In most regions, rice is also served for breakfast, in the form of a soft porridge called congee). The amount of rice eaten varies from person to person, normally between one and three bowls per meal. Quite often the tastiness of the other dishes determines how much rice one will consume along with them.

Four types of rice are available in China: long-grain, which absorbs more water and keeps the shape of the individual grains after cooking; short-grain, which loses its separateness and becomes mushy; unbleached rice, which is cheaper and considered to be a lower grade; and glutinous (sticky) rice, which is often used for stuffing poultry and making desserts. For the meals suggested in this book, I recommend long-grain rice.

In cooking rice, the Chinese never add anything but cold water to begin—no butter, salt, or other seasonings. The old-fashioned Chinese cook relies on experience and thus needs no measuring cup. After adding some water to the rice, she might stick her finger into the pot to judge whether the water level is high enough (up to the first joint would be about right). But perhaps this method seems unscientific now, as finger length may vary from person to person.

Several methods can be used to cook rice. Whatever method you choose, the most important step to ensure fluffiness is to wash the rice thoroughly first. (Instructions for preparing enriched rice usually say not to wash it because that would remove the vitamins in the coating. However, I feel it is worthwhile washing rice to ensure a fluffy result, which will entice diners to eat other dishes containing nutritional value.) Add cold water to the measured rice in a pot, and use your hand to swish the rice around in the water. Then pour off the water carefully so as not to lose any of the rice grains. Repeat this rinsing five or six times or until the water in the pot is no longer cloudy.

Boiling Method
1. Rinse rice.
2. For 1 cup long-grain rice, add 1¼ cups water; for 1 cup short-grain rice, add 1⅛ cups water.
3. Set pot on high flame and bring to a boil (this will take 4-5 minutes).
4. Reduce flame and simmer, covered, for 20 minutes.
5. Turn off heat and let covered pot sit another 20 minutes so that the steam will soften the cooked rice.

Using a Rice Cooker. In most Chinese restaurants, rice is cooked by an electric rice cooker. You just measure the rice, rinse it well, add the designated amount of water, plug in, and push the button. The rice is cooked automatically, and the result is fluffy and hot every time.

Steaming Method. I have developed this way of cooking rice on the stove by utilizing the hot steam principle of the electric rice cooker.
1. Measure 1 cup of rice into a heatproof dish, and rinse six times.

2. For long-grain rice, add 1¼ cups cold water for drier, more separate grains, or 1½ cups water for softer, stickier rice. For short-grain rice, add 1 cup water for drier rice, 1¼ cups for stickier rice.

3. Add 1 quart of cold water to a 6-quart dutch oven. Place the heatproof bowl inside the dutch oven, and cover it. Set on a high flame and cook the rice for 25 minutes.

4. Turn off the heat, but leave the cover on for another 25 minutes before serving.

Oven Method. Rice can also be cooked in the oven. My good friend Lillian Ing says that after rinsing her rice in a glass baking dish and adding the cold water, she covers it with a metal pie plate and cooks it in the oven at 375°F for 45 minutes.

NOODLES

Chinese noodles *(mein)* come in different sizes, shapes (flat, round, thick, thin, looped), and flavors (with egg or eggless, seasoned). Depending on the type of flour used, the cooking time is from five to ten minutes. If instructions are not given on the package, test the noodles with a fork or by tasting after five minutes of boiling.

Fresh noodles (lo mein), available in Oriental groceries, should be refrigerated and used within a few days. If stored in the freezer, they will keep up to six months.

Dried noodles come packaged or loose. They keep well in a cool, dry place without refrigeration. To cook them, always bring the water to a full boil first; then add noodles and stir. When they are done, rinse them under cold water and drain before stir-frying or adding to broth. If Chinese dried noodles are unavailable, you may substitute extra-thin spaghetti or vermicelli.

Instant noodles are sold in many Oriental groceries as well as supermarkets. They are packed in cellophane accompanied by a packet of seasonings for the broth. These noodles take only a few minutes to cook and can be served as a light lunch or a side dish.

Chow Mein noodles—canned fried noodles sold in supermarkets—are really an American invention, not an authentic Chinese food.

Rice noodles (or rice sticks) are fine, brittle, dried white noodles made of rice flour. They come in looped skeins. They are often soaked in water, drained, and then stir-fried as a noodle dish or cooked in soups with meat and vegetables. To deep-fry them, first cut them into two- to three-inch lengths. Dip them quickly in the hot oil-they puff up in seconds. They can be used as a garnish or as a crunchy addition to Chinese Taco. Store them in a cool, dry place.

Bean threads (cellophane noodles) are thin, dried white noodles made of mung bean flour. They come in looped skeins. Cut them into two- to three-inch sections and deep-fry in hot oil. Use them as garnishes or as a bed for stir-fried beef or similar dishes. To use them in soup or stir-fried dishes, first soak them in warm or cold water to soften the texture (they resemble whitish translucent rubber bands). They will absorb the flavors of other ingredients in a dish. Always add them to a soup last and then serve at once. Bean threads are also used in Chinese Fondue.

OIL

Lard or animal fat has traditionally been used in Chinese cooking. It gives meat and vegetables an added flavor and aroma, and ensures even browning in fried foods. Some restaurants advertise certain dishes cooked in lard or chicken fat as a special treat, such as fresh carp in chicken fat. However, because of the health hazards of animal fats in the diet, most people prefer to substitute vegetable oils. Delicious Chinese foods can be prepared with peanut, corn, safflower, cottonseed, or soybean oil. Peanut and corn oil are more expensive but give the best results in deep frying. A rule of thumb is that you may use any liquid oil that does not have a strong odor. With the rising costs of all foods, I sometimes choose whichever oil is on sale, and I use various oils in rotation to provide a variety of nutrients. For further tips on using oil, see pages 40 and 41.

SEASONINGS AND SPICES

Soy Sauce. An essential seasoning in Chinese food, soy sauce is also used for marinating and dipping. It not only enhances flavor, but also adds color and interest to a dish. There are many varieties of soy sauce, manufactured in the United States, Japan, the People's Republic of China, Taiwan, and Hong Kong. Each has its own color, aroma, grade, flavor, saltiness, and other variations. In general, soy sauce can be categorized in three ways. *Dark* or black soy sauce, which contains molasses, is darker and thicker than other types. Dark soy sauce comes in mushroom, shrimp, and other flavors as well as the regular flavor. *Light* or thin soy sauce is much lighter in color and more watery; it is used specifically for dipping. *Regular* soy sauce can be used for cooking as well as dipping. In my recipes, if the kind of soy sauce is not specified, any regular soy sauce available in supermarkets will do. *Tamari* soy sauce, sold in health-food stores, is a variety made without preservatives or additives.

Salt. Iodized salt or sea salt is recommended. Some people prefer a low-sodium salt substitute.

Cornstarch. An essential ingredient in Chinese cooking, cornstarch is used to tenderize meat or poultry in marinades, to thicken sauces, and to give a glossy appearance to a dish. When using cornstarch for thickening, always dissolve it first in a small amount of water to prevent lumps; then add the rest of the water and stir. Always be sure to stir the dissolved cornstarch well before adding it to the other ingredients, as cornstarch settles while sitting.

MSG (Monosodium Glutamate). This fine white crystal substance is a widely used flavor enhancer found in many food products. MSG was first discovered in the Orient and has long been used in Chinese and Japanese cooking, especially in restaurants. Excessive intake of MSG may cause some diners to have an unpleasant reaction including headache and other kinds of discomfort—a phenomenon known as "Chinese restaurant syndrome." MSG is *not* used in any of the recipes in this book.

Sichuan (Szechuan) Peppercorns. A dark reddish-brown tiny round seasoning. If you tasted it alone, you would find it mildly hot and numbing to the tongue. Used to flavor oil or in cooking, marinating, pickling, or curing, it lends a fragrant, aromatic, and unique flavor. A mixture of ground roasted Sichuan peppercorns and salt is often used as a dipping for fried food. Sichuan peppercorns are used in Sichuan Cucumbers, Cold-Plate Combination, Seasoned Turkey Slices, Peanuts for Beer Drinking, Red-Cooked Beef, Bean Sprouts and Leek, Bean Sprouts in Spicy Vinegar Sauce, Soy-Sauce Cornish Hen, and Fu Yang Salted Chicken.

Chili Powder. Pure ground red chili pepper is available in Oriental groceries. It does not contain cumin as Mexican chili powder does. Use it in Spicy Tofu.

Five-Spice Powder. This seasoning combines five ground spices: star anise, fennel, cloves, cinnamon, and Sichuan peppercorns. The powder has a pronounced aroma and is used with meat and poultry. Some manufacturers may use different substitutes for the ingredients, with the exception of star anise, which is a must in all cases. Common substitute ingredients are nutmeg, ginger, and orange peel. Recipes in this book that call for five-spice powder are Jiffy Egg Rolls, Oven-Barbecued Spareribs, Pan-Fried Meat Rolls, "Six Happiness" Beef Kabobs, and Steamed Meat Rolls.

Star Anise (Aniseed). This popular dried spice has a distinctive licorice flavor. It often comes broken into pieces, but a perfect star anise has a star shape with eight points. For this reason the Chinese call the spice "eight angles." It is used in Lu cooking (see recipe for Cold-Plate Combination), Soy-Sauce Cornish Hen, Red-Cooked Beef, and Marble Eggs.

Sesame Butter. This thick brown paste is made from ground roasted sesame seeds. (Do not confuse it with the Middle Eastern product known as tahini or taheeni, which is made from unroasted seeds.) It resembles peanut butter in texture, but is often diluted with water or sesame oil to produce a smooth consistency. Sesame butter can be used in cold-mixing noodle dishes, salads, marinades, and sauces. Store it either at room temperature or in the refrigerator; it will keep for several months. Sesame butter is an ingredient in two of my recipes: Chinese Fondue and Barbecued Pork Slices.

Sesame Oil. The thick, aromatic, golden oil extracted from roasted sesame seeds adds a delicate, subtle flavor to foods. It is available in Oriental grocery stores. (Do not confuse it with the light-colored sesame oil sold in Middle Eastern groceries and health-food stores. That variety is made from unroasted seeds and has less flavor and aroma.) Sesame oil is used as a seasoning in marinades and dipping sauces, in cold-mixing dishes (salads), in soups, and in stir-fried dishes. Be sure to use it sparingly, and never use it for frying.

Sesame Seeds. Unhulled seeds are used in two varieties—white and black. Sesame seeds appear mostly in candies, cakes, cookies, and pastries. Roasted sesame seeds are often added to hot and cold dishes for their flavor and their nutritional value. Sesame seeds are used in Sweet-Sour Pork, Chicken Fantastic, Suzhou Cakes, and Wonton Fritters.

Hot Pepper Oil. Hot chili pepper oil—called "red oil" in China—imparts a spicy flavor to various dishes. You can buy it bottled at an Oriental grocery or make it yourself, as follows.

1. Place 1 tbsp. crushed chili peppers in a heatproof bowl.
2. In a skillet, heat 1/4 cup vegetable oil to very hot. Turn off heat. Pour hot oil into the bowl.
3. Cool and strain the reddish oil, and store in a tightly sealed jar.

Use a spoon to scoop out the oil as needed. This oil will keep for a long time at room temperature.

Sherry. Sherry, cooking sherry, wine, and other alcoholic ingredients are used in Chinese cooking not only to enhance flavor but also to eliminate or diminish undesirable odors of meat, poultry, or fish. The inexpensive types of sherry (medium or dry) serve the purpose just as well as the more costly ones. If fish or shrimp are not fresh and have a strong odor, add one tablespoon sherry to two pounds of seafood, sprinkle with salt, let stand five to ten minutes, and then rinse with water. (Do not let it stand longer than ten minutes or the salt may penetrate the fish and make the texture too firm.)

Vinegar. Use your favorite vinegar in recipes that call for it. Apple cider vinegar is a good choice and nutritionally sound. In China, three kinds of rice vinegar are used—white, red, and black. White vinegar is used for sweet-sour dishes. Red and black vinegars are used in dipping sauces. Black vinegar is also used in braised dishes because of its full-bodied flavor.

Hoisin Sauce. This is a reddish-brown sauce made from soybeans, flour, sugar, salt, and garlic. Some brands contain chili peppers and other spices as well. The consistency is thick and creamy, and the taste is sweet, spicy, and piquant. Hoisin sauce is used in marinades or as a condiment for dipping. After opening the can, transfer the sauce to a glass jar and store it in the refrigerator, where it will keep indefinitely. I use it in Barbecued Pork Slices, Barbecued Ribs, Chicken Barbecue, Jade Beef, Oven-Barbecued Spareribs, and Red-Cooked Shrimp, and on Mandarin Pancakes with Peking Duck.

Oyster Sauce. A thick brown sauce made from oysters, soy sauce, and brine, oyster sauce has a rich, strong flavor. It is often used in Cantonese dishes as a seasoning or as a condiment for dipping. It keeps well stored in the refrigerator. I use oyster sauce in Barbecued Pork Slices, Barbecued Ribs, Beef with Broccoli and Onion, Oyster Beef, Oyster Chicken Wings, Oyster-Flavored Fried Rice, Oyster-Flavored Mushrooms, Oyster-Flavored Broccoli, Stir-Fried Asparagus, Boneless Pork Chops, Scallops Supreme, and Stuffed Mushrooms.

Plum Sauce (Duck Sauce). This thick reddish-brown sauce is made from plums, apricots, chili peppers, vinegar, and sugar. It has a sweet and pungent flavor. It is often served in Chinese restaurants with Peking duck, and can be used as a dipping sauce for egg rolls or crisp Wontons. It keeps indefinitely in the refrigerator.

Bean Sauce (Soybean Sauce, Yellow Bean Sauce). This thick, pastelike sauce is made of soybeans, flour, and salt. *Hot bean sauce* is bean sauce with the addition of chili peppers and spices; it sometimes contains kidney beans as well. Both sauces come in cans and should be transferred to glass jars for indefinite storage in the refrigerator. Bean sauce or hot bean sauce is used in Spicy Tofu, Red-Cooked Chicken Wings, and Sichuan Pork with Water Chestnuts.

Sweet Bean Sauce. This is a thick reddish-black pastelike sauce made from ground fermented soybeans, flour, sugar, and spices. It is used as a seasoning in Oven-Barbecued Spareribs.

Fermented Black Beans. These strong-flavored, salty preserved beans are soaked before use as a flavoring ingredient. They appear in Cantonese cuisine, with seafood or meat, in stir-fried or steamed dishes. Store them in a glass jar in the refrigerator, where they will keep indefinitely. They are an ingredient in Shrimp with Lobster Sauce and Spicy Tofu.

Sha-cha Sauce (Saté Paste). Sometimes called barbecue sauce, this bottled seasoning is made of minced garlic, minced shallots, dried shrimp, dried fish, dried green onion, chili peppers, and salad oil. It is the specialty of a region of Guangdong Province. Buy it in an Oriental grocery. It appears in recipes such as Sha-cha Beef and Chinese Fondue.

Chinese Soy Paste. This dark, thick syrup adds color to fried rice dishes. It is also used to thicken light soy sauce as a substitute for dark soy sauce. It is sold in Oriental groceries. (Gravy-making products such as Kitchen Bouquet and Gravy Master may be used instead of soy paste.) Use it in Ham Fried Rice.

OTHER PREPARED FOODS

Super Batter Mix. For best results when frying foods in batter, use my Super Batter Mix, sold at gourmet food stores or by mail from Pat Tung's Gourmet Delight, P.O. Box 16141, Rocky River, Ohio 44116. Made of wheat flour, rice flour, cornstarch, and baking powder, it is ideal for fish, shrimp, scallops, chicken, meat, vegetables, and cheese. (In my recipes, I also provide an alternative recipe for batter.) Use Super Batter Mix in Butterfly Shrimp and Sweet-Sour Pork.

Wrappers. Wonton and egg roll (spring roll) wrappers or skins are sold in Oriental groceries and in many supermarkets. They may be kept frozen, then thawed two or three hours before using. For further information, see the sections on wontons (page 160) and egg rolls (page 165). Recipes calling for these wrappers include Jiffy Egg Rolls, Shanghai-Style Egg Rolls, Crisp Wontons, Sweet Wontons, Wonton Chips, Wonton Fritters, and Wonton Soup.

Shrimp Chips. These thin, colorful dried chips are made of flour, baking powder, and shrimp seasoning. They resemble round pieces of plastic before cooking, but when they are deep-fried in very hot oil, they puff up in seconds like flowers blossoming. They are great to munch on as a snack or appetizer. Shrimp chips are available in Chinese groceries and some gourmet food stores. Instructions for cooking are on page 61.

TEA

Tea (*cha* in Chinese) is the most common beverage for adults in China, and hospitality requires, at the very least, offering a guest or visitor a cup of hot tea. The beverage is served throughout the day and especially after meals, but never during meals. It is felt that drinking tea with food will cause indigestion, for the tea will wash down rice that has not been properly chewed. Also, it is believed that drinking liquid will fill the stomach. Hot tea served after the meal, however, clears the system and washes down the oily foods that were consumed.

Chinese tea generally falls into one of three categories: black tea, green tea, and floral tea. Black tea is called "red tea" (*hong cha*) in Chinese because of its brownish-reddish color. Black tea leaves are fermented or semifermented, and the beverage has a full-bodied flavor. This tea is believed to have a warming effect on the body. The best-known and most popular black tea is oolong ("black dragon"), which is the type served in most Chinese restaurants in the United States. Other black teas are keemun, litchi-flavored black tea, black Iron Goddess of Mercy, and Yunnan's *pu-erh*.

Green tea (*lu cha* or *ching cha*) has a pale greenish color. The best parts of the tea plant—the young and tender leaves—are baked or sun-dried immediately after picking. Thus, green tea is unfermented, and it is the most expensive type in China. It is believed to have a cooling, refreshing effect on the body. Hangzhou's Dragon Well is the most famous green tea.

Floral tea (*hua cha*) is tea with flowers added to give it a special fragrance. The best-known floral teas are jasmine tea, rose tea, chrysanthemum tea, and orange tea. Floral tea is considered delicate and romantic.

To brew good tea, first clean the teapot and be sure it is free of oil. Then add good-quality tea leaves to the pot. Pour in water at a full boil—two to three cups water for every teaspoon of tea leaves. (According to preference, you may want to make the tea milder or stronger.) After you have poured out the tea, you may add more boiling water to the leaves in the pot to replenish the supply.

True connoisseurs of Chinese tea drink it without sugar, milk, or lemon. When drinking tea, if a few tea leaves have escaped into your cup, you may gently blow them away from your mouth as you sip.

For a large party, trying to serve tea to each individual's taste would be difficult. My suggestion is to brew one or two pots of very strong tea as a base, and have a separate pot of hot water. For those who prefer mild tea, dilute the strong brew with more hot water; for those who like strong tea, use less hot water to dilute the base.

HOW TO DETERMINE FRESHNESS

For good results, it is important that ingredients be fresh. Look for good color and firm texture in produce. Knowledge of the prime seasons for various vegetables and fish, and knowing the place of origin for seafoods, will also help you judge freshness.

Beef should be red, firm, and have a springy texture. Blood remaining in the package should be red; avoid meat showing dark blood.

Pork should have a pinkish color and be firm with a springy texture.

Lamb should have a pinkish color and be firm with a springy texture.

Organ meats (liver, kidney, etc.) should be dark and shiny, or purple. When touched, they should be firm and spring back.

Chicken and duck should have thin, smooth (not sticky) skin, firm and meaty flesh that is springy to the touch and a bright color (not dull or dark). For poultry parts, be sure the color is even. Avoid pieces surrounded by dark blood.

Eggs have a tough surface when fresh. When shaken, a fresh egg will make no sound. A fresh egg held to the light will be translucent, showing the round yolk. If placed in water, a fresh egg will sink.

Fish has a smooth and moist skin when fresh; it is not sticky or dry to the touch. The flesh should be firm and springy and the scales intact against the body. The eyes will be clear, transparent, full, and protruding. Gills should be a bright reddish-pink; head and tail are straight and stretched. The blood will be a bright red color.

Crabs are fresh when alive and lively. The shell is bluish and the stomach is white. The crab should turn over if placed on its back.

Clams and oysters should be tightly closed.

Prawns and shrimp should have a clear color, with shiny shells intact, and should have firm flesh, with head and tail intact.

Lobsters should be alive and lively. To test if a cooked lobster was alive before cooking, pull back the tail; it should spring back into a curl.

Vegetables should be crisp, plump, and have a shiny color; they should not be wilted or have yellowed leaves. Vegetables should have no dark or soft spots.

Equipment and Utensils

WOK

Wok is the Cantonese pronunciation for the name of a round-bottomed pan with sloping sides and handles. This useful and versatile utensil has been used by the Chinese for many, many centuries. The traditional wok is made of iron, which conducts heat rapidly and distributes heat evenly. Heat concentrated in the center radiates to the sloping sides. The wok's best use is for stir-frying. Cut or sliced ingredients are tossed in hot oil for just a few minutes. The result is tender meat with juices sealed inside and vegetables still fresh and crispy. Colors remain bright and flavors fresh. Thus, stir-frying in a wok is efficient and economical because it saves cooking time as well as fuel. The wok is also used for deep-frying, steaming, simmering, boiling, braising, smoking, and other methods.

The diameter of a wok ranges from ten to thirty inches. An ideal size for everyday cooking as well as for parties is fourteen inches. The wok usually comes with a high-domed lid to allow hot steam to circulate around food, and a round metal ring to use as a stand to steady the wok over the burner. (If the ring has openings of different sizes, place the smaller side around the gas burner, with the large opening above so that the flame can radiate to the side of the wok. For electric stoves, place the large ring down so that the heat will concentrate on the center.)

Woks are made of a variety of materials—aluminum, brass, copper, thin iron, or stainless steel with or without a copper (enameled) bottom. In the United States there are stainless-steel and aluminum electric woks made with a nonstick lining.

The best wok for authentic Chinese cooking is made of iron and is used on a gas range. Iron conducts heat very fast and evenly. Unfortunately, an iron wok will not stay as shiny and new-looking as a stainless-steel or copper one. After repeated usage, the intense direct heat will turn the wok bottom black, and the inside will also turn dark.

Stainless steel and copper do not conduct heat as rapidly as aluminum, so when woks made of those two materials are used on high heat, the sides above the oil level become burned because the heat radiates up from the sides, thus requiring scrubbing after use. Allow very little time to preheat a stainless steel wok. When adding oil, keep a low flame at first. Swirl the oil around to coat the pan above the oil level, then turn to high heat.

Electric woks work satisfactorily in conducting and distributing heat. Their automatically controlled heat is a plus for deep frying, but a minus for large-quantity stir-frying. To remedy this, food should be stir-fried in batches. The wok is portable, so food can be cooked in front of company, and the wok can also be used for serving. If your kitchen is equipped with an electric range, the electric wok is a good substitute for the iron wok on a gas range—unless you own a flat-bottomed iron wok, which sits firmly on the burner without a wok ring.

Wok Rack. Some woks come with a "tempura" rack. This is a rack placed on the top edge of the wok for holding morsels you have just deep-fried, such as egg rolls, wontons, or tempura (foods deep-fried in batter Japanese style). The rack serves two purposes: to drain fried food (the oil drips back into the wok) and to keep fried food warm while more food is being cooked in the wok.

Is the Wok a Must? Although the wok is the ideal cookware for stir-fried dishes, strictly speaking it is not a must, especially for those who are starting to introduce Chinese food to the family and do not yet know whether they will enjoy it, or for those who are not yet ready to invest in one. A ten- or twelve-inch-deep skillet, frying pan, or dutch oven will work well for stir-frying. In fact, with the even heat distribution of the electric range, it may be easier to stir-fry in a flat pan, as long as the food is stirred and turned constantly in a very quick motion. The drawback of using a skillet or frying pan is that the counter adjacent to the range and the range top may be splattered with oil. To remedy this, cover the counters with foil tightly folded under, and cover the burners not in use with a foil pie plate to prevent having to clean underneath the coil afterward. Dutch ovens are deeper, so oil does not splatter as much, and they are useful for preparing large amounts of food.

How to Season a Wok. First wash the wok with soap and water. With an iron work, it is sometimes necessary to use a heavy scouring pad and cleanser to remove the rustproof coating applied during manufacture. Rinse the wok well and dry it over a high flame while wiping dry. Add one cup of vegetable oil. Turn and rotate the wok to make sure the entire interior surface is coated with oil and heated through. Repeat oiling two or three times. Turn heat off; pour off oil and wipe dry.

Alternative ways to season wok are as follows: (1) Fill the wok with oil. Turn heat to very high, almost to the smoking point. Then turn heat off and let oil cool completely. Pour off oil and wipe dry. (2) If the first cooking project happens to be a deep-fried food, then the wok may be seasoned as the food cooks. Fill the wok two-fifths full with oil. Brush the top three-fifths with oil. First turn heat to very high; then, when ready to fry, reduce it to medium-high. After cooking is done, wait until oil is completely cooled; then remove oil and wipe wok dry (without washing). Food should not stick to a well-seasoned wok.

Care of the Wok. After each use, wash the wok with soap and water, rinse well, and place on direct heat, wiping dry at the same time. (If water remains on an iron wok, it will rust.) Moisten wok with a little oil, especially if it is not used frequently. In China, a whisk (made of thin strips of bamboo tied together at the top) is used to wash a wok thoroughly in hot water.

STEAMER

Two types of steamers are available, one made of bamboo and the other of aluminum. Both come in tiers with a lid. The bamboo woven tier has a latticed bottom, while the aluminum tier has a perforated bottom. Bamboo steamers, which may have from one to three tiers, must be placed on top of a wok or pot of a suitable size containing boiling water. The aluminum set comes with a base pot for water. Food is cooked by the hot, wet steam produced by the boiling water underneath.

The smallest bamboo steamer is about six inches in diameter; it is especially designed to steam dim sum snacks. The most useful one is about twelve to fourteen inches.

Lining a Steamer. If food cannot be placed on a heatproof plate or bowl, then line the steamer with double-folded cheesecloth or clean white cloth and put food directly in the steamer. I like to use lettuce, napa cabbage, or cabbage leaves as the lining. Less work is involved, and it is less expensive and easily disposed of. Wax paper or foil is not recommended.

Care of the Steamer. Clean aluminum steamers like any aluminum utensil. Wash with detergent, rinse, and wipe dry. After washing a bamboo steamer, shake it over the sink to get the water out. Wipe it dry, then put it on a dish rack to let it dry completely before storing.

CHOPSTICKS

It has been said that the dexterity of Orientals for fine, delicate handwork such as carving is partly due to the lifetime use of chopsticks. In Mandarin, the word for chopsticks is pronounced *kuai-zi,* which sounds the same as the words for "quick son." Therefore, in the olden days, a bride's parents would include ten pairs of chopsticks in the dowry, in the hope that she would soon have a son to carry on her husband's family name.

The size, shape, and length of chopsticks vary. They are usually nine to eleven and a half inches long. Extremely long chopsticks are used for cooking and barbecuing only only. The material of chopsticks ranges from plastic, bamboo, and lacquered wood to polished bone, ivory, coral, jade, silver, and gold. The most commonly used are those made of bamboo, which is nonslippery as well as economical. Bamboo chopsticks are very versatile and are widely used in the kitchen for processes such as mixing ingredients, stirring ground meat, whipping and beating eggs, sorting, picking, testing oil temperature, holding food for pan-frying or deep-frying, dotting, or piercing. They can even serve as a rack for steaming: you place two chopsticks parallel to each other or four chopsticks in a criss-cross arrangement in the wok, and then rest a plate on top of the chopsticks.

How to Clean Chopsticks. Bamboo chopsticks may be washed by hand or in a dishwasher. (Make sure they do not interfere with or fall into the machinery.) If chopsticks are too long to stand up in the silverware caddy, tie them with a band and lay them down in the top section. If they do fit in the silverware caddy, make sure they do not touch the top section, nor should they fall through the holes. Folded cheesecloth may be placed in one section for the chopsticks. Leaning chopsticks at an angle will require less clearance and also prevent them from slipping into the holes of the silverware caddy. Other kinds of chopsticks should never be washed in the dishwasher. The heat may cause lacquer chopsticks to peel, plastic ones to warp or crack, and ivory ones to discolor. Wash them by hand in detergent, rinse in very warm water, and wipe dry. Plastic and bamboo chopsticks may be washed simply by holding a bunch of them in your hand, adding detergent, rolling them against each other between your palms, and then rinsing. Air-dry or wipe with a clean kitchen towel. To sterilize bamboo chopsticks after washing, either pour boiling water over the eating ends or place them in a cup of boiling water.

Good-quality chopsticks should be dried by hand individually. To dry bamboo and plastic chopsticks in the authentic way, place them in the center of a clean kitchen towel, fold the towel over, and roll the chopsticks back and forth several times.

How to Use Chopsticks. Each person has a slightly different method of manipulating chopsticks. Since their primary function is to carry food to the mouth, as long as you can manage and achieve that, it is all right to use your own method if you have one.

If you do not know how to use chopsticks, first relax, then try the following instructions, and practice again and again. Don't give up! It takes a lot of practice to be proficient. Following is a detailed, slow-motion description.

1. Hold your right hand with palm facing you at an angle of forty-five degrees. Use your left hand to pick up one chopstick and place it in the curve between the right thumb and index finger one-third of the way down from the top of the chopstick. Close the thumb to hold and steady it.

2. Curve the ring finger inward (pointing to yourself), then let the lower part of the chopstick naturally drop and rest on the first joint. This chopstick will be the stationary one.

3. Curve the middle finger in the same direction as the ring finger, and rest the fingertip over the outside of the chopstick.

4. Pick up the other chopstick with the left hand and place it on top of the first joint of the middle finger. The upper portion of this chopstick will naturally fall onto the large joint of your forefinger. Make sure now that the two chopsticks are parallel to each other and with the tips even, about one inch apart. Relax the thumb

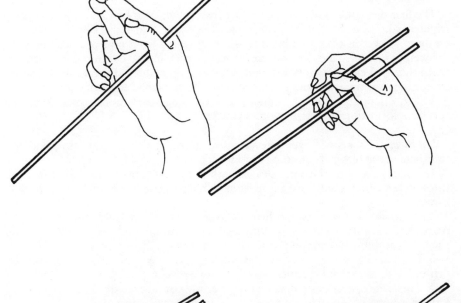

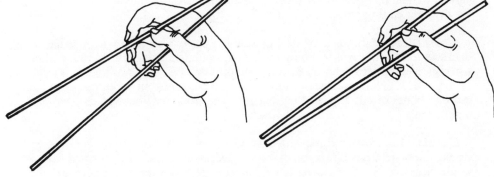

so that it will touch and hold the second chopstick as well. (Now you are holding it correctly.)

5. Separate the chopsticks by moving the middle and index fingers outward; your forefinger will naturally follow the same direction, as both are still holding the moving chopstick. The thumb is continuously holding the stationary chopstick as well as touching the moving one. Practice this open-and-close motion again and again.

6. To eat, hold the chopsticks about an inch apart at an angle to the food, then grasp a piece of food with the tip with a very steady hold, bring to the mouth, and enjoy! (The size of the morsel to be picked up determines the distance between the tips of the chopsticks.) Did you drop it? Try again and practice. In no time, you'll be an expert.

CLEAVER

The first sight of a cleaver—the cutting instrument used by Chinese cooks, may frighten you away. It is a big, clumsy-looking knife that looks like a dangerous weapon. However, once you learn to use it, you will soon find yourself enjoying the weight in your hand, for it makes cutting easier and saves you effort and time when slicing. A cleaver is versatile, and you will soon find it indispensable. It is used in cutting, slicing, shredding, cubing, dicing, mincing, tenderizing, crushing, grinding, chopping, boning, scaling, and carrying food. See pages 42-46 for specific information on cutting with a cleaver.

Kinds of Cleavers. Cleavers are classified according to weight, size, and the thickness of the blade. They come in four types:

1. The *chopper* is the heaviest cleaver with the thickest blade. It is used to chop through large bones and hard ingredients. Choppers are owned mostly by professionals.

2. A *regular cleaver* is not so heavy and large as the chopper, and its blade is narrower. A regular cleaver is multifunctional; it can be used for everything from slicing meat thinly to chopping chicken bones (but not hard bones).

3. The *slicer* has a narrow body, less weight, and a very thin blade. It is used by professionals to slice meat paper-thin, even transparent.

4. The *petite cleaver* has a blade with a slightly concave shape. Small in size and light in weight, it is ideal for cutting vegetables and can also be used to slice meat or for any light cutting work.

Blade. Cleavers are made of steel or stainless steel. Steel is heavier and harder than stainless steel. If you are going to chop through (chicken or duck) bones, then a steel cleaver is a better choice. Be sure to wipe it dry after each washing, as it tends to rust. The stainless-steel cleaver looks shiny all the time, but is not meant to cut through bones or cut any hard ingredients. The blade may become chipped and unrepairable.

Handle. Most cleavers come with a wooden handle for easy gripping. One steel cleaver imported from China comes in one piece, handle and blade formed from a single piece of steel. This cleaver has the advantage that water cannot get into the handle and cause the wood to split after long use. The blade of this particular cleaver is rather thin, and so it is not recommended for chopping through bones.

A wooden handle should never be immersed in water. Always wash and rinse it at a forty-five degree angle with the handle outside the water. Hold the handle with a dry hand so that water will not get into the wood or the joint. Immediately wipe the cleaver dry and let it stand in the dish drainer with the wooden handle up, so that water, if there is any, will drain away from the handle. Prolonged accumulation of water over the years may split or even rot the handle.

How to Sharpen a Cleaver. A good cleaver, like any other knife, should not be dull or have a nicked, chipped edge. The best way to sharpen a cleaver is with an old-fashioned abrasive stone with rough and smooth honing surfaces. The rough side is for dull and nicked edges, and the smooth one is for maintaining sharpness.

A steel is used to "set the edge." Regular and frequent use of the steel will help keep the cleaver and knife sharp. If the cleaver needs sharpening urgently and neither stone nor steel is available, use the knife-sharpener attachment on an electric can opener. Let the cleaver go through once or twice, starting from the heel tip (nearest to the handle), and move the cleaver in a backward motion (do not use a zigzag motion). Always be sure to rinse after sharpening to remove the metal particles. It is common in China to see a chef do a last-minute steeling of the tool before cutting, but turning over a china plate and, with swift, sure strokes, pulling the cleaver edge across the base edge of the plate.

CUTTING BOARD

A whole piece of thick, heavy, flat-surfaced solid wood is recommended as a cutting board. Such a board will not damage the blade of a cleaver or knife, and it produces a nice sound when you are chopping. Plastic cutting boards do not have these advantages but are more easily cleaned. To wash either type of board, first scrape any food particles from the surface with a cleaver. Wash and brush the board well, then rinse and wipe dry. Stand it up on the dish rack to air out the moisture within.

SKIMMER OR SLOTTED SCOOP

A skimmer or scoop is used to remove and drain foods from hot oil or hot liquid. Most often it is used to remove fried wontons, egg rolls, and shrimp chips or to drain wontons and noodles. When placed over a pot, it can serve as a drainer. It comes in various sizes. It is made of either wire with a bamboo handle or aluminum with a wooden handle.

CHINESE ROLLING PIN

The Chinese rolling pin is rather petite compared with its U.S. counterpart. It is a smooth section of solid wood with a three-inch diameter and a ten- to twelve-inch length. Some Chinese rolling pins are tapered at both ends; others have the same diameter throughout.

PASTRY MOLD

Pastry molds are specially designed to make desserts in uniform and identical shapes. Some molds are made of cast iron or aluminum with a piece of rubber at the top (for easy removal of the contents when tapped), and others are made of wood. Put sweet dough or dough with fillings into the mold, press, and even out with a knife. First tap once on the table to loosen the contents a bit, then turn the mold over while holding the handle, then tap or shake the dough out. Now the carved designs are on the top of the dough and ready to be baked or steamed. The most widely used mold is for moon cakes to be eaten at the Mid-Autumn Festival.

Methods of Food Preparation

Barbecuing. Cooking on a grill over hot charcoals.

Blanching. Ingredients are put into a pot of boiling water and cooked for thirty seconds to one or two minutes, then immediately rinsed under cold water to stop cooking and retain color. Blanched ingredients may be used for cold-mixing or stir-frying.

Boiling. Cooking in boiling broth or water.

Braising. Ingredients are fried or tossed in oil to coat the outside and seal the juices in. Seasonings and a little liquid are added, the pot is covered, and food is cooked over medium-low or low heat. Large pieces of meat or whole poultry take many hours to cook by this method.

Clear Simmering. Large cuts of pork or whole poultry are cooked in water with wine or sherry added. After the water comes to a boil, the heat is turned low and the food allowed to simmer for a long time. Salt is added at the end, or the cooked food is dipped in soy sauce to eat. The flavorful clear soup is served with the meat.

Cold-Mixing. Cold sliced vegetables are mixed with ingredients such as soy sauce, sugar, vinegar, and sesame oil, and served as a salad.

Deep-Frying. Frying in hot oil until food is golden. Since it is recommended that oil heated to a high temperature not be reused, I use one to one and a half cups of oil in a fairly narrow pot or wok, and then discard it after frying. To test the temperature of oil for deep-frying, stick an old wooden chopstick into it. The oil is ready if bubbles form around the chopstick, both at the surface of the oil and at the end of the chopstick. Turn the heat at once to medium-high; if the oil is allowed to stay very hot, the food will burn on the outside while remaining only partly cooked on the inside. Because the temperature drops after food is added to the oil, fry only four of five pieces at a time. Otherwise the food takes much longer to cook and absorbs too much oil.

To minimize splashing and splattering of oil while deep-frying, shield unused burners with foil or tin pie plates and cover countertops with foil paper. Also be sure that you have shaken any water from vegetables being prepared for frying.

To keep deep-fried food crispy, place the just-fried items on a rack with a foil-lined pan underneath to catch drippings. To reheat in the oven, also put the food on a rack over a foil-lined pan. If placed directly on foil paper or a pan, the reheated food will sit in the excess oil and become soggy and greasy.

Lu Cooking (Pot Stewing). Ingredients are immersed in a large potful of sauce made of water, soy sauce, sherry, green onions, ginger root, and spices such as star anise, Sichuan peppercorns, or fennel. The food is first brought to a boil, then simmered. When cooked, it is drained, cooled, and sliced to serve as an appetizer dish.

Oven-Roasting. Used for pork loin, ribs, and poultry.

Pan-Frying. Shallow-frying in a small amount of oil until both sides of the food are browned.

Poaching. Ingredients are placed in boiling water, then simmered for three to five minutes. In a variation of the poaching method, raw foods are placed in boiling water with or without seasoning ingredients; then the heat is turned off completely. The food is then cooked by the gradual decreasing heat.

Red Cooking. Ingredients are stewed in a reddish-brown sauce made of soy sauce, sherry, ginger root, and green onions. (Browning in oil beforehand is optional). This is a simple method that does not require constant attention. The dish can be cooked ahead of time and served cold or warm. It keeps well for many days. Red-cooking is thus one of the most popular home cooking methods in China.

Steaming. Raw foods are placed on a plate or bowl, which is then put on a rack standing in or above boiling water in a pot or steamer. The circulating hot steam cooks the food. Used for fish, meat, poultry, eggs, dim sum, and Chinese rolls and pastries.

Stir-Frying. With oil in the wok or pan, bite-sized pieces of food are tossed and turned very quickly over intense high heat until done. Every piece of food goes through the hottest part of the wok. This is a unique way of cooking that seals the juices in meat and poultry and keeps vegetables crisp. The cooking time is minimal if ingredients are cut beforehand and marinated or sauce is prepared ahead. In fact, preparing the ingredients takes more time than stir-frying them.

Before adding oil to your pan or wok for stir-frying, first preheat it for thirty seconds. After adding the oil, swirl it around so that the cooking surface will be evenly coated and food will not stick. When the oil and wok are both properly hot (and when the food to be fried contains little liquid), adding the food to the pan will produce the characteristic sizzling "cha" sound. (To minimize the mess from the splattering that may accompany the "cha," see the section on Deep-Frying, page 40.)

I recommend stir-frying meat in two or three batches for a specific reason. The highest flame you can get on a typical U.S. range is not intense enough for traditional stir-fried dishes. To make up for this, frying in batches makes the meat tender and ensures quick cooking. Otherwise, if the meat is added to the oil all at once, it immediately lowers the temperature and thus lengthens the cooking time.

TIPS FOR HEALTHFUL COOKING

- Wash or rinse meat, poultry, seafood, and vegetables regularly before preparation.
- Rinse residue blood from meats, poultry, etc., to eliminate undesirable odor and improve appearance. In making stews and soups, soak meat in cold water for 15 to 20 minutes to release blood before rinsing and cooking.

- Animal fats are hazardous to our health, so trim fat from meat to reduce both cholesterol and calories. In order to achieve a uniform tender texture in meat, also remove membranes before preparing.
- Remove scum and excess fat after cooking. (Using low heat can minimize its formation to begin with.) A double-folded cheesecloth or paper coffee filter in a funnel is ideal for straining broth to remove scum. You can skim fat from the surface of soups and other hot liquids with a large spoon or grease mop. However, if foods are not to be eaten immediately, cool them and then refrigerate overnight. The next day, the fat layer can be easily removed.
- To retain vitamins, rinse vegetables *before* cutting or slicing.
- Rinse fruits before slicing or eating.
- To rid leafy vegetables of sand or dirt, soak them in water, then wash under running water, and finally shake off excess water.
- For sanitary reasons, always wash the tops of cans before opening.

CUTTING METHODS

Please be extra-careful whenever you use a cleaver. Grasp the handle in the palm of your right hand, as you would hold any knife, but let your index finger fall naturally along the outside of the blade. (If it makes cutting easier, stretch your index finger to rest on the dull top edge of the blade.) When you are cutting a large or long piece of food into big chunks, hold the end of the ingredient with the

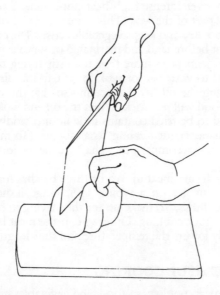

fingers of your left hand, and cut from right to left. The cleaver will be far from your left hand until it approaches the end of the food. When you are cutting a small piece of food into thin slices or slivers, hold the food in your left hand with fingers tucked under and the knuckles against the flat of the blade as a guide. With each cut, lift the cleaver a little and cut downward carefully.

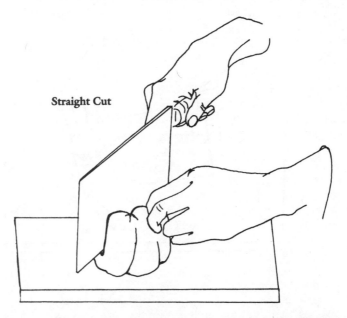

Straight Cut

Straight Cut. Use for vegetables and boneless meat. As the cleaver in your right hand advances (cutting downward), the left hand retreats at the same rate, like a crab crawling backward.

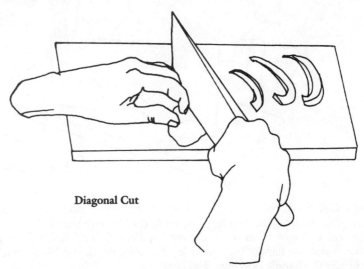

Diagonal Cut

Diagonal Cut (Push-Cut, Pull-Cut). Use for ingredients not suitable for a straight cut, or to produce a large cooking surface. Cut toward or away from you at an angle at regular intervals.

Sawing-Motion Cut (Shaving). Use for cutting meat into paper-thin slices, especially when it is still partially frozen; or for cutting cooked meat into very thin pieces. Cut downward while moving the cleaver in a sawing motion.

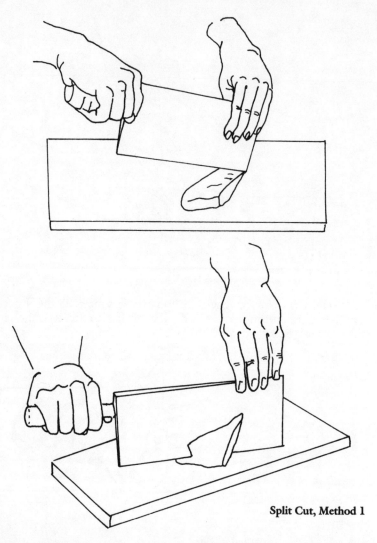

Split Cut, Method 1

Split Cut. Used for cutting small bones and tiny slippery items such as crabs, cooked chicken or duck, and eggs, or cooked food with shells.

Method 1: Right hand holds cleaver handle; left hand holds front top edge of cleaver. Raise the handle high, and let the front tip of the blade touch the food. Then press the handle downward to cut.

Method 2: Right hand holds cleaver handle, left hand holds front top edge of cleaver with fingers curved (not touching the blade). Cut through food back and forth with a sawing motion.

Roll Cut. Used for cutting carrots, turnips, and bamboo shoots. First cut diagonally at a forty-five degree angle. Then roll food toward you a quarter turn and cut again. Continue to roll and cut.

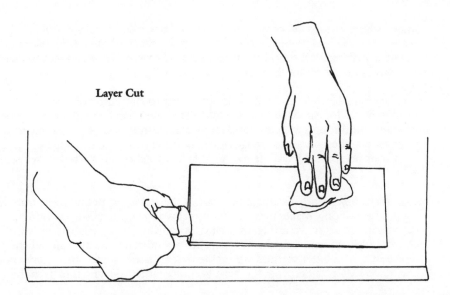

Layer Cut

Layer Cut. Used to make thin horizontal slices, often of boneless foods. This is the most difficult cutting method. However, with patience and practice, it will become easy. The trick is to lay the ingredients flat on the cutting board, hold the cleaver sideways (with the flat side of the blade parallel to the board), and hold the food firmly under the left palm or with fingers pressed close together. At the same time, with a very careful, slow sawing motion, move the cleaver toward the left, slicing horizontally. You will feel the cleaver working under your palm. As long as you press it steadily and keep the cleaver horizontal, there is no danger of cutting yourself.

Slanted Layer Cut. A variation of the layer cut. Instead of slicing horizontally, you slice thin layers at an angle, starting from one end. Lay the food flat on the board. Hold the cleaver at an angle, with the tip touching the board. Raise the back blade very slightly to determine the thickness of the slice; then cut.

Mincing. Used to grind or finely chop boneless ingredients for fillings or balls. You use the force of your wrist to chop systematically from left to right, then from right to left; or you flip ingredients over with the cleaver blade and chop repeatedly. Do not raise the cleaver too high—this not only avoids splatters but also helps you work more efficiently and save energy. Professional cooks usually hold one cleaver in each hand to chop. Before chopping, they dip the cleaver in cold water to keep meat from sticking to it. Some people prefer to use the flat side of the cleaver to crush the food and loosen up the texture before chopping. Another way to mince is to let the front tip of the blade touch the board; the left hand holds the top blunt edge, while the right hand moves the handle up and down.

Slitting. Among the purposes of slitting are (1) to speed up the cooking process, as the slits allow heat to penetrate the food, (2) to allow seasonings and flavors to penetrate the food, and (3) to beautify the food and add more interest to the dish, as by making various interwoven slits on squid or cuttlefish before cooking. Use the blade tip or the heel point of the cleaver to make slits without cutting through. For example, make several slits in the back of a fish before steaming, or cut through the tendons in meat but not through the meat itself.

Chopping Through. Use the force of the arm to chop through bones and joints, making neat, similiar-sized pieces. Hold the cleaver handle and aim at the desired location; cut through with one hard chop. If a second try is necessary, try to cut the same spot. Otherwise, rough edges or a double cutting line will appear. Be sure to keep your hand away from the moving blade. (To chop up a whole fowl, see page 48.)

Tenderizing. Gently use the blunt part of the cleaver to pound meat from left to right. This not only makes meat tender but also allows it to absorb seasonings more quickly and helps prevent it from curling up during frying. Alternatively, hold the cleaver sideways and use the flat part to pound hard on the ingredient to be tenderized. This latter method is suitable for pan-fried or deep-fried pork chops or beefsteaks. After tenderizing, the meat becomes rather thin and is of even thickness.

Crushing. A cleaver is an excellent tool for crushing garlic. Hold the cleaver sideways, with the blade to your right, and either (1) use the flat side to whack the garlic or (2) place your left palm on top of the cleaver and whack the garlic using both hands simultaneously. Once the garlic is crushed, the skin can be easily removed.

Other Cutting Methods. The cleaver can also be used for peeling (either holding the food in your hand, as when peeling an apple, or placing food on board), carving, scooping, and digging.

SHAPES

It is important to cut all cooking ingredients into uniform shapes and sizes so that the cooked foods are uniformly tender and attractive. Also, foods are usually cut into bite-sized pieces before cooking since knives are not used in the Chinese table setting. The following are the most commonly used shapes:

Chunks: 1- to 2-inch squares of meat, chicken, fish, or vegetables.
Cubes: $1/2$- to 1-inch size.
Diced pieces: $1/4$- to $1/2$-inch cubes.
Minced pieces: finely chopped pieces.
Thick slices: $1/2$- to 1-inch-thick slices.
Thin slices: flat pieces $1/8$ to $1/16$ inch thick, usually cut across the grain for meat. Straight cut, diagonal cut, or even layer cut may be used.
Diagonal slices: Harder vegetables such as bamboo shoots, broccoli spears, carrots, cauliflower, lobak, radish, and turnips, as well as coarse-grained meat, are often sliced diagonally in order to expose a larger surface to heat and flavoring during cooking.
Shreds: $1 1/2$-inch-long, $1/8$-inch thick matchsticks.

The Chinese cook always cuts in a very systematic, orderly way. In shredding, always cut ingredients into thin slices first, then stack five or six pieces together and cut them into one-eighth-inch-thick shreds. To chop, cut the shreds in half, stack together, and cut across in half. Then stack together again and thinly slice entire stack. For finely minced food, you may mince after the food is already cut into small pieces. For suggestions on chopping green onions, see page 23.

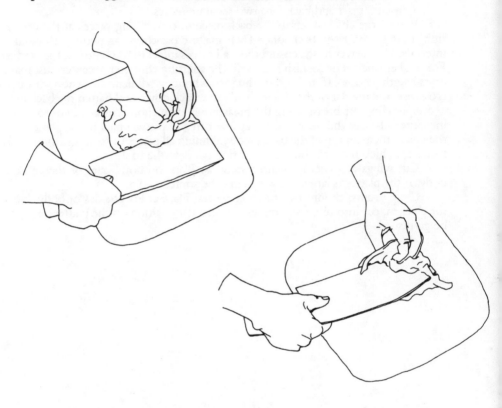

HOW TO BONE A CHICKEN BREAST

1. Place the half chicken breast flat so that the pointed part (tail portion) is directed away from you.

2. Holding the cleaver sideways, use the tip of the blade to make a slit on the right-hand side, separating the flesh from the soft bone, while the left hand holds and pulls the meat away.

3. With the cleaver blade against the bone, cut with a zigzag motion, while the left hand continues to pull the meat away until it is completely removed from the bone.

4. After boning, turn the breast over. Make slits on both sides of the tendon (the white-colored strip). Hold the tip end of the tendon, scrape the meat outward, and then use your left hand to pull out the tendon.

5. Remove the skin and visible fat.

HOW TO CHOP UP WHOLE FOWL

The Chinese prefer to serve a fowl whole, as this symbolizes completeness. The procedure for chopping into bite-sized pieces after cooking is as follows.

1. Cut off drumsticks at the joints.
2. Cut off wings at the joints.
3. Cut off tail. (Discard if no one likes it.)
4. Split-cut breast and back into two separate pieces.
5. For a large chicken, chop the back piece into two long pieces at the center, right next to the large backbone. Then make cross-chops at two- to three-inch intervals. Use cleaver to sweep and carry all pieces intact to the center of the platter. For smaller chicken or cornish hen, omit the splitting chop in the center; just make cross-length chops. If the protruding backbone is difficult to chop through crosswise, use the flat of the cleaver blade to whack down and flatten the back first.
6. Split-chop the breast along the breastbone, then chop across at two- to three-inch intervals. Use the cleaver to sweep and carry all pieces intact to the platter, but then place them on top of the back pieces, aligning all pieces in same direction. This forms the chicken body; the breast portion overlays the back.
7. Cut wings at joints into three sections. Place on both sides of the chicken body. If the platter is large, the wings may be stretched out.
8. Chop drumstick into two or three pieces. Place at lower sides of body. Now the chicken, cut into bite-sized pieces, lies in a flat position on the platter, ready to be garnished.

3

Recipes

Soups

CHICKEN BROTH

A basic chicken stock. Like many other peoples, the Chinese have long considered chicken broth to be a highly nutritious, healing beverage. It is served as a soup course at meals; it is also given to patients who are recuperating from operations or illnesses, for it is believed chicken will "make up the physical loss of strength and vigor." In the old days, women who had just given birth were supposed to stay home, preferably in bed, for a whole month. During this time the new mother was advised to stay out of drafts and avoid soaking her hands or feet in cold water. She was supposed to get plenty of sleep and rest, and was not to do any work. Most important, she was to eat chicken and drink chicken broth (made from a freshly killed chicken) each and every day, no matter how tired of it she became. In China it has always been believed that the period right after giving birth is the most opportune time to supply nutrients to the body to ensure future good health, and to cure old ailments.

> 1 whole chicken (2½-3 lbs.)
> 4 slices ginger root
> 2 green onions
> 6 cups water
> 1 tbsp. sherry
> 1½ tsp. salt

Preparation

1. Wash chicken and discard fatty parts and neck. Rinse gizzard and liver.
2. Pare ginger and slice. Tie green onions into knots or cut each into 6 sections.

Cooking

1. Put chicken breast side down into a large pot. Add all ingredients except salt and liver.
2. Bring to a boil, then turn to low heat, cover, and simmer for 2 hours.
3. Add salt and liver. Cook until liver is done (approximately 3-4 minutes).
4. Remove scum and fat if any. Also remove ginger and green onions.

Hints

- As an old cooking tradition, salt is always added last, after the broth has taken on the flavor of the chicken, to make the chicken meat tender.
- After the chicken broth is cooled, purify it by pouring it through a double-folded piece of cheesecloth or a funnel containing a coffee filter.

Variations

- Soak 6 Chinese dried mushrooms in warm water for 20 minutes. Remove stems and cook with chicken.
- For a tasty flavor, add a small piece of Smithfield ham to cook with the chicken.
- Add bamboo shoots if you happen to have some left over in the refrigerator.
- Add your favorite vegetable to the broth, or sprinkle 1 tsp. chopped green onions on top before serving.

EGG DROP SOUP

SOUP   SERVES 3-4

1 egg
1 tsp. pale dry sherry
1½-2 tbsp. cornstarch dissolved in 1½-2 tbsp. water
1 green onion
3 cups chicken broth
¼ tsp. sesame oil
bacon bits for garnishing (optional)

Preparation

1. Beat egg to a lemon-yellow color, and add sherry.
2. Dissolve cornstarch in water.
3. Chop green onion fine.
4. Skim fat from chicken broth.

Cooking

1. Bring chicken broth to boil.
2. Stir in dissolved cornstarch and cook until broth becomes smooth and transparent.
3. Pour beaten egg into broth gradually with one hand; at the same time, with a

wooden chopstick or fork in the other hand, stir the broth quickly as you add the egg. There should be no large lumps of egg in the soup. Turn off heat.

4. Sprinkle chopped green onion on top, and add sesame oil. Garnish with bacon bits if desired.

CUCUMBER SOUP

A simple and refreshing soup.

    2-3 oz. lean pork

    MARINADE
      1 tsp. sherry
      1 tsp. cornstarch

    2 green onions
    1 cucumber
    2 cups chicken broth
    1/8 tsp. pepper
    1/8 tsp. sesame oil

Preparation

1. Cut pork into strips 1 1/2 inches by 1/8 inch. Marinate for 5 minutes.
2. Chop green onions into 1/4-inch pieces.
3. Peel cucumbers thoroughly. Cut into halves lengthwise and remove seeds. Cut diagonally into 1/8-inch slices.
4. Remove fat from chicken broth.

Cooking

1. Bring broth to boil.
2. Add pork; cook until done (2-3 minutes).
3. Add cucumbers; turn off heat.
4. Sprinkle green onions on top; add pepper and sesame oil, and serve.

TOFU, TOMATO, AND SPINACH SOUP

A light, colorful soup. Without the pork, this is considered a vegetable soup. Adding a little pork not only adds flavor, but makes the soup a bit fancier. (In China all meats are a great deal more expensive than vegetables.)

    1 cake (12-16 oz.) tofu
    1 tomato
    5 spinach leaves
    2 oz. lean pork (optional)

MARINADE
    1 tsp. cornstarch
    1 tsp. sherry

4 cups chicken broth
1 green onion
1/8 tsp. pepper
1/8 tsp. sesame oil

Preparation

1. Rinse tofu and dice into 1/4-inch pieces.
2. Rinse tomato; cut into 8 wedges.
3. Rinse spinach well. Tear each leaf into 2 or 3 pieces.
4. Cut pork into 1/8-inch slices, then marinate for 5 minutes.
5. Remove fat from chicken broth.
6. Cut green onion into 1/8-inch pieces.

Cooking

1. Heat chicken broth to a boil. Add tofu and tomato. When soup boils again, add pork; cook until done (approximately 2 minutes). Turn off heat.
2. Immediately add spinach leaves and stir.
3. Sprinkle green onion on top; add pepper and sesame oil. Serve immediately.

Variation

Use 12 snow pea pods instead of spinach. Rinse and pat dry; remove strings from both ends. Cook for 1-2 minutes or until pods turn a deeper green.

SPINACH SOUP

SOUP   SERVES 4-5

A delightfully light soup with a subtle flavor enhanced by garlic.

    1/4 lb. fresh spinach
    2 cloves garlic
    4 cups chicken broth or water
    1/4 tsp. salt (1 tsp. if using water)
    1 tbsp. soy sauce
    1/8 tsp. white pepper
    1 tsp sesame oil
    1 tbsp. cooked ham or cooked meat slices
    1 tbsp. egg crepe shreds (See page 70.)

Preparation

1. Soak spinach in cold water and then rinse well to remove sand. Cut off stems and tear leaves in half.
2. Crush garlic.

Cooking

1. Bring broth or water to a boil in a large saucepan. Add garlic, salt, and soy sauce. Mix well.
2. Drop in spinach leaves and immediately turn off heat. Sprinkle with white pepper and then sesame oil. Stir well.
3. Garnish with ham and egg crepe shreds. Serve immediately.

Hints

- If you allow spinach to cook too long, it turns mushy and the soup tends to turn green.
- Sprinkling a little salt on the spinach will help in rinsing off the sand.

ZUCCHINI SOUP

SOUP   SERVES 4-5

A clear vegetarian soup, simple, quick, and inexpensive to make. This soup is especially appropriate when the other dishes on the table are oily or meaty.

1 large or 3 medium zucchini
1 green onion
4 cups water
3/4 tsp. salt
1 tbsp. soy sauce
1/8 tsp. white pepper
1/2-1 tsp. sesame oil

Preparation

1. Wash zucchini. Cut off both ends, and cut zucchini in half lengthwise, then slice crosswise into 1/8-inch pieces.
2. Rinse green onion, then chop into 1/8-inch pieces.

Cooking

1. Bring water to a boil in a saucepan. Add salt and soy sauce, then bring to boil again.
2. Add zucchini slices and cook, uncovered, for 3-4 minutes at high heat, until zucchini turns transparent. Turn off heat; add green onion, white pepper, and sesame oil. Stir well and serve immediately.

Variations

- Pare zucchini, slice into 1/8-inch pieces, and remove seeds.
- You may use cucumber slices, tomato, and tofu.

Appetizers, Snacks, and Side Dishes

STUFFED MUSHROOMS

APPETIZER/MAIN DISH   PAN-FRYING   YIELDS 30

Rich-flavored, meat-filled mushrooms

1 lb. large fresh mushrooms or 30 medium-sized Chinese dried mushrooms
8 water chestnuts
1 green onion
1/2 lb. ground lean pork

SEASONINGS
1 tbsp. soy sauce
2 tbsp. sherry
1 tsp. cornstarch
1/2 tsp. sugar
1/4 tsp. oil
1/8 tsp. pepper

1 1/2 tbsp. oil
2 tbsp. oyster sauce
1/4 cup water (or water used to soak dried mushrooms)

Preparation

1. Rinse fresh mushrooms and pat dry. Cut off and discard stems. Or soak Chinese dried mushrooms in warm water for 30 minutes until softened, then cut off tough stems. Save 1/4 cup of mushroom water for later use.
2. Mince water chestnuts and green onion.
3. Combine water chestnuts, green onion, ground pork, and seasonings. Stir in one direction, either always clockwise or always counterclockwise, for 1-2 minutes.
4. Fill mushroom caps with pork mixture. Use a knife to smooth edges for a neat appearance.

Cooking

1. Heat oil in frying pan over medium-high heat, and swirl it around to spread evenly in pan. Put mushrooms one by one into pan, stuffed side down. Turn heat to medium to brown them.
2. Add water (or mushroom water) and bring to a boil; then lower heat and cover. Simmer 4-5 minutes for fresh mushrooms, 6-8 minutes for Chinese dried mushrooms.
3. Uncover and turn mushrooms over. Stir in oyster sauce. Baste mushrooms and continue to cook over high heat for another minute, or until sauce is absorbed. Serve immediately while hot.

Hints

- Mushrooms may be filled ahead of time, placed on a plate, covered, and refrigerated until ready to cook.
- This dish can be prepared ahead through step 2 of cooking, then left in the covered cooking pan. Add the oyster sauce just before serving.
- When served as hors d'oeuvres, cooked mushrooms may be placed on a heated platter.

COLD-PLATE COMBINATION (LU DISH)

Beef, chicken, and eggs slow-cooked in a unique savory sauce and served cold. Lu means "pot-stewing" in a sauce.

BASIC LU SAUCE
¼ cup sherry
2 cups soy sauce
4 cups water
1 tsp. salt
3 tbsp. sugar
4 slices ginger root
3 green onions, tied in knots
1 tbsp. Sichuan peppercorns
2 whole star anise or 12 broken sections

2½-3 lbs. boneless beef shank, cross-cut by butcher
2 lbs. chicken wings
1 dozen eggs
Optional: duck, chicken, chicken gizzard, chicken liver, pork tripe, pork liver, pork ear, beef tripe

Preparation

1. Mix Lu sauce ingredients in large pot. Bring to a boil. If not using immediately, cool sauce and either freeze or store in refrigerator.
2. Soak beef in cold water for 15-20 minutes to release blood.

Cooking

1. Cook beef shank in boiling water for 5 minutes; remove and rinse off scum. Place beef shank in Lu sauce, cover, and slow-cook over medium heat for 2 hours or until meat is tender. Remove. Cut into bite-sized pieces and serve hot, or leave in refrigerator overnight, slice into very thin pieces, and serve cold.
2. Place chicken wings in the sauce and cook for 20 minutes. Remove and cut into three sections at the joints.
3. Hard-boil eggs. Remove shells. Place in Lu sauce and cook for 30 minutes. Soak in the sauce, remove when ready to serve, and cut into quarters.

Hint

After each use, skim fat off sauce and strain sauce through a coffee filter placed in a funnel. The sauce can be used three or four times. More soy sauce, sherry, sugar, and spices are added as needed. The more you use the sauce, the richer the flavor gets. Each food cooked in the sauce goes through a "give-and-take" process.

FRIED SHRIMP TOAST
APPETIZER   DEEP-FRYING   YIELDS 24-32 PIECES

This is a gourmet dish: a tasty shrimp paste piled on bread slices, then deep-fried. The result is meaty and crunchy.

> 1 lb. fresh raw shrimp in the shell or 12 oz. ready-to-cook frozen shrimp
> 10 large or 18 small water chestnuts
> 6-8 slices white bread (preferably slightly stale)
> 1 egg white
> 1 tsp. salt
> 1 tbsp. sherry
> 2 tbsp. cornstarch
> oil for deep-frying

Preparation

1. Shell and devein shrimp, wash, pat dry, and mince.
2. Mince water chestnuts.
3. Trim crusts from bread and cut each slice into four triangles.
4. Combine minced shrimp and water chestnuts with egg white, salt, sherry, and cornstarch. Mix well, stirring in one direction only.
5. Spread shrimp mixture on bread with a knife, smoothing it up to the edges. (The amount of mixture used can be varied according to taste and budget.)

Cooking

1. Heat oil to medium-high (375°F). Using tongs to hold one corner of the bread, deep-fry with the shrimp side down first.
2. When edges of bread turn to golden brown, turn over to brown the bread side. (If the bread "resists" being turned, wait a while and try again.)
3. Remove and drain on a rack or paper towel.

Hints

- Do not use cooked shrimp. After frying it will be tough.
- Using somewhat stale bread is the secret of success, as fresh bread absorbs a lot of oil and gets a greasy taste. If you have to use fresh bread, dry it in the air, on a clean counter or board, before starting the recipe. Press out excess oil against the wok or frying pan before removing from pan.
- The cornstarch and egg white are what make the bread and shrimp stick together.

- You may cook this ahead of time, then reheat on a rack with a pan underneath to catch the oil drips. Or cook, cool, and freeze Shrimp Toast. It may be taken directly from the freezer and warmed on a rack in the oven at 425°F for 12-15 minutes. But it tastes the best when freshly made and served immediately.
- For hors d'oeuvres, serve Shrimp Toast on a heated platter; each triangle may be cut into smaller triangles, which can be pierced with cocktail picks for easy handling.

Variations

- Add minced carrots to the mixture.
- Sprinkle sesame seeds on top before frying.

BUTTERFLY SHRIMP

APPETIZER/MAIN DISH   DEEP-FRYING   YIELDS 30

Scrumptious deep-fried shrimp, Cantonese style, with a light, crispy crust.

1 lb. raw medium or large shrimp in the shell
1 tsp. salt
½ tsp. pepper

BATTER
  1 bag Super Batter Mix (see page 31) or:
    ¾ cup flour
    ¼ cup cornstarch
    1½ tsp. baking powder
    1 egg
    7 oz. water
    2 tsp. oil

oil for deep frying

Preparation

1. Shell shrimp but leave the tails on.
2. Cut each shrimp open from the back all the way to the inner curve, but do not cut through.
3. Open shrimp flat into a large piece. Devein, rinse, and pat dry. Pound shrimp with the blunt edge of a cleaver or knife.
4. Place shrimp on a plate, and gently and evenly sprinkle first with salt and then with pepper.
5. Mix batter.
6. Blot the shrimp dry again with a paper towel.

Cooking

1. Heat oil to medium-high (375°F). To test temperature, put a little batter in the oil; when it sizzles, the oil is ready for deep-frying. Or test by sticking a wooden

chopstick in the center of the oil; if bubbles form around chopstick, the oil is ready for deep-frying.

2. Dip shrimp into batter either one or five at a time, by holding the ends of the tails. Remove from batter; then immediately drop shrimp into oil. Deep-fry to a golden-brown color; or until tails turn pink and crust is formed; or until shrimp rise to surface. Remove and serve immediately.

Hints

- Cooked shrimp may be served plain or with ketchup, sweet-sour sauce, mustard sauce, or plum sauce.
- Cutting shrimp open from the back provides a large round shape. If cut from the inner (leg) part, the shape is smaller and the sandy vein is more difficult to remove.
- Do not deep-fry more than five shrimp at a time, as the temperature will drop and the cooking process will be lengthened.
- If there is a rack attached to the top of your wok, place the cooked shrimp on the rack so that the oil drips back into the wok and the shrimp are kept warm.
- Use a slotted spoon or wire strainer to remove crumbs of batter occasionally. These fried crumbs make a good snack.
- Shrimp taste best when freshly cooked. If you have to make this dish ahead of time, deep-fry until crust forms, remove, cool, and freeze. When ready to use, do not thaw, and deep-fry in the oil once more. Drain and serve.

PAPER-WRAPPED CHICKEN   *APPETIZER   DEEP-FRYING   YIELDS 24 PIECES*

Seasoned chicken wrapped in paper and deep-fried. The chicken will be tender, as it is cooked by indirect heat. This dish can be a conversation piece. However, you have to open the paper to eat the contents, so it's better to serve it at an informal sit-down occasion.

2 chicken breast halves, filleted

MARINADE
  2 1/2 tbsp. soy sauce
  1 tbsp. sherry
  1/2 tsp. sugar
  1/4 tsp. salt
  1/4 tsp. black pepper
  1 tsp. sesame oil

6 Chinese dried mushrooms (optional)
1 piece leek or 4 green onions, sliced lengthwise
24 slices of water chestnut
24 squares (5" × 5") parchment paper or foil paper
oil for deep-frying

Preparation

1. Layer-cut each chicken breast into two pieces. Then cut each piece into 6 slices.
2. Combine marinade ingredients. Marinate chicken for 15 minutes.
3. Soak Chinese dried mushrooms in warm water for 20 minutes, then remove stems. Cut each mushroom into 4 thin strips.
4. Cut leek or green onions into 6 sections; then cut each leek section into 4 pieces.
5. Place parchment paper before you in a diamond shape. Place a slice of leek (or green onion), mushroom, water chestnut, and chicken in the center. Fold paper into an envelope to enclose slices, and tuck the top corner into the fold.

Cooking

1. Heat oil to 375°F and deep-fry wrapped chicken 1½-2 minutes each side.
2. Place on platter and serve.

WINE CHICKEN   *APPETIZER/MAIN DISH   STEAMING   SERVES 8 AS APPETIZER/4 AS MAIN DISH*

Juicy, tender chicken with a wine aroma and flavor.

> 1 whole chicken (2½-3 lbs.) or 2 whole breasts or 4 drumsticks and 1 whole breast or 4 thighs and 1 whole breast
> 1 tbsp. salt for whole chicken or 2 tsp. salt for drumsticks and breasts (1 tsp. for each pound)
> 2 green onions
> 4 slices ginger root
> 1½ cups sherry or white wine

Preparation

1. Rinse chicken, pat dry, and remove fat. Rub salt on chicken and let stand one hour.
2. Cut each green onion into 6 sections. Pare ginger root.
3. Put chicken in a bowl. Put ginger slices and green onion pieces on top of chicken.

Cooking

1. Steam chicken over boiling water—20 minutes for whole chicken, 15 minutes for parts. Turn off heat and cover for another 15-20 minutes. This method uses the remaining heat to finish cooking the chicken so that the meat is done but tender.
2. Remove chicken; cool. Chop whole chicken into 8 large pieces.

3. In a large glass mixing bowl, place chicken pieces and add sherry. (You may add the chicken juice from the steaming bowl, but defat and strain or clarify the juice first.) Cover and refrigerate overnight or until ready to serve.

4. Remove chicken from liquid. Bone it if you wish, and chop into small pieces (1″ × 2″).

Variation

Instead of steaming the chicken, you may put green onions, ginger, and water into a large pot and bring to a boil. Add chicken and cook over medium heat for 15-20 minutes. Turn off heat and leave lid on for another 15-20 minutes. Remove chicken; salt it and let it stand for 2-4 hours. Then pour sherry and purified chicken broth over it.

SEASONED TURKEY SLICES　　　　　*APPETIZER/SIDE DISH　STEAMING　SERVES 4*

2 turkey legs or 1 turkey breast (2 lbs.)
2 tbsp. sherry
1 tbsp. salt
1 tsp. Sichuan peppercorns

Preparation

1. Remove visible fat. Rinse turkey and pat dry.
2. Rub sherry over turkey.
3. Rub salt and peppercorns on turkey.

Cooking

1. Put turkey into a large heatproof bowl. Steam in a pot or wok on a rack over boiling water for 50 minutes. Replenish water in pot or wok to prevent burning. Keep covered for another 10 minutes after turning off heat.

2. Remove and cool. Scrape away any scum and bone. Slice at an angle into very thin slices.

Hints

- This dish can be served either warm or cold.
- A gravy to serve over turkey may be made by blending cornstarch with the juices that have accumulated in the bowl, but remove fat first. Cook until thickened.

A crunchy snack with a unique flavoring, ideal for munching with beer.

8 oz. shelled raw peanuts or Spanish peanuts
3 cups water
½ tsp. Sichuan peppercorns
2 tsp. salt

Preparation

Wash peanuts and drain.

Cooking

1. Put peanuts, water, peppercorns, and salt in a pot. Bring to a boil, then turn to medium-low heat and cook, uncovered, for 40-45 minutes. (Large peanuts require a little more time.)
2. Drain immediately. Serve warm or cooled.

Hint

Raw peanuts can be purchased at Oriental grocery stores, health-food stores, and some supermarkets.

SHRIMP CHIPS

SNACK/APPETIZER   DEEP-FRYING

shrimp chips (see page 31)
oil for deep frying

Heat oil to the highest temperature. Drop in a few pieces at a time and deep-fry for a few seconds until chips puff up. Remove and place on a paper towel to drain.

WONTON CHIPS

SNACK/APPETIZER   DEEP-FRYING

Crisp, crunchy delights.

wonton wrappers
oil for deep-frying

Preparation

Tear wonton wrappers into small, bite-sized pieces, in regular or irregular shapes.

Cooking

Heat oil to high, then turn to medium-high. Drop in wonton pieces and deep-fry until brown and crisp. Turn off heat and remove chips with a wire strainer or slotted spoon. Serve as a snack or appetizer either alone or with Sweet-Sour Dipping Sauce (see page 170).

Variation

Take several pieces of wonton wrapper, fold in half, and cut into thin slices. Deep-fry. Use them as fried noodles to munch on or to add crispy texture to a salad.

TASTY CHICKEN LIVERS
JIFFY SIDE DISH   BOILING   SERVES 4

Tender chicken livers dipped in garlic sauce.

1 lb. chicken livers

DIPPING SAUCE
3 cloves garlic
1 tbsp. soy sauce
1 tsp. sesame oil

2½ cups water
1 tsp. sherry

Preparation

1. Rinse chicken livers until the water is clear.
2. To make dipping sauce, crush garlic and place in saucer or dish. Mix in soy sauce and sesame oil.

Cooking

1. Bring water to a boil in a saucepan over high heat. Add chicken livers and sherry. Cook for 5 minutes.
2. Drain chicken livers and serve with garlic sauce for dipping.

BASIC DOUGH FOR CHINESE ROLLS *SIDE DISH/DIM SUM   STEAMING   YIELDS 16-24*

You will need a bamboo steamer to make these rolls.

1 package dry yeast
1 tbsp. sugar
⅓ cup very warm water
3 cups sifted all-purpose flour
⅔ cup lukewarm milk

Preparation

1. Put yeast and sugar into a large bowl. Add ⅓ cup very warm water (110°-115°F). Place bowl in a draft-free place. Let stand a few minutes, and then stir to dissolve sugar and yeast. In 10-15 minutes yeast will bubble up and the foamy mixture will double in volume.
2. Sift flour into large mixing bowl. Gradually pour in yeast mixture and add lukewarm milk. First use chopsticks, a wooden spoon, or a mixer to blend. Then use hands to form dough.
3. Sprinkle flour lightly on working surface. Knead dough for 8 minutes for best volume. Sprinkle more flour if dough starts to stick to working surface.
4. Place dough in a bowl, cover, and place in a warm place or in the unheated oven with the pilot light on (or with a pan of hot water on the shelf below it) for 1½-2 hours, or until dough doubles in size.
5. Punch down and let rise for another 30 minutes (optional).
6. Knead dough for 5 minutes, until smooth and elastic.
7. Now dough is ready to be divided into small portions, rolled out, and filled with your choice of mixtures. Or you may roll the dough into a cylindrical shape and slice off circles 1 to 1½ inches thick.
8. Allow rolls to rise 20-30 minutes. When holding a roll in your palm, it should feel very light. Then it is ready to steam.
9. Line steamer with cabbage leaves or a piece of clean white cloth, or a double piece of cheesecloth. Place rolls on leaves or cloth and steam over boiling water for 20 minutes.

Hints

• Hot plain steamed rolls may be served as the main staple in place of rice, as is the custom in northern China.
• Cold cooked rolls can be sliced into thin pieces and pan-fried until brown and crispy or popped into the toaster. Serve for breakfast with jam.
• Cooled cooked rolls can be frozen. When ready to use, do not thaw. Steam frozen rolls in a rack over boiling water, or place in a heatproof container on a rack in hot water for 5-6 minutes, or heat them in microwave oven.

The Chinese answer to the hamburger!

FILLING
   3 green onions
   2 slices ginger root
   10 water chestnuts
   1 lb. ground pork
   1 tbsp. soy sauce
   1 tbsp. sherry
   2 tsp. salt
   2 tbsp. sesame oil
   1/2 tsp. five-spice powder (optional)
   1/4 cup water

1 recipe Basic Dough (page 63)

Preparation

1. Finely chop green onions, ginger, and water chestnuts. Mix with other filling ingredients. Stir in one direction until smooth.

2. Divide dough into 4 equal parts. Take out 1 part and leave the other 3 covered. Roll dough between your palms into a 6-inch-long cylinder. Slice into six 1-inch-thick pieces.

3. Roll each piece into 4½- to 5-inch circle with the center part thicker than edges. (Cover the other 5 pieces with a damp cloth while working on one piece.)

4. Add 1 tbsp. meat filling in the center of a circle of dough. Use fingers to gather loose folds on sides of dough; folds meet at the top. Pinch and twist top of dough to be sure that fillings are firmly sealed. Use palms to rotate roll base into a round shape. Repeat with remaining circles of dough.

5. Place each roll in the bamboo steamer on top of a leaf of lettuce or cabbage or a white cloth, leaving 1 inch of space between rolls. Cover. Allow rolls to rise approximately 20-30 minutes.

Cooking

When water boils in wok, place steamer on top, cover, and steam for 15-20 minutes over high heat.

Hints

- Steamed rolls may be frozen for later use. To reheat, steam again over boiling water on high heat for 4-5 minutes, or warm in microwave oven.
- Ready-to-bake (uncooked) buttermilk rolls from the supermarket may be used in place of basic dough. Use 2 of these rolls overlapping for each Chinese steamed roll.

Crusty-bottomed rolls with the same meat filling used for the steamed version.

> 1 recipe Basic Dough (page 63)
> Filling for Steamed Meat Rolls (page 64)
> 2 tbsp. oil
> 1 cup cold water

Preparation

1. Divide basic dough into 4 equal portions. Take one portion (cover the other three), roll into a 10-inch-long cylinder, and cut into 1-inch-thick pieces.
2. Using a rolling pin, flatten each piece of dough into a 4-inch circle.
3. Fold as for Steamed Meat Rolls on page 64 to enclose the meat filling.
4. Repeat process with the other 3 portions of dough.

Cooking

Heat oil in a skillet. Add rolls, keeping them 1 inch apart. Cook at medium-low heat for 2 minutes. Add cold water, cover, and turn heat to medium-high to cook for 8-10 minutes, or until water is all absorbed. (Rolls may have to be cooked in batches.) Serve hot.

Hint

Rolls may be frozen after preparation. Place them on a lightly floured plate in a large plastic bag, or on a lightly floured cookie sheet covered with foil. When ready to cook, do not thaw, but place directly in skillet.

SWEET BEAN ROLLS   *DIM SUM/SNACK STEAMING YIELDS 24*

> 1 recipe Basic Dough (page 63)
> 1 can red bean paste

Preparation

1. Same as steps 2 and 3 of Steamed Meat Rolls recipe (page 64).
2. Use 1 tbsp. red bean paste as the filling for each roll.
3. Continue with steps 5 and 6 of Steamed Meat Rolls recipe.

DOUGH
2 cups all-purpose flour
²/₃ cup warm water
6 tbsp. (3 oz.) vegetable shortening

FILLING
2 cups chopped green onion
1 tsp. salt
2 tbsp. vegetable shortening

Preparation and Cooking

Same as for Suzhou Cakes (page 133).

SUZHOU MEAT CAKES   *DIM SUM/SNACK/MEAL-BY-ITSELF   PAN-FRYING   YIELDS 20*

Pastry cake filled with seasoned ground pork.

1 recipe dough (see Green-Onion-Filled Suzhou Cakes)

FILLING
¹/₂ lb. ground lean pork
¹/₂ tsp. salt
1 tbsp. sherry
1 tsp. soy sauce
1 tsp. sesame oil
2 green onions, chopped fine

Preparation and Cooking

Same as for Suzhou Cakes (page 133).

Eggs

SCRAMBLED EGGS

A jiffy egg dish with green onions. In China, food is not prepared on an individual-serving basis, and there is always plenty of cooked rice for each meal. Therefore, adding an extra bowl, a serving plate, and a pair of chopsticks is all that is necessary when an unexpected guest is asked to stay for a meal. To ensure that there is enough to eat, the polite hostess will add a scrambled egg dish at the last minute.

> 5 large eggs
> 1 tsp. sherry
> 1/2 tsp. salt
> 1 green onion
> 3 tbsp. oil

Preparation

1. Beat eggs in a bowl to lemon-yellow color. Add sherry and salt. Mix well.
2. Chop green onion into 1/8-inch pieces. Add to egg mixture.

Cooking

Heat oil in wok to high. Pour egg mixture into hot oil. Scramble and stir until done. Serve immediately.

Variation

Chopped chives may be added to egg mixture.

POACHED EGG

A whole egg poached and seasoned. It can be a side dish or a breakfast dish.

> 2 cups broth or water
> 1 egg
> 1 green onion (white bulb part only)
> 1/2 tsp. soy sauce
> 1/4 tsp. sesame oil

Preparation

Chop green onion fine.

Cooking

1. Bring broth or water to a boil over medium-high heat.
2. Break egg directly into the boiling water and simmer for 3-4 minutes.
3. In a serving bowl, place soy sauce, sesame oil, and green onions. Ladle poached egg into bowl and add some broth or water from the pot. Serve immediately.

Variation

Add button mushrooms, 2-3 torn pieces of spinach, or croutons to the bowl with the seasonings before adding the poached egg and liquid.

Hint

When poaching more than 1 egg, use a larger pot or deeper rim skillet to cook 2 or 3 eggs at a time. Add seasoning to individual bowls.

EGG CUSTARD *SIDE DISH   STEAMING   SERVES 3-4*

Steamed eggs are eaten in place of soup as a snack, at breakfast, or even when ill. In this form, eggs are easy to digest.

> 1 can (about 14 oz.) chicken broth
> 3 eggs
> 1/8 tsp. sherry
> salt (if necessary)

Preparation

1. Skim fat from top of chicken broth.
2. Beat eggs in a heatproof bowl. Add sherry and chicken broth. Mix well.

Cooking

Put 1/2-inch of water in bottom of a dutch oven. Place the heatproof bowl containing the egg mixture on a rack in the dutch oven. Cover and steam egg mixture for 25 minutes over medium-low heat. Custard is ready when eggs are no longer liquid. Do not stir.

Hints

- To make one egg for an individual serving, add ½ can of water or chicken broth to egg in a heatproof bowl. Place it in a saucepan to steam for 6-8 minutes.
- If you like custard a little thicker, use 4 or 5 eggs.

MARBLE EGGS (TEA EGGS)   *SIDE DISH/APPETIZER/SNACK BOILING SERVES 12-18*

Whole eggs cooked in seasoned tea, with a marbled appearance and a very subtle taste.

> 1-1½ dozen eggs
> 2 tsp. salt
> 5 tbsp. soy sauce
> 1 whole star anise or 5 broken sections
> 3 cups water
> 1 tea bag or 1 tsp. loose black tea
> 1 tsp. oil

Cooking

1. In a saucepan, cover eggs with cold water. Hard-boil for 20 minutes.
2. Chill cooked eggs in cold water until cool enough to handle. Pour off water.
3. Crack each egg with the back of a tablespoon until shells are covered with fine cracks.
4. Place eggs in saucepan and add remaining ingredients. Bring to a boil over high heat, then reduce heat to medium, cover, and cook for 50 minutes. Turn off heat. Let eggs soak overnight.
5. Eggs can be served hot or cold. Remove shell and slice into quarters.

Hints

- For a stronger flavor, let cooked eggs refrigerate in cooking liquid for 1 or 2 days. Serve either warm or cold. To reheat, warm up in original liquid.
- After 2 days, uneaten eggs should be drained and can be kept in refrigerator another week. You may warm them by reheating in water.

EGG CREPES

Egg crepe shreds are an ingredient in dishes such as Spinach Soup and Cold-Style Noodles. They may be made ahead of time and refrigerated.

> 1 egg
> ¼ tsp. oil

Cooking

1. Beat egg to lemon-yellow color.
2. Preheat pan at medium heat for 1 minute. Use a brush to apply oil.
3. Pour in egg and swirl to make a very thin crepe. Remove.

Salads

CUCUMBER SALAD

SALAD   COLD-MIXING   SERVES 4

Cool, crisp, and refreshing.

> 2 lbs. cucumbers
> 1 tsp. salt
>
> DRESSING
> 1 tbsp. sugar
> 1 tbsp. vinegar
> 1 tsp. sesame oil or salad oil

Preparation

1. Wash and peel cucumbers, and cut them in half lengthwise.
2. Use a knife to cut off seed portion, or scrape it off with a spoon.
3. Cut cucumber pieces crosswise into ¼-inch slices.
4. Sprinkle salt over cucumbers. Mix well and let stand for 10-15 minutes. Rinse and drain.
5. Combine dressing ingredients and add to cucumbers. Mix well and serve.

RADISH COLD-MIXING SALAD

Raw, crisp radish in a sweet-sour dressing.

1 1/2 lbs. radishes

DRESSING
4 tsp. sugar
4 tsp. vinegar
1 tbsp. soy sauce
1 tbsp. oil
1 tsp. sesame oil

Preparation

1. Wash each radish and scrape off the black dirt.

2. Cut off both ends of each radish. Crush each radish individually with a cleaver. Place in a bowl.

3. Combine dressing ingredients and pour over crushed radishes. Mix thoroughly. Serve immediately or 15-30 minutes later.

Hints

- Radishes become discolored and less crisp but more flavorful if soaked for several hours or overnight.
- To prepare ahead of time: Crush, cover, and refrigerate radishes, and mix dressing. Don't combine radishes with dressing until 15-30 minutes before serving.

COLD-MIXING CELERY

Celery slices with a flavorful dressing.

1 lb. celery hearts
1 1/2 tsp. salt
2 green onions
2-3 cloves garlic
3 tbsp. oil

Preparation

1. Wash individual celery ribs. Cut off the root end, stack 3 or 4 ribs together, and slice diagonally into 1/8-inch pieces. Place in a serving dish.

2. Sprinkle salt evenly over celery slices, mix well, and let stand for 10-20 minutes. Drain water from celery.

3. Cut each green onion into 6 sections, then sliver them. Crush garlic.

Cooking

1. Sprinkle green onion slivers on top of celery.
2. Heat oil in pan and add garlic. Remove garlic when oil is flavored.
3. Pour hot oil over celery, mix well, and serve.

Hints

- This dish may be prepared ahead of time, even refrigerated overnight.
- The minimum time for leaving salt on the celery is 10 minutes. After 20 minutes celery becomes soft and produces water, which should be drained off.

COLD-MIXING KOHLRABI
SALAD   COLD-MIXING   SERVES 4

An enticing salad course.

1 lb. kohlrabi

DRESSING
5 tsp. soy sauce
1 tsp. sugar
¼ tsp. salt
1 tbsp. sesame oil
hot pepper oil (optional)

Preparation

1. Pare and rinse kohlrabi. Pat dry and slice into ⅛-inch pieces. Stack several pieces together and slice into ⅛-inch shreds. Place in a bowl.
2. Combine dressing ingredients and add to kohlrabi. Mix well and serve.

Variations

- Add green pepper shreds or sweet red pepper slices for color and texture contrast.
- Mix prepared kohlrabi with a sweet-sour sauce by adding 2 tsp. sugar and 1 tbsp. vinegar to the dressing.

BEAN SPROUT SALAD
SALAD   COLD-MIXING   SERVES 4

A summertime favorite.

1 lb. fresh bean sprouts
2 oz. cooked ham (optional)
1 green onion

DRESSING
2 tbsp. vinegar
1 tsp, salt

2 tsp. sugar
2 tsp. soy sauce
2 tsp. sesame oil

Preparation

1. Rinse bean sprouts and drain.
2. Slice cooked ham into matchstick-sized pieces.
3. Cut green onion into slivers.
4. Combine dressing ingredients.

Cooking

1. Parboil bean sprouts in boiling water for 2 minutes. Immediately rinse under cold water to stop the cooking process. Drain and shake off excess water in a colander.
2. Pour dressing over bean sprouts and mix well. Drain dressing and pour over sprouts again and again (3 times in all).
3. Place ham slices on top of bean sprouts, and arrange green onion slivers around ham.
4. Chill for at least 10 minutes, and serve.

Hint

May be prepared several hours ahead.

HAM AND ASPARAGUS SALAD   SALAD   COLD-MIXING   SERVES 4

1 lb. fresh asparagus
4 oz. cooked ham

DRESSING
   1-2 tbsp. soy sauce
   1 tsp. sugar
   1 tsp. vinegar
   1 tsp. sesame oil
   1 tsp. oil

¼ tsp. pepper

Preparation

1. Wash asparagus. Cut off and discard tough ends. Cut asparagus into 4 sections.
2. Slice cooked ham into strips about the size of the asparagus sections.
3. Combine dressing ingredients.

Cooking

1. Blanch asparagus in boiling water for 2 minutes, then immediately rinse under cold water. Place in a mixing bowl.
2. Pour dressing over asparagus. Drain dressing and pour over again and again (3 times in all). Sprinkle with pepper and then refrigerate.
3. Drain asparagus and place in the center of a serving plate. Arrange ham around asparagus.

Variation

For ham-olive-asparagus salad, add pitted canned olives in a ring between ham and asparagus.

ASPARAGUS SALAD
SALAD   COLD-MIXING   SERVES 4

Fresh asparagus delicately seasoned with Oriental dressing.

> 1 lb. fresh asparagus
> 3 cloves garlic (optional)
>
> DRESSING
> 2 tbsp. soy sauce
> 2 tsp. vinegar
> 2 tsp. sugar
> 1 tsp. sesame oil

Preparation

1. Wash asparagus. Cut off and discard tough ends. Cut each stalk into 1½- to 2-inch lengths.
2. Mince garlic.

Cooking

1. Blanch asparagus in boiling water 2-3 minutes, then immediately rinse under cold water. Drain and pat dry. Scatter minced garlic on top.
2. Combine dressing ingredients and add to asparagus. Mix well. Chill for 20 minutes. Serve cold.

Cooled cooked broccoli with an Oriental dressing.

1 ½ lb. fresh broccoli

DRESSING
1 tbsp. soy sauce
2 tsp. sugar
2 tsp. vinegar
1 tsp. sesame oil
1 ½ tsp. oil

Preparation

1. Rinse broccoli and pat dry. Break off small branches one by one, about 1 inch below florets. Peel off the tough skin, and cut stems into half lengthwise. Then quarter each half.
2. Combine dressing ingredients.

Cooking

1. Drop broccoli pieces into boiling water and cook for 2-3 minutes. Immediately rinse under cold water. Drain in colander.
2. Add dressing and mix well. Drain dressing and pour it over broccoli again and again (3 times in all).

Vegetables

SICHUAN CUCUMBERS

Cool, crunchy cucumber sections sealed with hot sauce.

1½ lbs. large cucumbers or dill cucumbers

SAUCE
   3 tbsp. vinegar
   3 tbsp. sugar
   1 tsp. salt
   ½ tsp. sesame oil

5-8 dried chili peppers
¼ cup oil
1½ tsp. Sichuan peppercorns

Preparation

1. Wash cucumbers and pat dry. Cut off both ends, and cut cucumbers in half. Cut each half into quarters lengthwise. Scrape off seeds. Cut each quarter into 2-inch pieces (2" × ¾").
2. Combine sauce ingredients.
3. Cut chili peppers into ¼-inch strips.

Cooking

1. Heat oil. Add Sichuan peppercorns and chili peppers. Cook until oil is flavored, then discard peppercorns and peppers.
2. Add cucumber pieces and stir-fry for a few turns. Add sauce and mix well. When sauce bubbles, remove pan from heat.
3. Transfer cucumbers to serving dish and let stand for 30 minutes. Serve cold.

Hints

• If you let cooled cucumbers stand overnight, the flavor will be stronger.
• Wear rubber gloves when cutting chili peppers; otherwise they may sting the fingertips. Never touch eyes or mouth after handling chili peppers with bare fingers; wash hands thoroughly.

OYSTER-FLAVORED MUSHROOMS

1 lb. fresh mushrooms
2 cloves garlic
1 green onion

SAUCE
  1 tsp. cornstarch dissolved in 2 tsp. water
  1/4 tsp. sugar
  1 tsp. soy sauce
  1 tbsp. oyster sauce

6 tbsp. oil

Preparation

1. Wash each mushroom thoroughly. Slice the small ones in half and the bigger ones into thirds.
2. Crush garlic. Cut green onion into 6 sections.
3. Combine sauce ingredients.

Cooking

1. Heat oil. Stir-fry garlic and green onion; remove them when brown.
2. Add mushrooms and stir-fry for a few turns.
3. Add sauce and mix well. Serve either on rice or as a separate vegetable.

TOFU WITH FRESH MUSHROOMS

Soybean curd with mushrooms and ground pork, to be served over rice.

1 lb. tofu
6 oz. fresh mushrooms
1 clove garlic
2 green onions
1 tbsp. cornstarch dissolved in 3 tbsp. water or chicken broth
2 tbsp. oil
2 tbsp. ground lean pork
1/2 tsp. salt
1 tbsp. soy sauce
1/2 cup chicken broth
1/4 tsp. white pepper
1/2 tsp. sesame oil

Preparation

1. Cut tofu into 1-inch cubes.
2. Wash mushrooms and slice vertically into 2 or 3 pieces.
3. Crush garlic. Finely chop green onions (¼-inch length).
4. Dissolve cornstarch in water or broth.

Cooking

1. Heat 2 tbsp. oil to medium-high temperature. Add garlic, removing when oil is flavored.
2. Add ground pork and stir-fry until fully cooked. Add tofu and cook 15 seconds, gently turning cubes once. Add mushrooms, stir once or twice, and cook for another 15-20 seconds.
3. Add salt, soy sauce and ½ cup chicken broth; cover and cook for 2 minutes.
4. Add cornstarch mixture. When sauce bubbles, add white pepper and sesame oil; sprinkle chopped green onions on top. Gently mix. Serve over cooked rice.

Hint

This may be cooked ahead of time, then either kept warm in oven or reheated.

SPICY TOFU

VEGETABLE STIR-FRYING SERVES 4

This popular dish, known in Chinese as *ma-la* tofu, is hot in both taste and temperature. *Ma* means "numbing," referring to the sensation on the tongue produced by the peppercorn powder. *La* means "hot."

1 lb. tofu
1 leek (2 oz.)
2 tsp. cornstarch dissolved in 2 tbsp. water
1 tbsp. fermented black beans (optional)
1 tbsp. oil
3 tbsp. (2 oz.) ground pork or beef
1-2 tbsp. hot bean sauce or 1 tbsp. bean sauce plus ½-1 tsp. chili powder
½ cup chicken broth or water
2 tbsp. soy sauce
1 tsp. Sichuan peppercorn powder

Preparation

1. Cut tofu into 1-inch cubes.
2. Rinse leek leaves separately to remove sand; pat dry. Slice into 2-inch sections, then cut each section into 4 strips. Separate leek pieces.
3. Dissolve cornstarch in water.
4. Soak fermented black beans in warm water for 10 minutes; then drain.

Cooking

1. Heat oil over high heat. Stir in ground meat for 1 minutes, then add hot bean sauce (or add bean sauce, turn meat 5 or 6 times, and immediately add chili powder). Turn 2-3 times, then add broth or water.

2. Add tofu, fermented beans, and soy sauce; gently turn over. When liquid boils, turn to low heat, cover, and simmer 5 minutes.

3. Uncover, add leek, and turn tofu over gently. Raise heat to medium-high. Add dissolved cornstarch and mix well. Sprinkle Sichuan peppercorn powder on top. Serve immediately with rice.

BEAN SPROUTS AND LEEK   *VEGETABLE   STIR-FRYING   SERVES 2-4*

12 oz. fresh bean sprouts
1 leek (2 oz.) or 5 green onions
3 tbsp. oil
10 Sichuan peppercorns (optional)
1 tsp. salt

Preparation

1. Rinse bean sprouts in cold water, drain, and pat dry.

2. Rinse leek leaves separately to remove sand; pat dry. Cut leek into 8 pieces, each about 2 inches long, then sliver each slice into matchstick size (approximate size and shape of bean sprouts).

Cooking

1. Heat oil to high temperature. Add peppercorns, removing when oil is flavored or peppercorns turn black.

2. Stir-fry bean sprouts about 1 minute. Add leek and salt, and stir-fry another 2 minutes. Serve hot or cold.

Hints

- Canned bean sprouts tend to be soggy, so they are not recommended for use in this dish.
- Fresh bean sprouts should be plump and light in color.

Variation

If you prefer a hot, spicy taste, add 1 tsp. Tabasco sauce or ½ tsp. hot pepper oil (see pages 29-30) after removing peppercorns.

12 oz. fresh bean sprouts
1/2 carrot (1/4 cup shredded)
3-6 dried chili peppers or 1-2 fresh chili peppers
2 green onions
3 tbsp. oil
10 Sichuan peppercorns
1 tsp. salt
1/2 tsp. sugar
2 tsp. vinegar

Preparation

1. Rinse bean sprouts in a colander. Shake off excess water.
2. Pare carrot and slice diagonally into 1/8-inch pieces, then shred into matchsticks.
3. Slice dried chili peppers or fresh pepper in half. Slice green onions into thin strips either diagonally or straight into 6 sections; then slice each section into thin strips.

Cooking

1. Heat oil over medium-high heat. Add dried chili peppers and Sichuan peppercorns, removing them when they turn black or oil is flavored. Turn off heat just before removing.
2. Turn heat to high. Stir-fry bean sprouts and carrot in oil and add salt, sugar, and vinegar. Continue to stir-fry for 2-3 minutes.
3. Remove and garnish with thin slices of green onion. Serve hot or cold.

Variation

Omit peppercorns and peppers if you prefer a nonspicy flavor.

OYSTER-FLAVORED BROCCOLI   *VEGETABLE   STIR-FRYING   SERVES 4-5*

Tender broccoli spears and florets stir-fried in oyster sauce.

1-1 1/4 lbs. fresh broccoli
2 cloves garlic
2 slices ginger root
2 tbsp. oil
1 tbsp. water or broth
3 tbsp. oyster sauce

Preparation

1. Rinse broccoli and pat dry. Break off small branches about 2 inches below florets. Peel tough skin off stems and slice stems diagonally into ⅛-inch pieces.
2. Crush garlic. Pare ginger.

Cooking

1. Heat oil to medium-high. Add garlic and ginger, removing when they turn brown or oil is flavored.
2. Turn heat to high. Stir-fry broccoli for 1 minute, then add water, cover, and cook for 1 more minute. Uncover.
3. Stir in oyster sauce and mix well. Serve immediately.

SWEET-SOUR GREEN PEPPERS *VEGETABLE STIR-FRYING SERVES 4-5*

3-4 (12-16 oz.) medium green peppers or mixture of green and sweet red
   peppers
2 cloves garlic

SAUCE
   1 tsp. cornstarch dissolved in 1 tbsp. water
   2 tbsp. sugar
   3 tbsp. vinegar
   1 tbsp. soy sauce

3 tbsp. oil

Preparation

1. Wash peppers and slice into ⅛-inch shreds. (If you slice peppers on the inner side instead of the skin side, the cleaver or knife is not so apt to slip.)
2. Crush garlic.
3. Combine sauce ingredients.

Cooking

1. Heat oil to high. Add garlic; remove when it turns brown.
2. Turn heat to medium-high. Stir-fry green peppers until they turn a deep green. Add sauce and cook until thickened a little. Serve hot or cold.

1 lb. cauliflower
20-24 snow pea pods (optional)
1 green onion
3 cloves garlic
2 tbsp. oil
1 tbsp. soy sauce
1/2 tsp. sugar
1/4 cup chicken broth

Preparation

1. Rinse cauliflower. Cut off any dark spots. Pat dry. Break off small individual branches of cauliflower. Peel any tough skin off the stems.
2. Rinse snow pea pods. Snip strings from both ends.
3. Cut green onion into 6 sections.
4. Crush garlic.

Cooking

1. Heat oil in a pan or wok. Stir-fry cauliflower for 1 minute. Add soy sauce and sugar, and mix well. Pour in chicken broth, then add green onion and garlic. Cover and cook for 3-5 minutes over medium-high heat.
2. Uncover, add fresh snow pea pods, and cook another minute. When snow peas turn a deep green, remove pan from heat and discard green onion and garlic. Serve hot.

Hint

Cauliflower can be cooked ahead of time, then left in a covered pan or wok. Right before serving, warm up cauliflower first, then add snow peas.

BROCCOLI AND CAULIFLOWER   *VEGETABLE   STIR-FRYING   SERVES 4*

Colorful vegetables cooked in a light garlic sauce.

1/2 lb. cauliflower
1/2 lb. broccoli
1/2 carrot (2 oz.)
2 cloves garlic
2 tbsp. cornstarch dissolved in 2 1/2 tbsp. water
3 tbsp. oil
1 1/2 cups chicken broth
1 tsp. salt

Preparation

1. Rinse cauliflower and pat dry. Break into small florets, with ½ inch of stem.
2. Rinse broccoli and pat dry. Break off small branches one by one about ¼ inch below florets; peel tough skin from stems. Cut stems into ½-inch pieces.
3. Peel carrot and cut into ¼-inch pieces. (Or cut carrot into flower shapes by making vertical indentations around it before slicing.)
4. Crush garlic.
5. Dissolve cornstarch in water.

Cooking

1. Heat oil over medium-high heat. Add garlic, removing when garlic turns brown or oil is flavored.
2. Stir-fry cauliflower, broccoli, and carrot for 1 minute.
3. Add chicken broth and salt. Cook for 2-3 minutes.
4. Thicken with cornstarch mixture. When sauce is transparent, remove and serve immediately over hot rice.

Variation

Add shrimp for a one-dish meal. Peel and devein ½ lb. fresh shrimp. Marinate for 15 minutes in 1 tsp. sherry, ⅛ tsp. white pepper, ½ tsp. cornstarch, and ½ tsp. sesame oil. Stir-fry shrimp first, removing it when it turns pink; then stir-fry vegetables. Put shrimp back into pan before adding dissolved cornstarch.

WATERCRESS OR KALE   *VEGETABLE STIR-FRYING SERVES 4*

1 lb. watercress or kale or spinach
3 cloves garlic
1½ tbsp. oil
½ tsp. salt

Preparation

1. Rinse watercress in a colander. Shake off excess water.
2. Bunch together and cut into 2-inch-long pieces.
3. Crush garlic.

Cooking

1. Turn heat to high. Heat wok or skillet for 30 seconds, then add oil; swirl to coat pan evenly. Add garlic, then watercress. Stir-fry for 10 turns.
2. Add salt and mix well. Remove garlic before serving.

Hint

To prevent vitamin loss, wash vegetables *before* cutting.

Variation

If a hot, spicy taste is preferred, add chili peppers first to the oil, then proceed with garlic, etc.

SNOW PEA PODS WITH MUSHROOMS

VEGETABLE   STIR-FRYING   SERVES 4

A delicious combination.

> 1/2 lb. fresh mushrooms or 10-12 Chinese dried mushrooms
> 1/2 lb. fresh snow pea pods
> 1 tsp. cornstarch dissolved in 2 tsp. water
> 2 tbsp. oil
> 1/2 tsp. salt
> 1/2 cup chicken broth or 1/4 cup broth plus 1/4 cup strained mushroom water
> 1/4 tsp. sesame oil

Preparation

1. Wash fresh mushrooms and cut large ones in half; or soak dried mushrooms in warm water for 20 minutes, then remove stems.
2. Rinse fresh pea pods, snip off the strings from both ends, and pat dry.
3. Dissolve cornstarch in water.

Cooking

1. Heat oil over high heat. Stir-fry snow pea pods for 30 seconds or until they turn deep green. Remove pods but leave oil in wok or pan.
2. Reheat oil. Stir-fry mushrooms for 5-6 turns. Add salt and soy sauce, mixing well.
3. Add chicken broth and strained mushroom water. Bring to a boil and return the snow pea pods. Stir in dissolved cornstarch and cook until sauce becomes transparent.
4. Add sesame oil, stir well, and serve immediately.

STIR-FRIED ASPARAGUS

VEGETABLE   STIR-FRYING   SERVES 4

> 1 lb. fresh asparagus
> 3 tbsp. oil
> 1/4 tsp. salt
> 1 tsp. oyster sauce

Preparation

Wash asparagus, and cut off and discard tough ends. Slice diagonally into pieces ⅛ inch thick and 2 inches long.

Cooking

Heat oil on high in wok or pan. Stir-fry asparagus for about 10 turns. Add salt and oyster sauce. Stir-fry until the asparagus changes to a deep green.

VEGETARIAN'S GARDEN

Assorted vegetables stir-fried and then cooked in a flavorful sauce.

> 8 wood ears or 4 cloud ears (optional)
> 20-24 fresh or frozen snow pea pods
> 6 oz. broccoli
> 4 oz. cauliflower (20 small florets)
> 2½ oz. canned button mushrooms or fresh mushrooms or canned straw
>   mushrooms
> ½ carrot
> 8 water chestnuts
> 1 tbsp. cornstarch dissolved in 2 tbsp. water
> 1 tbsp. oil
> 1 tsp. salt
> 1 cup chicken broth

Preparation

1. Soak wood ears in warm water for 20 minutes; when softened, snip off hard tips, rinse, and drain. Or slice cloud ears into 4 pieces.
2. Rinse fresh snow pea pods. Snip strings from both ends. If frozen pea pods are used, pat them dry.
3. Rinse broccoli and pat dry. Break off the small branches one by one about 1 inch below florets. Peel tough skin off stems, and slice diagonally into ⅛-inch pieces. Rinse cauliflower and pat dry. Break off cauliflower 1 inch below florets.
4. If large fresh mushrooms are used, rinse them and cut each in half. Drain canned mushrooms.
5. Peel carrots and slice diagonally into ⅛-inch pieces.
6. Slice water chestnuts into quarters or thirds.
7. Dissolve cornstarch in water.

Cooking

1. Heat oil. Stir-fry cauliflower and broccoli for 1 minute.
2. Add mushrooms, wood ears, carrots, and water chestnuts. Add salt. Stir well.
3. Add chicken broth and pea pods. Cook until vegetables are tender. When broth is boiling, stir in dissolved cornstarch, cooking until sauce becomes transparent (approximately 1-2 minutes).

Variations

- A variety of vegetables may be used in this dish, such as radishes, canned young baby corn, potatoes, bok choy, asparagus, various types of canned mushrooms, etc. They should be cut into slices or different shapes, then cooked in the chicken broth.
- For a dish that is truly vegetarian (though it will be less tasty), you may substitute water for chicken broth.

EIGHT PRECIOUS VEGETABLES
VEGETABLE STIR-FRYING SERVES 4-6

A traditional Chinese New Year dish. The eight kinds of vegetables stir-fried together symbolize perfection. Authentically, fresh soybean sprouts are used in this dish. Because of their color, the Chinese call them "yellow bean sprouts." Soy sprouts are big and chewy. Their shape resembles the old-fashioned ornament called *ru yi,* meaning "May your wish come true." The bean sprouts available in U.S. supermarkets are mung bean sprouts, which the Chinese call "green bean sprouts."

> 1/2 oz. (30) tiger lily buds
> 1/2 oz. (14) small wood ears or 8 cloud ears
> 6 Chinese dried mushrooms
> 2 (4 oz.) carrots
> 9 white radishes or 4 oz. lobak
> 1/4 cup (1 oz.) slivered celery
> 1/4 cup (1 oz.) bamboo shoots
> 3 1/2 cups (12 oz.) fresh soybean sprouts or mung bean sprouts
> 3 tbsp. oil
> 1 tbsp. soy sauce
> 1 tsp. salt
> 2 tsp. sesame oil

Preparation

1. Soak tiger lily buds, wood ears, and dried mushrooms in warm water for 20 minutes, then drain. Cut tiger lily buds in half. Remove tough ends of wood ears; rinse and sliver. Remove stems from mushrooms and sliver.

2. Rinse carrots, radishes, and celery. Pare carrots and radishes. Sliver carrots, radishes, bamboo shoots, and celery to approximate size of bean sprouts.

3. Rinse bean sprouts in colander and shake off excess water. (In China, for a neat appearance, the root tips of the bean sprouts are snipped off one by one—a very time-consuming process.)

Cooking

1. Heat oil in wok or skillet and stir-fry bean sprouts for 1/2 minute. Add tiger lily buds, mushrooms, wood ears, and vegetables. Add soy sauce and salt, and mix well. Continue to stir-fry over high heat until liquid has evaporated.

2. Add sesame oil to cooked vegetables and mix. Serve hot or cold. For the Chinese New Year the dish is often served cold.

Main Dishes

PEPPER STEAK

Thin slices of marinated steak stir-fried with onion, green pepper, and tomato.

1 lb. flank steak

MARINADE
   1 tbsp. pale dry sherry
   4 tbsp. soy sauce
   ½ tsp. sugar
   2 tsp. cornstarch
   1 tbsp. sesame oil

2 medium green peppers
1 medium onion
2 medium tomatoes
4 slices ginger root
2 cloves garlic
6 tbsp. oil

Preparation

1. Rinse steak and pat dry. Trim off fat and membrane. Cut into 3 strips lengthwise. Then cut across grain into ⅛-inch slices.
2. Combine marinade ingredients. Marinate meat for at least 20 minutes or up to 24 hours.
3. Cut green peppers, onion, and tomatoes lengthwise into 8 strips. Separate onion into slivers.
4. Pare ginger root. Crush garlic.

Cooking

1. Heat 5 tbsp. of the oil over high heat. Add ginger and garlic; remove and discard when they turn brown. Stir in half the meat; when about 90 percent done (in approximately 50-60 seconds), remove the meat. Leave oil in pan.
2. Heat oil again and cook rest of the meat. Remove meat from pan.
3. Heat 1 tbsp. oil for 30 seconds. Lower heat to medium-high and stir-fry onion and green peppers until cooked to taste.
4. Stir in tomatoes very quickly (about 10 seconds), add meat, and mix well. Then serve.

Hints

- If the meat is cooked in one batch, the temperature of the oil drops drastically, so cooking will take much longer and the meat pieces will not be evenly cooked.
- To reheat oil without splattering, cover wok for 15-30 seconds.

Variation

This is the authentic way to stir-fry a dish. If gravy is desired, dissolve 4 tsp. cornstarch in 1 cup beef broth, then add to the dish after cooking step 4, and cook until sauce becomes transparent.

OYSTER BEEF

Tender stir-fried beef in an oyster-flavored sauce.

1 lb. flank steak

MARINADE
- 1/2 tsp. baking soda
- 2 tsp. cornstarch
- 2 tsp. sherry
- 2 tsp. water
- 2 tbsp. oil
- 1 tbsp. soy sauce

1 green onion
4 slices ginger root
2 cloves garlic

SAUCE
- 1 1/2 tsp. cornstarch dissolved in 2 tbsp. broth or water
- 1/8 tsp. pepper
- 1/4 tsp. sugar
- 1 tsp. sesame oil
- 1 tsp. dark soy sauce or 2 tsp. regular soy sauce
- 2 tsp. sherry
- 1 tbsp. oyster sauce

1/3 cup oil for stir-frying

Preparation

1. Rinse beef and pat dry. Trim off fat and membrane. Cutting with the grain, slice into 3 long strips. Then slice each strip cross-grain into slices about 1/8 inch thick.

2. Combine marinade ingredients and marinate steak for 20 minutes or up to 24 hours.

3. Cut green onion into 6 sections. Pare ginger. Crush garlic.

4. Combine sauce ingredients.

Cooking

1. Heat wok or pan until very hot. Add oil, swirling it around to coat evenly. Add green onion, ginger root, and garlic, removing them when they turn brown. Stir-fry half the beef (separating slices if necessary) until about 90 percent done (it should be brown, with no streaks of blood showing). Remove and drain beef.

2. Reheat oil and stir-fry second batch of beef. Remove and drain.

3. Turn off heat and drain oil from wok. Return wok to high heat, and add cooked beef and sauce mixture. Mix well, and serve at once with cooked rice.

Hints

- This is a quick stir-fry dish. If the movement is slow, the beef will be tough.
- The beef is cooked in two batches to avoid overcooking.
- The baking soda in the marinade tenderizes the meat.

Variation

One bunch (1 lb.) broccoli may be added around the beef. Prepare as follows:

1. Rinse broccoli and pat dry. Break off small branches one by one about 2 inches below florets. Peel tough skin off stems and slice diagonally into 1/8-inch pieces.

2. Blanch broccoli for 2 minutes in 2 cups of boiling water with 1/2 tsp. salt added. Remove and immediately rinse under cold water. Drain.

3. Arrange broccoli florets around a serving plate, stem pieces in the center. Then place oyster beef on top of the stem pieces so that it is ringed by the florets.

ONION BEEF   *MAIN DISH   STIR-FRYING   SERVES 4*

Succulent beef stir-fried with crispy onions.

> 1 lb. flank steak, sirloin, or round steak
>
> MARINADE
> 1/2 tsp. sugar
> 1/4 tsp. baking soda
> 1 tbsp. cornstarch
> 2 tsp. sherry
> 2 tbsp. soy sauce
> 1 tsp. sesame or vegetable oil
>
> 4 medium onions
> 2 green onions
> 4 slices ginger root
> 2 cloves garlic
> 5 tbsp. oil
> 4 tsp. soy sauce

Preparation

1. Rinse steak and pat dry. Trim off fat and membrane. Cut steak lengthwise into 3 strips. Slice each strip across the grain into slices about 1/8 inch thick.

2. Combine marinade ingredients and marinate meat at least 20 minutes or up to 24 hours.

3. Cut onions into 6-8 wedges; separate pieces.

4. Cut green onions into 6 sections. Pare ginger. Crush garlic.

Cooking

1. Heat wok or skillet first. Add 4 tbsp. of the oil and swirl it around. Add ginger, garlic, and green onions. Remove them when the oil is flavored.
2. Stir-fry beef in two batches; use the highest heat and stir quickly. Remove beef when 90 percent done (in approximately 50-60 seconds). Reheat wok and stir-fry the second batch. Drain, leaving oil in wok or skillet.
3. Heat 1 tbsp. oil to medium-high. Stir-fry onions to preferred doneness and crispness. Add soy sauce and mix well. When onion becomes transparent, add drained beef and quickly mix well. Remove food but leave oil in wok. Serve immediately with cooked rice.

Hints

- Baking soda is used in the marinade to tenderize the meat.
- In step 3 of preparation, if you refrigerate the onions and cut the root part last, the irritation to your eyes will be less.

JADE BEEF   *MAIN DISH   STIR-FRYING   SERVES 4*

Beef and green pepper stir-fried in hoisin sauce.

1 lb. flank steak or tenderloin, sirloin, round steak, etc.

MARINADE
1 tbsp. sherry
3 tbsp. soy sauce
½ tsp. sugar
2 tsp. cornstarch
1 tbsp. sesame or vegetable oil

3 medium green peppers
4 slices ginger root
2 cloves garlic
2 tsp. cornstarch dissolved in 4 tbsp. water
5 tbsp. oil
2 tbsp. hoisin sauce

Preparation

1. Rinse steak and pat dry. Trim off fat and membrane. Cut lengthwise into strips 1½ to 2 inches wide. Then cut strip across into ⅛-inch slices.
2. Combine marinade ingredients and marinate meat for 15 minutes or up to 24 hours.
3. Wash green peppers. Cut in half, remove seeds, and cut each half into ⅛-inch slices (or 1-inch squares).
4. Pare ginger. Crush garlic.
5. Dissolve cornstarch in water.

Cooking

1. Heat wok or skillet to high heat for 30 seconds. Then add 4 tbsp. oil and swirl it around. Add ginger and garlic. Remove them when oil is flavored.
2. Stir-fry half the meat until about 90 percent done (in approximately 50-60 seconds). Remove, leaving oil in the wok.
3. Reheat oil and stir-fry rest of meat. Remove.
4. Heat 1 tbsp. oil on medium heat to stir-fry green peppers for 1-2 minutes. Add hoisin sauce and mix well.
5. Return meat to wok. Stir well, and add dissolved cornstarch mixture. Stir to thicken juices.

BEEF WITH BROCCOLI AND ONION

MAIN DISH   STIR-FRYING   SERVES 4

1 lb. flank steak

MARINADE
   1 tbsp. sherry
   4 tbsp. soy sauce
   1/4 tsp. pepper
   1 tsp. sugar
   2 tsp. cornstarch
   1 tbsp. oil

6 stalks (1/2 lb.) broccoli
1 large or 2 medium onions
4 cloves garlic
1 tbsp. cornstarch dissolved in 2 tbsp. water
6 tbsp. oil
1 tsp. oyster sauce
1/2 cup water or beef broth
1 tsp. sesame oil

Preparation

1. Rinse steak and pat dry. Cut lengthwise into 3 strips. Slice each strip cross-grain about 1/8 inch thick.
2. Combine marinade ingredients and marinate meat for 20 minutes or up to 24 hours.
3. Rinse broccoli and pat dry. Break off small branches about 2 inches below florets. Peel tough skins from stems, and slice diagonally into 1/8-inch pieces.
4. Cut onions lengthwise into 8 parts and separate pieces.
5. Crush garlic.
6. Dissolve cornstarch in water.

Cooking

1. Heat wok or skillet first, then add 4 tbsp. oil. Add garlic until it flavors the oil; then remove.

2. Over high heat, stir in half the meat. Remove it when no sign of pink remains.

3. Stir-fry second half of the meat and remove.

4. Add 2 tbsp. oil to wok. Stir-fry broccoli and onions. Add oyster sauce and cook for 2 minutes. Then add beef; mix well. Add water or broth. When liquid boils, push food to sides. In the center, thicken liquid with cornstarch mixture; then mix with food.

5. Add sesame oil and serve immediately.

Variation

A sweet red pepper may be added to this recipe for a more colorful appearance.

SWEET-SOUR STEAK

1 lb. round steak or sirloin tip steak

MARINADE
  1/2 tsp. salt
  1/2 tsp. baking soda
  2 tbsp. cornstarch
  1 tbsp. soy sauce
  1 tbsp. sherry
  3 tbsp. oil
  1/4 cup water

1 whole onion
1 green pepper
8 cherry tomatoes or 1 tomato
1 green onion
2 slices ginger root
2 cloves garlic

SWEET-SOUR SAUCE
  2 tbsp. soy sauce
  3 tbsp. sugar
  2 tbsp. vinegar
  1 tbsp. sherry
  2 tsp. cornstarch dissolved in 2 tbsp. pineapple juice

5 tbsp. oil
2 oz. unsweetened pineapple chunks, drained

Preparation

1. Rinse steak and pat dry. Tenderize by pounding. Then cut into 8 or 9 pieces about 2 by 3 inches.
2. Combine marinade ingredients and marinate steak for 2 hours.
3. Cube onion and green pepper. Wash tomatoes. If one large tomato is used, cut into 6-8 sections.
4. Cut green onion into 6 sections. Pare ginger root. Crush garlic.
5. Make sweet-sour sauce by measuring ingredients into a small bowl.

Cooking

1. Heat 3 tbsp. oil in skillet. Pan-fry meat until both sides turn brown, approximately 2-3 minutes.
2. Heat 2 tbsp. oil in another skillet or wok. Add green onion, ginger root, and garlic, removing when oil has become flavored. Add green pepper and onion cubes. Stir-fry for 1-2 minutes, then add cherry tomatoes and pineapple chunks. Mix well.
3. Add sauce and cook until thickened.
4. Pour sauce over hot steak pieces and serve.

Variation

Marinated steaks can be served alone (after cooking step 1) as a meat dish, without sauce or vegetables.

BEEF CHOP SUEY
MAIN DISH   STIR-FRYING   SERVES 2

Succulent meat stir-fried with fresh vegetables.

1/2 lb. flank steak or round tip

MARINADE
   4 tsp. soy sauce
   1 tsp. cornstarch
   1 tsp. sesame oil

1/4 lb. bok choy
3 ribs (4 oz.) celery
8 water chestnuts
4 oz. fresh bean sprouts (optional)
1 tbsp. cornstarch dissolved in 2 tbsp. water
3 tbsp. oil
1/2 tsp. salt
1 tsp. soy sauce
1/2 cup beef broth
1/4 tsp. mild curry powder
1/8 tsp. pepper
1/8 tsp. sesame oil
1 oz. fried almond chips (See hint.)

Preparation

1. Rinse steak and pat dry. Cut flank steak lengthwise into 3 strips, then cut across into ⅛-inch pieces. Marinate beef for 20 minutes.
2. Rinse bok choy and celery, and pat dry. Slice them diagonally into ⅛-inch slices. Cut each water chestnut into 2 or 3 slices.
3. Rinse bean sprouts and drain.
4. Dissolve cornstarch in water.

Cooking

1. Heat oil in wok or pan on high heat, swirling oil around. Stir-fry half of beef for 1 minute, then remove. Stir-fry remaining meat and remove. Drain oil into wok or pan.
2. Stir-fry bok choy, celery, water chestnuts, and bean sprouts for 1 minute. Add salt and soy sauce, and mix well.
3. Add meat and broth; cook for another minute. Stir in cornstarch and mix well.
4. Sprinkle curry powder and sesame oil on top; mix again.
5. Sprinkle almond chips on top and serve immediately over rice.

Hint

Deep-fry almond chips in oil, removing with a slotted spoon. Drain and cool. Almond chips may be fried ahead of time, then when cooled, placed in a covered clean jar. Use as a garnish or snack.

RED-COOKED BEEF

MAIN DISH   RED-COOKING   SERVES 4

Tender, chunky meat simmered in a rich, aromatic sauce. It can be served either hot or cold.

> 2 lbs. beef stew or boneless shank or beef chuck
> 3 green onions
> 2 slices ginger root
> 1 whole star anise or 4 broken sections
> ½ tsp. Sichuan peppercorns
> 6 tbsp. soy sauce
> 2 cups beef broth or water
> 1 tsp. salt
> 1½ tsp. sugar
> 1 tbsp. sherry

Preparation

1. Cut beef into bite-sized cubes, each 1-1½ inches.
2. Soak beef in cold water for 15 minutes to release blood. Rinse.
3. Wash green onions and tie into knots. Pare ginger.

Cooking

1. Put beef in a pot, cover with water, and cook for 5 minutes. Pour off water and rinse scum from meat.

2. Put beef and all other ingredients into a clean pot. Cover and simmer for 2½ hours. Discard green onions, ginger, star anise, and peppercorns.

Hint

Beef may be cooked a few days ahead.

Variation

Whole dried chili peppers may be added for a hot, spicy flavor. Remove them after cooking.

SWEET-SOUR PORK
MAIN DISH   DEEP-FRYING   SERVES 4

A favorite Cantonese dish. Batter-dipped and deep-fried cubes of lean pork, topped with sesame seeds served with colorful vegetables and in a sweet-sour sauce.

> 1 lb. pork tenderloin or boneless lean loin
> 1 tbsp. sherry
> 1 tsp. salt
> ¼ tsp. pepper
> 2 green or sweet red peppers
> 2 tomatoes or 15 cherry tomatoes
> 1 cup (8-oz. can) unsweetened pineapple chunks
>
> SAUCE
> 2 tbsp. cornstarch dissolved in 2 tbsp. water
> ½ cup water
> ½ cup sugar
> 6 tbsp. vinegar
> ¼ cup ketchup
> 4 tsp. soy sauce
> 2 tsp. sesame oil
>
> BATTER
> 1-1½ bags Super Batter Mix (see page 31) or:
> ¾ cup flour
> ¼ cup cornstarch
> 1½ tsp. baking powder
> 1 egg
> 7 oz. water
> 2 tsp. oil
>
> 2 tbsp. sesame seeds
> oil for deep-frying

Preparation

1. Tenderize pork by pounding, and cut into 1-inch cubes. Pour sherry over cubes, add salt and pepper, and let stand for 15 minutes.
2. Cube green peppers. Cut tomatoes into 6 or 8 parts. Drain pineapple.
3. Combine sauce ingredients.
4. Mix batter.
5. Toast sesame seeds in a clean pan over medium-high heat, shaking pan often, until they are lightly browned.

Cooking

1. Heat oil to very high, then turn to medium heat. Dip pork into batter and deep-fry until it turns a bit brown (about 3 minutes). Remove pork and drain on a rack or in a strainer, with a pan or pot underneath to catch the dripping oil.
2. Reheat oil to high. Ladle out crumbs and return pork pieces to oil for crispness. Remove and drain. Put meat in a serving dish. Sprinkle toasted sesame seeds on top.
3. Add 3 tbsp. oil to another wok or pan (or use the deep-fry wok but drain all oil except 3 tbsp.). Stir-fry pepper, pineapple, and tomatoes in oil, then add sweet-sour sauce and cook until thickened. Reserve sauce for dipping.

STOVETOP SWEET-SOUR
SPARERIBS
MAIN DISH/APPETIZER   RED-COOKING   SERVES 2-3

Tender ribs braised in a savory sauce.

1 lb. pork back ribs or spareribs (Ask butcher to cross-cut ribs in half.)
2 slices ginger root
2 tbsp. sherry
3 tbsp. sugar
3 tbsp. vinegar
3 tbsp. water
4 tbsp. dark soy sauce or 6 tbsp. regular soy sauce

Preparation

1. Rinse ribs well. Put them in a pan of boiling water and cook for 1 minute. Remove and rinse ribs.
2. Cut ribs between bones.
3. Either wash pot clean or have another pot ready.

Cooking

Place the ribs in a pot and add all the ingredients. Cover and cook over medium-low heat until ribs are tender and sauce is mostly absorbed, approximately 1 hour.

- This dish may be cooked ahead of time and refrigerated. Before serving, remove fat and reheat.
- To cook 1½-2 lbs. spareribs, prepare 1½ times the seasonings.

BONELESS PORK CHOPS

MAIN DISH   PAN-FRYING   SERVES 4

Crusty, bite-sized pieces. Delicious!

1-1½ lbs. pork loin chops (5 chops)
1 tbsp. sherry
1 tsp. garlic salt
1 tsp. pepper
5 tsp. oyster sauce or soy sauce
2 tbsp. flour
1 cup dried bread crumbs
1 egg
½ cup oil for frying

Preparation

1. Rinse pork chops and pat dry. Remove bones from chops. Pound meat with a mallet or the blunt side of a cleaver to tenderize and loosen texture, until meat is twice the size of original chop and much thinner.
2. Arrange pieces of meat side by side. Add sherry, then sprinkle garlic salt and pepper on both sides of each piece.
3. Use pastry brush to brush oyster sauce or soy sauce on both sides of the first piece of meat; then stack another piece and brush only the top. Continue to stack, brushing only the top of each piece.
4. Spread flour and bread crumbs on two separate plates or pieces of wax paper.
5. Beat egg to a lemon-yellow color.
6. Coat meat with flour, then dip in beaten egg, and finally coat with bread crumbs.

Cooking

Put oil in frying pan and turn heat to high for 30 seconds. Turn heat down to medium; fry pork chops 2 or 3 at a time until browned on both sides. Cut each pork chop into 5-6 bite-sized pieces.

Hints

- The preparation work can be done to step 5. Refrigerate until ready for step 6 and cooking.

- Cutting pork chops into bite-sized pieces makes them easy to eat. At a Chinese meal there are no knives on the table, as everything has been precut to bite-size. A pair of chopsticks, a soup spoon, a plate, a soup bowl, and a rice bowl are sufficient. If your table is set in the Western style with knife and fork, then there is no need to cut the meat into pieces.
- The bones from the pork loin can be saved and used in making broth or stock, together with chicken or more pork bones.

SICHUAN PORK WITH WATER CHESTNUTS   *MAIN DISH   STIR-FRYING   SERVES 2*

Shredded pork sautéed in a hot, spicy sauce.

1/2 pound lean pork

MARINADE
  1/2 tsp. salt
  1 tsp. soy sauce
  1 tsp. sherry
  1 1/2 tsp. cornstarch

12 wood ears or 8 cloud ears
8 water chestnuts
2 green onions
4 slices ginger root
2 cloves garlic

SAUCE
  1/2 tbsp. cornstarch dissolved in 2 1/2 tbsp. water
  2 tsp. sherry
  1 tbsp. soy sauce
  1 tsp. sesame oil
  1 tbsp. sugar
  1 tbsp. vinegar
  1-2 tbsp. hot bean sauce

1/4 cup oil for stir-frying

Preparation

  1. Rinse pork and pat dry. Slice across grain into very thin slices about 1/8 inch thick, then cut them into matchstick size.
  2. Combine marinade ingredients and marinate pork for 15-30 minutes.
  3. Soak wood ears in warm water for 15 minutes. Snip off hard tips. If cloud ears are used, slice into thin pieces.
  4. Cut each water chestnut into 2 or 3 slices.
  5. Cut green onion into 6 sections. Pare ginger and crush garlic.
  6. Combine sauce ingredients.

Cooking

1. Heat oil until very hot. Add green onion, ginger root, and garlic, removing when oil is flavored.

2. Add pork and stir-fry until pork turns color. Remove pork, leaving oil in wok. (Pork may be cooked in two batches to ensure high cooking temperature.)

3. Use remaining oil in wok (add 1 tsp. oil if necessary) to stir-fry wood ears and water chestnuts. Turn several times.

4. Add pork and mix well. Add sauce and stir well. Serve with rice.

PEARL BALLS

APPETIZER/MAIN DISH   STEAMING   YIELDS 20

Delectable steamed meat balls rolled in pearly glutinous rice.

½ cup glutinous rice
12 Chinese dried shrimp (optional)
8 water chestnuts
2 green onions
4 leaves of cabbage or lettuce
¼ carrot
½ lb. ground pork

SEASONINGS
1 tsp. salt
1 tsp. sherry
1 egg
2 tsp. cornstarch
1 tsp. sesame oil
¼ tsp. pepper
¼ tsp. sugar

Preparation

1. Rinse glutinous rice until water runs clear. Soak in cold water for 1 hour. Drain and spread on a plate.

2. Soak dried shrimp in warm water for 20 minutes. Drain and chop fine.

3. Chop water chestnuts and green onions fine.

4. Cut each cabbage or lettuce leaf into 5 triangles.

5. Grate carrot. Set aside.

6. Mix pork, dried shrimp, water chestnuts, and green onions with seasonings, stirring in one direction only.

7. Use a spoon to scoop up the meat and make balls 1 inch in diameter. Roll in glutinous rice until coated. Place one ball on each cabbage or lettuce leaf.

8. Place on steamer rack or on a heatproof plate, spacing the balls ¾ inch apart.

Cooking

1. Bring 3 cups water to boil in wok. Then put in steamer rack or heatproof plate on top of rack, and cover. Steam at high heat for 20 minutes.

2. Remove lid, sprinkle specks of grated carrot on top of each ball, cover, and continue steaming for another minute. Serve hot in the steamer or on a plate.

Hints

- The preparation work can be done ahead of time. Or the meat balls can be cooked days ahead, then reheated by steaming for 5 minutes after the water comes to a boil.
- Make sure the water level is lower than the rack so that when water boils it will not get into the plate. If you need to add more water to the wok, just pour boiling water in.

OVEN-BARBECUED SPARERIBS

MAIN DISH/APPETIZER   OVEN-ROASTING

SERVES 4 AS MAIN DISH/6 AS APPETIZER

Finger-licking ribs marinated in an Oriental sauce.

3 lbs. spareribs or back ribs or country ribs
1 tbsp. salt
4 slices ginger root
2 green onions, tied in knots
2 tbsp. sherry

MARINADE
1/2 cup soy sauce
1/2 cup ketchup
1/4 cup sherry
6 tbsp. hoisin sauce
2 tbsp. sweet bean sauce
1 tbsp. oil
2 tbsp. sugar
1/4 tsp. five-spice powder (optional)
3 cloves garlic, crushed
3 slices ginger root, minced

GLAZE
1/3 cup honey
2 tbsp. pineapple juice

Preparation

1. Put spareribs in a saucepan with enough water to cover. Add salt, ginger, green onions, and sherry. Bring to a boil. Lower heat and simmer for 1 hour.

2. Pour off water. Rinse spareribs to remove scum.

3. Combine marinade ingredients and marinate spareribs for 2-24 hours,

covered and refrigerated. Make sure the meaty side of the ribs soaks in the marinade.

    4. Combine glaze ingredients.

Cooking

    1. Place spareribs in oven on a rack above a baking pan with 1 cup water in it. Bake at 375°F for 35 minutes.

    2. Use a pastry brush to glaze ribs on both sides with glaze mixture. Set oven at 450°F and put ribs back in for 5 minutes on meaty side, then 2 minutes on bony side. Serve immediately when hot. (Ribs may be kept warm in oven if not served right away.)

Hint

    The leftover marinade can be used for an oven-roasted chicken or refrigerated for later use.

CHICKEN WITH SNOW PEA PODS   *MAIN DISH   STIR-FRYING   SERVES 4*

4 chicken breast halves (1¾-2 lbs.) or 4 filleted breast halves (14-16 oz.)
4 oz. fresh or frozen snow pea pods
1 rib celery
4 oz. bamboo shoots
10 water chestnuts
1 green onion
3 cloves garlic
2 slices ginger root

SAUCE
    ½ tbsp. cornstarch dissolved in 2 tbsp. water
    1 tbsp. sherry
    2 tbsp. soy sauce
    ½ tsp. salt
    ½ tsp. sugar
    ⅛ tsp. pepper
    1 tsp. sesame oil

5 tbsp. oil for stir-frying

Preparation

    1. Bone chicken breasts. Make 2 layer cuts through each piece to form 3 thin slices. Stack all slices, then cut against the grain into strips about ¼ inch wide.

    2. Rinse snow pea pods and pat dry. Snip off strings from both ends.

    3. Rinse celery and pat dry. Slice diagonally into thin pieces ¼ inch thick.

    4. Slice bamboo shoots into thin ¼-inch pieces.

    5. Slice water chestnuts into 3 pieces.

    6. Cut green onion into 6 sections. Crush garlic. Cut ginger into ⅛-inch slices.

    7. Combine sauce ingredients.

Cooking

1. Heat 4 tbsp. oil to high heat. Add green onion, garlic, and ginger, removing when seasoning turns brown or when oil is flavored.
2. Stir-fry chicken in two batches, each batch about 45 seconds to 1 minute. Remove when chicken pieces turn white.
3. Add 1 tbsp. oil to wok, then add vegetables and stir-fry until snow peas turn a deeper green (approximately 30-45 seconds).
4. Return chicken to wok; immediately add sauce, then stir thoroughly for 30 seconds. Serve with rice.

Hint

If frozen snow pea pods are used, be sure to pat them completely dry, or they tend to become soggy.

Variation

If several slices of pork, a few shrimp, and a greater variety of vegetables are added to this dish, it then becomes a chicken sub gum dish.

CHICKEN FANTASTIC

MAIN DISH/APPETIZER   DEEP-FRYING

YIELDS 20-24 APPETIZERS/SERVES 2 AS MAIN DISH

Tender chicken fillets covered with crunchy sesame seeds and almonds.

2 filleted chicken breast halves (approx. 7-8 oz.)

MARINADE
  1 tsp. sherry
  1/2 tsp. cornstarch
  1/2 tsp. salt
  1/8 tsp. black pepper
  1 egg

1/2 cup cornstarch
1/2 cup sesame seeds
1/2 cup slice almonds
1 egg
1 cup or more oil for frying

Preparation

1. Rinse chicken and pat dry. Tenderize by placing chicken within fold of wax paper and gently pounding with mallet or blunt edge of cleaver. Cut each breast into 10-12 pieces.
2. Combine marinade ingredients and marinate chicken pieces for 20 minutes.
3. Measure 1/2 cup cornstarch into a plate. Mix sesame seeds and sliced almonds in another plate. Beat egg in a small bowl.

4. Lightly coat each chicken piece first with cornstarch on both sides, then dip in the beaten egg, and finally coat with sesame seeds and almonds.

Cooking

Heat oil to medium-high (375°F). Deep-fry chicken pieces 4 or 5 at a time until golden brown (about 45 seconds to 1 minute). Remove and drain, and serve hot.

Hints

- The preparation work may be done ahead of time. Deep-frying should be done just before serving for best results.
- Chicken may be fried, refrigerated, and then reheated on rack over foil-lined pan just before serving.
- Cooked chicken may be dipped into ketchup, mustard, or a sweet-sour sauce.
- For a large group, or to save time and effort, omit the cutting into serving pieces (preparation step 1) until after deep-frying. Or serve as a whole piece in an American-style dinner.

GONG BAO CHICKEN

MAIN DISH   STIR-FRYING   SERVES 4

A traditional Sichuan dish of stir-fried diced chicken with peanuts. Gong Bao is said to have been either the name of the man for whom this dish was first created, or the official title he held in the Ching dynasty.

2-3 oz. shelled raw peanuts or dry-roasted peanuts
1 cup oil
4 filleted chicken breast halves (14-16 oz.)

MARINADE
⅛ tsp. baking soda
1 tsp. sherry
2 tsp. cornstarch
1 tsp. oil

2 slices ginger root
3 cloves garlic
8-12 dried chili peppers

SAUCE
1 tsp. cornstarch dissolved in 1 tbsp. water
1 tbsp. sherry
2 tbsp. soy sauce
1 tsp. salt
2 tsp. sugar
2 tsp. vinegar
1 tsp. sesame oil

Preparation

1. Soak shelled raw peanuts in boiling water for 5 minutes. Remove skin and blot dry with paper towel. (Omit this step if you use dry-roasted peanuts.)
2. Heat oil in wok or pan. Deep-fry raw peanuts over medium heat till brown, then drain. (Can be done ahead of time.)
3. Pound chicken breasts with a mallet or the blunt edge of a cleaver. Dice chicken and marinate for 20 minutes or up to 24 hours.
4. Pare ginger and crush garlic; cut chili peppers into sections.
5. Mix sauce.

Cooking

1. Heat oil to high. Stir-fry chicken in two batches, separating pieces if necessary. Remove chicken when it turns white.
2. Drain oil, leaving only 2 tbsp. oil in wok. Add chili peppers and stir-fry until they turn to dark brown; then add ginger and garlic, and stir-fry for 10 seconds. Remove ginger, garlic, and chilis. Add drained chicken and sauce, and mix well.
3. Turn off heat, immediately add peanuts, mix well, and serve.

Variation

For a nonspicy taste, omit dried hot peppers.

PEPPER CHICKEN DIN

MAIN DISH   STIR-FRYING   SERVES 4

Succulent chicken cubes with vegetables. *Din* is the Cantonese word for "diced."

4 filleted chicken breast halves (14-16 oz.)

MARINADE
1 tbsp. sherry
1/2 tbsp. soy sauce
1 egg white
1 tbsp. cornstarch
1/4 tsp. salt

1 small green pepper
1 sweet red pepper
10 large or 16 small water chestnuts
2 green onions
4 slices ginger root
3 cloves garlic

SAUCE
2 tsp. cornstarch dissolved in ¼ cup chicken broth
2 tbsp. soy sauce
2 tbsp. vinegar
1½ tsp. sugar
1 tbsp. sherry

6 tbsp. oil for stir-frying

Preparation

1. Rinse chicken, pat dry, remove fat, and cut into ½-inch cubes.
2. Combine marinade ingredients and marinate chicken for 20 minutes.
3. Cut peppers into ½-inch cubes.
4. Cut water chestnuts into quarters.
5. Chop green onions. Pare ginger root. Crush garlic.
6. Combine sauce ingredients.

Cooking

1. Heat wok first, then add oil and swirl it around. Add green onions, ginger, and garlic, removing when oil is flavored or they turn brown.
2. Stir-fry chicken in two batches, each for 1 minute. Add pepper and water chestnuts for another minute, or until green pepper turns a deeper green. Add sauce and mix well. Serve with rice.

Variation

If a spicy flavoring is desired, add 6-10 dried chili peppers to the oil together with green onion, ginger, and garlic.

HUNAN CHICKEN

MAIN DISH   STIR-FRYING   SERVES 2

Tender chicken shreds stir-fried in a hot, spicy sauce.

2 chicken breast halves (approx. 14 oz.) or 2 filleted breast halves (approx. 7-8 oz.)

MARINADE
1 egg white
½ tsp. cornstarch

½ lb. (2½ cups) fresh bean sprouts
2-4 fresh chili peppers or 4-6 dried chili peppers
5 cloves garlic

SAUCE
   1 tsp. cornstarch dissolved in 1 tbsp. sherry
   ½ tsp. salt
   2 tbsp. soy sauce
   1 tbsp. vinegar

¼ cup oil
½ tsp salt (for bean sprouts)
1 tsp. sesame oil

Preparation

1. Rinse chicken and pat dry. Remove skin, and bone. Layer-cut each breast into 2 or 3 slices. Slice each piece into ⅛-inch shreds. Marinate in combined egg white and cornstarch for 20 minutes.
2. Rinse bean sprouts and drain; shake off excess water.
3. Slice chili peppers into 3 thick slices. Crush garlic.
4. Combine sauce ingredients.

Cooking

1. Heat wok or frying pan, then add ¼ cup oil. Stir-fry chicken shreds at high heat. Remove chicken when it turns white, leaving oil in wok.
2. With wok still at high heat, add chili peppers, garlic, bean sprouts, and ½ tsp. salt; mix well. Stir-fry for 1 minute. Then add chicken shreds; turn 4-5 times, add sauce, and stir well. Sprinkle sesame oil on top, remove garlic, and serve immediately with rice.

Hints

- The hot flavor of this dish depends upon the amount of chili pepper used. The fresh green hot pepper or dried red chili pepper may be used.
- Chicken may be cut into 1-inch cubes instead of shreds.

SHANGHAI-STYLE RED-COOKED CHICKEN   *MAIN DISH   RED-COOKING   SERVES 4*

Chicken cooked in a rich brown sauce.

   2-2½ lbs. chicken legs and thighs
   2 green onions
   3 slices ginger root
   2 tbsp. oil
   2 tbsp. sherry
   3 tbsp. soy sauce
   1 tbsp. sugar

Preparation

1. Rinse chicken, pat dry, and remove fat. Cut drumsticks and thighs in half.
2. Cut green onions into 6 sections. Pare ginger.

Cooking

1. Heat oil in a pot or wok. Add ginger root and green onion and stir for 15 seconds. Add chicken pieces; turn and toss until thoroughly coated with oil. (Or deep-fry chicken pieces until brown.)
2. Add sherry, soy sauce, and sugar, cover, and cook on medium heat, stirring occasionally (especially during the last 5 minutes of cooking), until tender (about 30-35 minutes).
3. Remove ginger and green onions. Serve with rice.

Hints

- This dish may be prepared ahead of time. Warm before serving.
- Spoon off fat after cooling. Sauce can be served with rice or noodles.

RED-COOKED CHICKEN WINGS   *MAIN DISH/APPETIZER   RED-COOKING   SERVES 3-4*

15 chicken wings
3 green onions
4 slices ginger root

SAUCE
  1 tbsp. bean sauce (optional)
  2 tbsp. sherry
  3 tbsp. soy sauce
  1 tsp. sugar
  2 tbsp. water

1 tbsp. oil

Preparation

1. Rinse chicken wings. Pat dry. Cut joints into 3 sections, discard the wing tips or save for broth.
2. Wash green onions, pat dry, and tie into knots. Pare ginger root.
3. Combine sauce ingredients.

Cooking

1. Heat oil to medium high, add ginger and green onions, and cook for 30 seconds.
2. Add chicken wings and turn to coat with oil. Add sauce, cover, and cook on low heat until done, about 20-25 minutes.
3. Remove green onions and ginger.

12-15 chicken wings (1 1/2-2 lbs.)
1 green onion
2 slices ginger root

SAUCE
  1 tbsp. soy sauce
  1 cup water
  1/2 tsp. salt
  1/4 tsp. pepper

1 tbsp. cornstarch dissolved in 1 tbsp. water
oil for deep-frying
1 tbsp. oyster sauce
1 tsp. sesame oil

Preparation

1. Cut chicken wings into 3 sections at joints. Discard wing tips or save for broth. Rinse chicken and pat dry.
2. Cut green onion into 6 sections. Pare ginger root.
3. Combine sauce ingredients.
4. Dissolve cornstarch in water.

Cooking

1. Deep-fry chicken wings in hot oil until golden-brown; remove.
2. Put 1 tbsp. oil in pot or wok. Stir in green onion and ginger root. Add chicken; then add sauce. Mix, cover, and cook on medium-low heat for 20 minutes.
3. Add oyster sauce and sesame oil, and mix well. Thicken a little with the dissolved cornstarch mixture. Remove green onion and ginger root. Serve with rice or noodles.

Hints

• Chicken wing tips can be frozen and cooked later to make broth.
• This dish may be cooked ahead of time. Refrigerate. Serve either hot or cold.

Variation

Add 3 peeled potatoes (1 lb.), cut into chunks, and cook together with chicken. Omit cornstarch.

Whole Cornish hen cooked in dark brown soy sauce and spices.

1¼ cups soy sauce
¼ cup water
2 tbsp. sherry
2 whole star anise or 8 broken sections
1 tsp. Sichuan peppercorn
1 Rock Cornish hen or 6-8 drumsticks (1½ lbs.)
1 whole green onion, tied in a knot
1-2 tsp. sesame oil

Preparation

1. Measure soy sauce, water, sherry, star anise, and peppercorns into a 1½-qt. pot large enough to hold hen.
2. Rinse hen, remove fat, and then soak hen in seasonings in pot for 20-30 minutes. Be sure to turn it once during this time.

Cooking

1. Remove hen from pot.
2. Add green onion to mixture in pot. Bring to a boil; then replace hen in mixture, breast side down. Cover. Cook 8-10 minutes over moderate heat.
3. Turn hen over, cover, and cook for another 7-8 minutes.
4. Turn off heat. Let pot stand, covered, for 10 minutes.
5. Remove hen from sauce. Let cool, then brush with sesame oil. Cut into pieces and serve.

Hints

- Cooked hen may be placed in a plastic bag or covered dish and refrigerated for several hours or overnight, then cut or chopped into pieces before serving cold.
- Another Cornish hen may be cooked with the remaining juice and frozen for future use. After complete thawing, brush with sesame oil and cut into pieces.
- The remaining juice can be frozen or refrigerated after being strained through a coffee filter either in a funnel or in a strainer.

Steamed chicken with a subtle flavor. Fu Yang is a town situated on the beautiful Fu Chun River in Zhejiang (Chekiang) Province. The Chinese consider it my hometown even though I was born in Shanghai and have never been to Fu Yang. In China, when people ask you where you are from, you name the place your ancestors were from instead of the place where you were actually born. (Suppose you were born in Chicago, but your ancestors were born in New York City and had lived in New York City for generations; according to Chinese, you would be a New Yorker, not a Chicagoan.) I assume that in olden days the family lived in a place for generations, as there was little mobility. It is easy in China to trace one's family tree. In large cities in China and overseas, if a large group of people are from the same town, they often form an association for social gatherings and to do some charitable work.

> 4 chicken legs and thighs or other chicken parts (1 ½-2 lbs.)
> 1 tbsp. salt
> 1 tsp. Sichuan peppercorns
> 1 tsp. sherry

Preparation

1. Rinse chicken and remove fat. Sprinkle salt over chicken legs and thighs on both sides.
2. Refrigerate overnight.

Cooking

1. Place chicken in a bowl. Add Sichuan peppercorns and sherry. Put bowl in a bamboo steamer or on a rack in a wok to steam over boiling water for 20-25 minutes.
2. Turn off heat and keep covered for 10 more minutes.
3. When cool, chop into 2-inch pieces, or remove the bone, cut into pieces, and serve.

Hint

Traditionally, salt and peppercorns are first stir-fried without oil in the wok until the peppercorns have released their fragrance (about 3-4 minutes); then they are rubbed onto meat or poultry. The recipe here omits this step, as the flavor of peppercorns are released through the steaming process, although to a lesser extent.

Tender chunks of chicken stir-fried with vegetables. *Kow* is the Cantonese word for "chunks."

4 filleted chicken breast halves (14-16 oz.)
2 medium green peppers
1 medium sweet red pepper
2 medium onions
10 fresh mushrooms
6 water chestnuts
1 green onion
3 cloves garlic
2 slices ginger root

SEASONINGS
  1 tbsp. sherry
  2 tbsp. soy sauce
  1/2 tsp. sugar
  1/4 tsp. salt
  1/8 tsp. pepper
  1 tsp. sesame oil

1 1/2 tbsp. cornstarch dissolved in 1 cup chicken broth
1/4 cup oil

Preparation

1. Rinse chicken and pat dry. Cut into chunks.
2. Wash green and red peppers and cut into cubes.
3. Cut onions into 6 wedges and then cross-cut.
4. Wash mushrooms and cut large ones in quarters. Cut water chestnuts into quarters.
5. Cut green onions into 6 sections. Crush garlic. Pare ginger root.
6. Combine seasoning ingredients.
7. Dissolve cornstarch first with 3 tbsp. chicken broth; then add the rest of the broth and mix well.

Cooking

1. Heat oil to high and swirl it around to coat wok. Add green onion, garlic, and ginger root, removing when they turn brown or when oil is flavored.
2. Stir-fry chicken in two batches. Remove pieces when they turn white, draining oil into wok or pan.
3. Stir-fry green and red peppers, onion, mushrooms, and water chestnuts for 1 minute.
4. Add chicken and seasonings; mix well. Immediately add the cornstarch-broth mixture and stir until thickened. Serve hot over rice.

MOO GOO GAI PAN

In Cantonese, *moo goo* means mushrooms, *gai* means chicken, *pan* means slices. Therefore, this is a dish of chicken slices with mushrooms.

4 filleted chicken breast halves (14-16 oz.)

MARINADE
2 tsp. cornstarch
$1/2$ tsp. salt
1 tsp. sherry
1 egg white

2 ribs celery
$1/4$ cup (2 oz.) bamboo shoots
8 water chestnuts
$4^{1}/_{2}$ oz. canned mushrooms, sliced
3 slices ginger root
2 cloves garlic

SAUCE
2 tbsp. soy sauce
2 tsp. sherry
$1/2$ tsp. sesame oil
$1/4$ tsp. black pepper

2 tsp. cornstarch dissolved in $1/2$ cup chicken broth
5 tbsp. oil

Preparation

1. Layer-cut each chicken piece into 2-3 slices, and slice against the grain into 1-inch pieces.

2. Combine marinade ingredients, marinate chicken for 20 minutes.

3. Cut celery diagonally into slices about $1/2$ inch thick. Slice bamboo shoots into $1/8$-inch pieces.

4. Slice water chestnuts into halves. Drain canned mushrooms.

5. Pare ginger. Crush garlic.

6. Combine sauce ingredients.

7. Dissolve cornstarch in chicken broth.

Cooking

1. Heat oil to high heat. Add garlic and ginger; remove when oil is flavored.

2. Stir-fry chicken in two batches until pieces turn white, then remove.

3. Stir-fry mushrooms, water chestnuts, and bamboo shoots. Add sauce and mix well. Add chicken and cornstarch-broth mixture until sauce bubbles. Serve hot over rice.

BEER DUCK

4-5 lbs. duck
¼ cup sherry
1½ tbsp. salt
2 green onions, tied in knots
4 slices ginger root
3-4 cabbage leaves
12 oz. beer

Preparation

1. Rinse duck well and remove fat. Pat dry.

2. Rub sherry all over duck, both inside and out.

3. Rub salt all over duck, inside and out. Place knotted green onions and ginger root slices inside the cavity. Let duck stand in refrigerator for 30-60 minutes.

Cooking

1. Turn oven to 400°F. Line roasting pan with cabbage leaves. Place duck in pan, breast side up. Pour half of beer over duck slowly as you rub beer into skin; then turn duck over and use remaining beer, rubbing it into back. Leave beer in baking pan. Slide pan into oven and roast for 1 hour. After an hour the beer will have evaporated.

2. Remove roasting pan from oven, and remove duck and lining. Drain oil from pan and duck cavity. Place duck on an oiled rack. Add 3 cups water to pan to eliminate oil fumes; turn heat to 425°, and roast for 50 minutes, then turn duck over for 10-15 more minutes. Remove duck. Take green onion and ginger from cavity and discard.

3. Garnish whole duck with parsley, cherry, and pineapple pieces, and serve. Or chop the duck into bite-size pieces and serve with rice or Mandarin pancakes, or dip in hoisin sauce.

Hints

- Lining the baking pan with cabbage leaves prevents the duck's skin from sticking to the pan.
- Oiling the baking rack prevents the skin from tearing.
- If dinner is delayed, the duck can be kept in oven at 250° for another 30 minutes; turn it occasionally.

Roast duck with crispy aromatic skin and tender, juicy meat. Long Island duckling is the preferred choice for this dish. It is believed to be the descendant of the Peking duck, for in the 1870s a sea captain brought twenty-one ducks from China to the United States, and a few of them ended up in Long Island.

> 4-5 lb. duck
> 2 tsp. salt
> 1/4 cup vodka or gin
> 1/3 cup sugar dissolved in 2/3 cup water
> 1 bunch green onions

Preparation

1. Wash duck to rinse off residual blood. Remove fat. Wipe duck thoroughly dry.
2. Rub duck cavity with salt.
3. Rub duck skin with vodka or gin. Let stand 2-3 hours. Then hang duck up to dry in a cool, drafty place for 4-6 hours. (Place a large foil-lined pan below the duck to catch the drippings.)
4. Dissolve sugar in 2/3 cup water and rub it evenly all over duck. Hang duck up again in a cool, drafty place until it is dried out (at least 12 hours and up to 24 hours).

Cooking

1. Put 3 cups of water in a baking pan, and place duck on an oiled rack well above the pan, breast side down. Wrap wings with foil. Turn oven to 250°F and roast for 1 hour. The pan will catch the fatty drippings.
2. Turn heat up to 375°, turn duck over, and roast for another hour. Turn off heat, remove rack with duck, and set aside while emptying grease from pan.
3. Add 2 cups water to pan. Turn duck over (breast down) and roast 1/2 hour at 400°. Then turn over and roast another 1/2 hour.
4. Remove duck from oven and let stand for 5 minutes for easier handling. (The skin will become crisper.) Remove foil. Slice the skin off into large pieces, then cut into pieces 1 1/2 by 2 1/2 inches. Carve meat into bite-sized pieces.

Hints

- Serve with Mandarin pancakes, a dish of Green Onion Brushes (see below), and hoisin sauce. Take a pancake and split it into two separate round pancakes (if you have not already separated them before serving). Place one piece of pancake on the plate or in the left palm. Dip onion brush in the hoisin sauce, and brush the sauce on the pancake. Then place the onion brush in the center of the pancake. Add 1 or 2 pieces of duck skin and/or duck meat, roll the pancake up, tuck in the ends, and eat.
- Instead of Mandarin pancakes, you can serve steamed rolls with this dish.

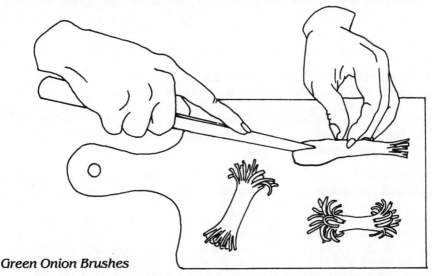

Green Onion Brushes

Wash green onions. Use the lower 3½-inch length of the white part of the onion. Using either end of a cleaver blade (or any knife), slash one or both ends of the onion through the outer skin to the center in 1-inch-long cuts as fine as possible. Then soak the onion ends in ice water. The brushes will form almost immediately. The longer they soak in water, the curlier the onion tips become; sometimes they look like cascades.

CRAB EGG FU YUNG

MAIN DISH   PAN-FRYING   SERVES 4

A delectable omelet filled with crab meat and vegetables.

½ cup (2 oz.) bamboo shoots
1 medium onion (½ cup sliced)
4 oz. fresh mushrooms
6 eggs
1 tbsp. cornstarch
1 tbsp. sherry
1 tbsp. soy sauce
1 tsp. salt
½ tsp. pepper
2 tbsp. oil for stir-frying
6½ oz. canned crab meat or 6 oz. frozen crab meat
3½ tbsp. oil for pan-frying

Preparation

1. Shred bamboo shoots to matchstick size (⅛″ × 1½″).
2. Cut off both ends of onion and slice lengthwise into thin strips.
3. Slice each mushroom into 3 or 4 slices.
4. Beat eggs in a bowl.
5. Mix cornstarch with sherry, then add soy sauce, salt, pepper, and eggs. Mix well.

Cooking

1. Heat 2 tbsp. oil. Stir-fry vegetables for 1 minute. Remove and cool.
2. Add vegetables and drained crab meat to eggs; mix well.
3. Heat 3½ tbsp. oil in a frying pan, then turn to medium heat. Pour egg mixture into the oil as you would pancakes. (You may pan-fry in two batches.) When edge becomes brown, turn over once. Remove when both sides are browned. Cut into wedges and serve.

POACHED TROUT

MAIN DISH   POACHING   SERVES 2-3

Tender fish in a flavorful light sauce. The cooking method used here is actually a variation of poaching in which the heat is turned off immediately after coming to a boil, so that the fish cooks in the retained heat of the cooling water. Because of its symbolic meaning, fish is a "must" dish for the Chinese New Year. The Mandarin word for fish is *yu*, which sounds the same as the word meaning "plenty, and some to spare." To serve fish symbolizes the auspiciousness of the coming year and the eternal abundance of the material needs in life.

2-3 frozen rainbow trout (10-16 oz.)
1 tbsp. sherry
3 green onions
3 slices ginger root

SAUCE
  3 tbsp. soy sauce
  1 tbsp. sherry
  2 tbsp. water
  ½ tsp. sugar
  ⅛ tsp. white pepper

2 tbsp. oil

Preparation

1. Defrost and rinse trout. Pour sherry over them.
2. Shred green onions into thin strips. Pare ginger root.
3. Combine sauce ingredients.

Cooking

1. Place a large pot (or a pan or enamel roaster large enough to hold entire fish) on stove. Add ginger slices and water to a depth of 2½ inches, then bring to a rapid boil.
2. Place trout in the rapidly boiling water and immediately cover. Turn off heat. Keep covered for 6-8 minutes or until eyes turn white. Carefully transfer trout to a serving dish. Sprinkle shredded green onions on top.

3. In a saucepan or wok, heat oil, then add the sauce. Immediately cover with a lid to prevent splatters. Cook sauce for 30 seconds, then pour over the trout and green onions. Serve immediately.

STEAMED FISH

Tender, succulent fish in a light, green-onion-flavored sauce.

1-1½ lbs. fresh catfish, shad, any white-meat fish, or any fish fillets
1 tbsp. sherry
3 slices ginger root
3 green onions
1 tsp. salt
1-2 tsp. soy sauce
¼ tsp. salt (optional)
3 tbsp. oil

Preparation

1. Rinse fish and place on a heatproof plate. Add sherry to fish, and place ginger slices on top.
2. Shred green onions and mix well with 1 tsp. salt.

Cooking

1. Put 2-3 inches of water into a wok, large pot, or enamel roaster. Turn heat to high and bring water to a rapid boil.
2. Place fish plate on the steam rack or on a rack or stand, cover, and steam 12-15 minutes. (For fish fillets, steam 6-8 minutes.)
3. When fish is cooked, remove plate from steamer and pour excess liquid from the plate.
4. Sprinkle ¼ tsp. salt if desired on both sides of fish, and add soy sauce. Then place salted green onion shreds on top of the fish.
5. Heat oil in a frying pan until very, very hot. Turn off heat and pour oil over fish. Serve immediately.

Hints

- To serve one person, use a ½-lb. fish, divide the seasoning ingredients in half, and steam for 8 minutes.
- If fish has a very strong odor, do the following before preparing recipe: Rinse fish under cold water, pat dry, and place on a plate. Sprinkle 1 tbsp. sherry and 1 tsp. salt over both sides of fish. Let stand for 3 minutes. Rinse off salt and sherry. This will help to eliminate the fishy smell.

Scrumptious shrimp coated with a brown garlic sauce.

> 1 lb. fresh shrimp in the shell
> 2 green onions
> 2 slices ginger root
> 3 cloves garlic
> 2 tbsp. oil
> 1 tbsp. sherry
> 1 tbsp. soy sauce
> 2 tsp. sugar
> 1 tsp. hoisin sauce

Preparation

1. Use a knife or scissors to cut open the back of the shells enough to devein. Wash and pat dry.

2. Chop green onions into ⅛-inch pieces. Pare ginger. Crush garlic.

Cooking

1. Heat oil to high. Add ginger and garlic, removing when they turn brown.

2. Add shrimp; turn them over when they turn pink. Add sherry, soy sauce, sugar, and hoisin sauce directly to the shrimp. Stir-fry for 1-2 minutes, then turn off heat. (Large shrimp require a little more time). Sprinkle chopped green onions on top and mix well. Serve immediately as a main dish.

Hints

- The Chinese prefer to cook shrimp in the shell for two reasons: (1) Shrimp shells produce a savory flavor and thus enhance the taste of the shrimp, and (2) cooking in the shell seals in the juice of the shrimp.
- If kept refrigerated overnight, with shells peeled off, this dish can be served with cocktails as an appetizer.

There is no lobster in this Cantonese dish, which is a blend of shrimp and pork in a seasoned egg sauce. (The sauce is designed to be served with lobster, hence its name.)

1 lb. medium fresh shrimp
1 tbsp. fermented black beans
1 egg
1/2 tsp. sherry
1 green onion
3 slices ginger root
2 cloves garlic
1 1/2 tbsp. cornstarch dissolved in 3 tbsp. water
3 tbsp. oil
1/4 lb. lean ground pork
1 tbsp. soy sauce
1/2 tsp. salt
1/8 tsp. black pepper
1 cup chicken broth
1/4 tsp. sesame oil (optional)

Preparation

1. Shell shrimp completely. Cut the back of the shrimp halfway and devein. Wash and pat dry.
2. Soak fermented black beans in warm water for 10 minutes. Drain and pat dry.
3. Beat egg. Add sherry to egg.
4. Chop green onion. Pare ginger and crush garlic.
5. Dissolve cornstarch in water.

Cooking

1. Heat 3 tbsp. oil. Stir in ginger and garlic, removing when they turn brown. Add fermented black beans and stir for a few seconds. Add ground pork and stir-fry. When pork is half-cooked, add shrimp and soy sauce, salt, and pepper. Stir well.
2. Add chicken broth; cover and bring to a boil. Stir cornstarch mixture again and add to the shrimp mixture.
3. When sauce becomes transparent, slowly pour in egg. Mix with shrimp mixture. Turn off heat.
4. Sprinkle green onions on top; add sesame oil if desired. Serve with rice.

Scrumptious crab meat treats.

> **3-4 lbs.** king crab or queen crab legs or crab claws
> **2 tbsp.** sherry
>
> DIPPING SAUCE
> 1 piece (2″ × 2″) fresh ginger root
> ¼ cup vinegar

Preparation

1. Rinse crab legs or claws. For large legs, cut at the joint.

2. Pare ginger root. Either grate it fine or cut into ⅛-inch slices, stack, and cut into ⅛-inch shreds. Place in a dish and add vinegar; seal with plastic wrap until ready to use.

Cooking

1. Put 1½ inches of water in an enamel roasting pan and place pan on both front and rear burners, or add water to dutch oven, or wok. Bring water to a boil.

2. Place a rack in pan, dutch oven, or wok and place crab legs on a heatproof plate on top of rack. Cover and steam for 4-5 minutes. Or use a steamer to steam. Serve immediately with vinegar-and-ginger dipping sauce.

Hints

- Provide a nutcracker and nut picks to help diners crack the shells and remove the meat.
- Left-over crabmeat can be used as a salad dish, for garnishing, or for crab omelet.
- A ginger-vinegar dipping sauce is traditionally served with crab. Fresh ginger is said to give a warming effect to the body, and crab is said to be a cooling food. Therefore, the dipping sauce not only enhances the flavor of the crab meat, but also neutralizes the cooling effect on our body.
- The favorite crab dish in China is steamed fresh blue crab, preferably the female crabs, especially in the fall season since the roe contained in the shell delight a gourmet's palate. One tells the female from the male crab by looking at the flap over the abdomen. The female's flap is round and wide, with several horizontal lines on it; the male crab has a long, narrower and pointed flap. Sometimes I steam Maryland blue crab for about 20-25 minutes with beer and seafood seasoning, which is also delicious.

Scallops with mushrooms and snow pea pods in oyster sauce.

1 lb. fresh scallops
1 tsp. baking soda
4 oz. fresh mushrooms
24 snow pea pods
1 green onion
2 slices ginger root
3 cloves garlic

SAUCE
1/2 tbsp. cornstarch dissolved in 1 tbsp. water
1 tbsp. sherry
1/2 tbsp. sesame oil
1/2 tsp. salt
1/2 tsp. sugar
1/4 tsp. vinegar
1 tbsp. oyster sauce
1 tbsp. soy sauce

3 tbsp. oil for stir-frying

Preparation

1. Rinse scallops well. By making two layer cuts, slice each scallop into 3 thin pieces. Toss with baking soda and let stand for 30 minutes. Rinse well.
2. Rinse mushrooms and pat dry. Making two vertical cuts, slice each mushroom into 3 pieces.
3. Rinse snow pea pods and pat dry. Snip strings from ends.
4. Cut green onion into 3-inch pieces. Pare ginger. Crush garlic.
5. Combine sauce ingredients.

Cooking

1. Heat oil to very hot. Add ginger and garlic, removing when they turn brown.
2. Stir-fry scallops and snow pea pods about 7-8 turns. Add mushrooms and green onion; continue to stir-fry for 1 or 2 minutes. Add sauce and mix well.

Hint

Mixing baking soda with scallops gives the scallops a smooth texture and makes them tender.

Flavorful rice stir-fried with ham, egg, and water chestnuts.

> 4 oz. cooked Danish ham or ¾ cup diced leftover ham, chicken, pork, or turkey
> 8 water chestnuts
> 1 large onion
> 3 green onions
> 3 eggs
> 1 tsp. sherry
> 5 tbsp. oil
> 4 cups cold cooked rice
> ½ tsp. salt
> 2 tbsp. soy sauce
> 1 tsp. Gravy Master or Kitchen Bouquet or Chinese soy paste for coloring (optional)

Preparation

1. Dice ham. Dice water chestnuts.
2. Cut onion into wedges, then dice them.
3. Chop green onions into ¼-inch pieces.
4. Beat eggs to lemon-yellow color. Add sherry.

Cooking

1. Heat 3 tbsp. oil on high heat. Stir-fry eggs very fast, as for scrambled eggs. While stirring, cut into tiny pieces. Remove egg from pan.

2. Stir-fry diced onion and water chestnuts to desired doneness. Remove.

3. Add 2 tbsp. oil and stir-fry rice 2-3 minutes. Add ham, onion, water chestnuts, green onions, salt, soy sauce, and Gravy Master. Mix well, add eggs, and serve warm.

Hints

- To make a good fried rice, the rice has to be cold. Leftover rice is ideal. If freshly cooked, hot rice is stir-fried in hot oil, the rice absorbs the oil and sticks together in a glob.
- Drier rice is preferred. Use a little less water to cook. Rinse 2 cups of long-grain rice 6 times. Add 2¼ cups water and bring to a boil (approximately 5 minutes). Then simmer for 25 minutes. Turn off heat and let it stand covered for another 25 minutes to let the cooked rice "relax." Yields 6 cups. (For steaming method, see pages 26-27.)
- Fixing fried rice is the best way to clean out refrigerator by using raw or cooked leftover ingredients.
- Fried rice served in Chinese restaurants in the United States is brown in color. Chinese soy paste is added for the coloring. It is actually optional.
- Leftover fried rice can be refrigerated for a few days. Just reheat it.
- To serve this dish as a meal-by-itself, add more meat and vegetables.

8 water chestnuts
1/4 cup frozen green peas
2 whole green onions
4 eggs
1 tsp. sherry
5 tbsp. oil
4 cups cold cooked rice
3 tbsp. oyster sauce
1 tbsp. soy sauce
1/2 tsp. salt

Preparation

1. Dice water chestnuts.
2. Blanch frozen green peas in boiling water for 1 minute, then rinse under cold water.
3. Chop green onions into 1/4-inch pieces.
4. Beat eggs to a lemon-yellow color; add sherry.

Cooking

1. Heat 3 tbsp. oil on high heat. Stir-fry eggs very fast, as for scramble eggs. While stirring, cut into tiny pieces. Remove eggs.
2. Heat 1 tbsp. oil and stir-fry water chestnuts and green peas for 1 minute; then remove from pan.
3. Add 1 tbsp. oil to pan, then add rice and stir-fry until rice is flavored (approximately 2-3 minutes). Add eggs, water chestnuts, peas, and green onions. Add oyster sauce, soy sauce, and salt; mix well.

Hint

This may be cooked ahead of time, then left covered in the pan or wok. Heat before serving.

Fried rice with beef slices and vegetables.

¼ lb. flank, round tip, sirloin tip, or top round steak

MARINADE
    1 tsp. sherry
    1 tbsp. soy sauce
    ¼ tsp. sugar
    ½ tsp. cornstarch
    ½ tsp. oil

1 medium onion
1 rib celery
2 green onions
3 eggs
½ tsp. sherry
4 cups cold cooked rice
4 tsp. soy sauce
5 tbsp. oil

Preparation

1. Rinse steak and pat dry. Cut cross-grain into ⅛-inch slices. Combine marinade ingredients and marinate steak for 15 minutes.
2. Cut onion and celery into cubes.
3. Cut green onions into ⅛-inch pieces.
4. Beat eggs; add sherry.

Cooking

1. Heat 2 tbsp. oil on high heat, and swirl it around. Scramble eggs; remove, leaving oil in wok or pan. Cut eggs into small pieces.
2. Heat 3 tbsp. oil on high heat. Stir-fry beef until brown. Remove beef, leaving oil in wok.
3. Stir-fry onion and celery for 1 minute, removing while still crisp. Leave oil in wok.
4. Stir-fry rice for 2-3 minutes, adding 1 tbsp. oil if needed. Then add soy sauce and mix well.
5. Add green onions, eggs, beef, onion, and celery. Mix well and serve warm.

One-Dish Meals

CHINESE TACO

Tasty, multitextured fillings wrapped in lettuce leaves make a satisfying meal. In China this dish is customarily made with pigeon. This recipe substitutes chicken.

4 filleted chicken breast halves (14-16 oz.)
4 oz. lean ground pork

MARINADE
 1 tbsp. sherry
 2 tbsp. soy sauce
 1 tsp. salt
 2 tsp. cornstarch
 1/2 tsp. sugar
 1/4 tsp. pepper

10 water chestnuts
1 medium green pepper
2 small onions
10 fresh mushrooms or 4 Chinese dried mushrooms
12 lettuce leaves
2 oz. rice stick noodles
1 cup oil for deep-frying
1 tbsp. soy sauce
1 tbsp. sesame oil

Preparation

 1. Mince chicken breast meat. Combine marinade ingredients, and marinate chicken and pork for at least 20 minutes.
 2. Dice water chestnuts, green pepper, onions, and mushrooms. (If Chinese dried mushrooms are used, soak them in warm water for 20 minutes. Remove stems before dicing.)
 3. Rinse lettuce and pat dry. Cut the edges into a round shape. Stack lettuce leaves like bowls (with the curved side down) in a serving dish. (This can be done ahead of time, the leaves refrigerated and arranged on a serving plate just before serving.)

Cooking

 1. Heat 1 cup oil to very high. Deep-fry rice noodles for 3 seconds. Remove, drain, and place in a serving bowl. When cool, crush noodles to the size of large crumbs. (This can be done ahead of time.)

2. Leave only 4 tbsp. oil in wok, and turn to very high heat. Stir-fry chicken and pork in two batches, each for 1-2 minutes. Remove, draining oil into wok.

3. Reheat wok (add 1 tbsp. oil if needed), then stir-fry vegetables. Add soy sauce. Return the meat to wok, add sesame oil, and stir well. Remove contents to a serving bowl, but drain juice in wok.

4. Place some fried rice noodles on a lettuce leaf, then cover with some hot meat and vegetables. Fold in half. Repeat for remaining leaves. Hold in hand and eat like tacos.

Variations

- This filling dish may be served with Mandarin pancakes instead of lettuce leaves.
- Ground beef may be substituted for the chicken and pork.
- For a fancier dish, use crabmeat.
- Try putting potato chips on top of the filling in lettuce leaf. Or substitute crushed potato chips for rice noodles.
- Fresh puffed rice cereal may be substituted if rice noodles are not available.

COLD-STYLE NOODLES   *MEAL-BY-ITSELF   BOILING   SERVES 4-5*

½ lb. cooked chicken, pork, ham, turkey, or other meat
2 egg crepes (see page 70)
2 cucumbers
½ lb. fresh bean sprouts
1 lb. Chinese dried noodles or very thin spaghetti
2 tbsp. sesame oil
¼ cup soy sauce
2 tbsp. vinegar
1 tsp. salt
2-4 tsp. hot pepper oil (optional)
½ tsp. mustard (optional)

Preparation

1. Shred cooked meat, then refrigerate.
2. Make egg crepes. When cool, shred to matchstick size.
3. Peel cucumbers and shred into thin strips, matchstick size.

Cooking

1. Boil water and blanch bean sprouts for 1 minute. Remove and rinse under cold water. Drain.

2. Cook noodles or spaghetti in boiling water until tender. Immediately rinse noodles under cold water in a colander. Drain off excess water. Mix noodles with sesame oil so that they will not stick together.

3. Cover noodles with meat, egg shreds, and vegetables.

4. Mix with soy sauce, vinegar, salt, hot oil, and mustard. Mix well and serve cold.

Hint

This dish can be prepared ahead of time and refrigerated.

BEEF CHOW MEIN

MEAL-BY-ITSELF   STIR-FRYING   SERVES 2-3

An authentic fried noodle dish.

½ lb. flank steak

MARINADE
   1 tsp. cornstarch
   1 tbsp. dark soy sauce or 2 tbsp. regular soy sauce
   1 tbsp. oil
   1 tbsp. sherry

4 Chinese dried mushrooms or 8-10 fresh mushrooms
4 ribs bok choy
1 oz. bamboo shoots
6 water chestnuts
½ carrot
2 green onions
10 snow pea pods
½ lb. Chinese dried noodles or very thin spaghetti or egg noodles
1 tbsp. sesame oil
5 tbsp. oil
¼ tsp. salt
¼ tsp. pepper
2 tbsp. soy sauce

Preparation

1. Rinse beef and pat dry. Cut into 3 strips, then cut each strip across into ⅛-inch slices. Combine marinade ingredients, and marinate steak for 20 minutes.

2. Soak Chinese mushrooms in warm water for 20 minutes; remove stems, then cut into slices. If you are using fresh mushrooms, rinse and slice them.

3. Cut bok choy, bamboo shoots, water chestnuts, and carrots diagonally into ⅛-inch slices. Cut green onions into 6 sections.

4. Snip both ends from snow pea pods and remove strings.

Cooking

1. Cook noodles in boiling water. Rinse under cold water and drain. Add sesame oil and mix well.

2. Heat 4 tbsp. oil over high heat, then stir-fry beef. Remove when cooked.

3. Add 1 tbsp. oil, then stir-fry vegetables for 1 minute. Add salt, pepper, and noodles, and stir. Add soy sauce. Mix well.

4. Add beef, mix well, and serve.

BEEF SHAO MAI   *MEAL-BY-ITSELF/DIM SUM/SNACK   STEAMING   YIELDS 32 DUMPLINGS*

Cantonese-style steamed beef dumplings.

2 Chinese dried mushrooms (optional)
2 oz. (¼ cup) bamboo shoots
8 water chestnuts
2 green onions
¼ lb. fresh or cooked shrimp
32 wonton wrappers
½ lb. lean ground beef

SEASONINGS
  1 tbsp. sherry
  4 tbsp. water
  1 tbsp. soy sauce
  ½ tsp. salt
  ⅛ tsp. pepper
  1 tsp. cornstarch
  1 tsp. sesame oil

3 leaves of lettuce, cabbage, or napa cabbage

Preparation

1. Soak dried mushrooms in warm water for 20 minutes. Drain, then mince.

2. Mince bamboo shoots, water chestnuts, and green onions.

3. Devein shrimp, rinse, pat dry, and chop fine.

4. Trim corners of wonton wrappers into round shape. Cover with a damp cloth or white paper towel to keep moist.

5. Mix beef, shrimp, bamboo shoots, water chestnuts, and green onion. Add seasonings and stir vigorously in one direction (either always clockwise or always counterclockwise) until mixture is smooth.

6. Place wonton wrapper on left palm. In center, place 2 tsp. of filling. Use fingers of right hand to make 8-10 pleats on the side of the wonton wrapper around the filling. Let the cylinder-shaped dumpling stand on a flat surface. Squeeze the center part gently. A small portion of meat mixture will be pushed up in the center. Flatten the bottom and smooth the base by gently tapping the dumpling between your palms as you turn it around.

7. Sprinkle finely chopped mushrooms on top if desired.

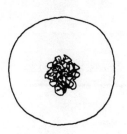 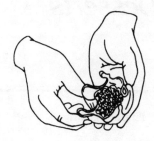 

Cooking

Place dumplings on a heatproof plate, or put directly into a bamboo steamer lined with lettuce leaves. Steam with high heat over boiling water for 10 minutes. Serve immediately.

Hints

- Ground pork may be used instead of ground beef.
- All the preparation work can be done ahead of time; cover and refrigerate before steaming.

Desserts

ALMOND DELIGHT

A refreshing gelatin with an almond flavor.

2 envelopes unflavored gelatin
1 cup sugar
pinch of salt (optional)
2 cups boiling water
$1/2$ cup evaporated milk plus $1 1/2$ cups milk (or 2 cups milk)
2-3 tbsp. almond extract
1 large can of fruit cocktail or Mandarin oranges
litchis or kumquats (optional)

Cooking

1. In a 9 × 11-inch glass baking pan, mix gelatin, sugar, and salt. Add boiling water and stir until dissolved.
2. Scald milk, then add to gelatin mixture and stir well.
3. Stir in almond·extract.
4. Cool, then chill in refrigerator until gelled. (This takes some time, so it is best to make the dessert in advance.)
5. Make crisscross cuts so that each piece will be a diamond shape.
6. Top with fruit cocktail or Mandarin oranges with a little juice. Add litchi fruits or kumquats if you wish. (See garnishing instructions below.)

Variations

- Use fresh pineapple, banana slices, and/or fresh cherries to garnish.
- For a refreshing taste, mix $1/2$ tsp. peppermint extract with 1 cup water and pour over gelatin. Garnish with fresh mint leaves instead of fruit.
- Serve in individual dishes with creme de menthe.
- Garnish with fresh fruit, as follows.

To Garnish Almond Delight

1. Rinse 7 large or 9 medium strawberries, 12 seedless grapes, 4 kumquats, and 1 blueberry.

2. Remove hulls from strawberries. Cut 6 large (8 medium) strawberries in half. Arrange them cut side down in an oblong shape 1½ inches from the rims of the dish.

3. After removing the hull from the remaining strawberry, make a flat cut at the end; then cut lengthwise into 8 sections (6 sections for medium size). To form a flower, use 5 sections with tips out. Put flower in center of gelatin.

4. Place a blueberry in the center of the flower.

5. Place a kumquat in each corner, and arrange 3 grapes around each kumquat.

6. For a moist appearance and taste, pour 4 tablespoons of juice from canned fruit cocktail onto the Almond Delight.

SWEET WONTONS
DESSERT YIELDS 24

Sweet filling sealed in a crispy wrapping.

> ½ cup chopped walnuts or pecans
> ¼ cup sugar
> ¼ cup sweet bean paste
> 24 wonton wrappers
> oil for frying

Preparation

1. Mix chopped walnuts, sugar, and sweet bean paste well.

2. Lay a wonton wrapper on a clean surface in a diamond position. Add 1½ tsp. filling in the lower center of the wrapper. Lift the lower triangle flap over the filling with the point tucked under. Fold both sides toward center, like an envelope; continue to roll. Wet the top triangle with water to seal. (Fold like an envelope.)

Cooking

Deep fry 5-6 at a time in hot oil till brown.

WATERMELON BASKET

1 large watermelon
1 cantaloupe
1 honeydew melon
seedless grapes
cherries
strawberries

Preparation

1. Wash all fruits and pat dry.
2. Cut watermelon horizontally across, leaving 2 inches in the center as a handle (as for grapefruit basket illustrated on page 187). Remove portions around handle on top.
3. Cut the edges of the watermelon basket into a zigzag design.
4. Scoop out watermelon into balls.
5. Make cantaloupe and honeydew melon balls, or slice into bite-sized pieces.
6. Place all the fruits into the watermelon basket and serve with cocktail picks.

LITCHIS ON ICE

Litchis are really fruits, although they are often called litchi (or lychee) "nuts."

1 large can litchi fruits
1 large can Mandarin oranges, drained
8-12 kumquats
crushed ice

Preparation

Serve litchi fruits, drained Mandarin oranges, and kumquats on a bed of crushed ice in a large serving bowl.

Hint

Fresh strawberries or cherries may be added for extra color.

Pastry cake coated with sesame seeds with a sweet filling.

DOUGH
- 2 cups all-purpose flour
- ⅔ cup warm water
- 6 tbsp. (3 oz.) vegetable shortening

1 can sweet red bean paste, or apricot or prune filling for pastry
white sesame seeds

Preparation

1. Mix flour, warm water, and shortening well. Let stand 15 minutes.
2. Divide dough into 20 equal portions.
3. On a floured working surface, roll each portion into a circle about 3 inches in diameter. Put 2 tsp. sweet bean paste in the center, gather edges toward the center, pinch it to enclose the filling, then press down gently.
4. Turn cake over (with the gathering folds on the bottom) and shape it into a round cake by turning it counterclockwise between your palms.
5. When 20 cakes are done, pour sesame seeds onto a piece of wax paper. Gently stick the smooth top of each cake onto the sesame seeds until it is evenly covered.

Cooking

Place 8-10 cakes in a large ungreased skillet or frying pan, leaving a little space between each cake. Place over medium to medium-low heat, cover, and cook for 8-10 minutes or until the bottom turns brown, or until you can hear the cakes moving freely when you shake the pan. Turn to the other side and heat for 7-10 minutes. Total cooking time is about 15-20 minutes. When both sides are brown, remove cakes from pan. Serve warm or cold.

Hints

- These cakes can be prepared in advance. After doing the preparation, fold the uncooked cakes in foil paper and seal well; store in freezer until ready to cook.
- The dough and the uncooked cakes can be refrigerated for a few days.
- The cakes may be baked in oven at 400°F for 18-20 minutes, but baked cakes tend to be a little drier than pan-fried ones.
- Cooled cooked cakes may be warmed up in 250°F oven for 10-12 minutes.

Variations

- You may want to serve a variety of fillings, but using different sesame seeds on the outside to identify the cakes. For example, use white sesame seeds for sweet bean paste filling; use black sesame seeds for prune filling.
- See page 66 for nonsweet versions filled with green onion and meat fillings.

Munchable crisp chews.

24 wonton wrappers
oil for deep-frying
syrup (optional)
powdered sugar (optional)

Preparation

1. Stack 6 wonton wrappers at a time, then cut in half.
2. For each stack of half-wonton wrappers, use the tip of a knife blade to make a slit in the center, stopping 1 inch from each end.
3. Hold the top corners together and push them into the slit. Then open the corners and lightly stretch them apart.

Cooking

1. Heat oil in wok or pan to high, then turn to medium-high (375°) and deep-fry 5-6 pieces at a time. Use wire strainer or slotted spoon to remove. Drain
2. Serve ungarnished as chips; or drizzle on maple or other pancake syrup, then sprinkle with toasted sesame seeds; or simply sprinkle with powdered sugar.

4

Menu Planning for All Occasions

In China, a family meal typically consists of four dishes plus soup to go with rice. Dishes are placed in the center of the table and shared communally, each person bringing food from a dish to his serving plate or directly to his own rice bowl with chopsticks.

As mentioned earlier, rice is considered the main part of the meal. Because of its heartiness, rice is even served for breakfast in certain farming areas. The most common at-home breakfast in China is rice congee—rice cooked in large amounts of water and simmered for a long time. It is served with small dishes of fried peanuts, canned pickled cucumbers and vegetables, eggs (salty or "thousand-year-old" or fresh-cooked ones), dried shredded meat, various canned goods, or freshly deep-fried long Chinese crullers.

A major difference between U.S. and Chinese eating habits lies in the status of vegetables. In the United States the price of vegetables is close to that of meat or poultry; sometimes fresh produce costs more than meat. In China, the difference between the prices of vegetables and meats is like day and night. Meat products are much more expensive. Thus the main ingredients of the traditional four-dish meal vary according to what a family can afford. Everyone can afford vegetables, and consequently they are considered "cheap" dishes. Traditionally, no vegetable dishes are served alone at a formal banquet, or to guests at any time. If there is a vegetable in a dish, it should be the most tender part of the choicest greens.

Tea is always served at the end of the meal. The Chinese do not serve water with the meal, because it is believed by the old folks that cold water consumed with rice will cause indigestion. Also, it is not advisable to add soup to rice, because people tend to swallow the rice whole without chewing. In a home-style meal, soup is served with the meal. However, in Chinese restaurants in the United States, soup is always served as the first course.

The Chinese usually serve fresh fruit as dessert. You may serve fresh or canned fruit. For a formal banquet, fruits are sliced into bite-size pieces and placed in a serving dish. For an informal occasion, you may place various fruits in fruit bowls or serving platters with paring knives for the guests to help themselves.

In figuring the amount of food to be prepared for a party, the Chinese usually count one person for one dish, then add one extra dish. In other words, for five people, you'd serve six dishes; for eight, you'd serve nine dishes. All the dishes are shared, and each person samples a portion of each dish to go with the rice.

At a formal banquet, only one dish of food is served at a time, thus it is called a "course." Twelve to sixteen courses are offered, depending upon the fanciness and extravagance desired. Liquor and/or wine are served. Normally, the four cold-plate dishes placed on the table before the guests sit down are appetizers to be eaten with drinks.

Speaking of banquets and parties, I am reminded of an interesting point of difference between Oriental and Occidental etiquette. Oriental culture emphasizes extreme modesty as a virtue. With a tableful of good food in front of you, the polite Oriental host and hostess will still apologize for not having prepared many good dishes to entertain an honorable guest like you. If compliments are paid to the cook, the gracious American hostess will accept with a simple thank-you, whereas a humble Chinese hostess would acknowledge the praise by saying, "Not that good" (meaning not adequate for exalted company like you) or "You are most kind to say that." The Chinese are taught that showing off, boasting, bragging, or exaggerating one's ability is in very bad taste.

In menu planning, variety is the basic principle to keep in mind.

Kind of food: Choose each dish's main ingredient from one of the following categories: pork, beef, chicken, duck, shelled fish, unshelled fish, dried seafood, vegetables. Avoid repetition.

Cooking methods: Use various methods so not all foods are of the same nature.

Texture: Aim for contrast, with textures that are soft, smooth, tender, crispy, crunchy, resilient, etc.

Flavor: Use sweet natural flavor, fresh, delicate, savory, rich, robust, salty, sweet, sour, hot, bitter, and spicy flavors to avoid monotony.

Shape and size of ingredients: To make foods attractive, present different sizes and shapes—whole, chunky, cubed, diced, minced, sliced, shredded, even fancy designs. The ingredients in any one dish should be about the same size and shape.

Color: Balance and contrast are used not only within one dish but for the whole meal.

Also take seasonal needs into consideration—prepare cool, light, refreshing dishes for summer, warm, heavier, stronger-flavored dishes for winter. Try to use fresh products in season.

Keeping the above in mind while considering individual preferences, total working time, and do-ahead possibilities, you can plan and synchronize a well-balanced, appetizing meal that your family and guests will rave about.

The following menus for various occasions have been planned to accommodate American custom and taste:

- Dinners for one person (8 suggestions).
- Home-style dinners, with the emphasis on balanced meals with a minimum of preparation time (50 suggestions).
- Jiffy dinners for two cooks to prepare, with enough food to serve two adults and two children (5 menus). These are designed for people who decide to cook

Chinese food on the spur of the moment. With two people working in the kitchen, the meal can be prepared in less than 30-45 minutes.

- American-style Chinese dinners for four people (2 menus).
- Dinner parties for two to six people (6 menus). For such parties I adopt the Chinese fashion of offering a variety of dishes for guests to sample, and offer some "do-ahead" suggestions for the busy hostess. Stir-fried dishes are usually done last, so that they are still warm when served. Unless food is served course by course, no more than two stir-fried dishes are recommended. Otherwise the hostess will miss all the fun and conversation while she is working in the kitchen. Combinations of two sets of home-style dinner menus can be served for four people, and three sets may be served for six. For a family gathering, you might enjoy deciding on the menu by letting everyone choose and cook his or her favorite dish.
- Buffet-style meals in which all the food is prepared ahead of time, with some warming up and steaming just before serving (3 elaborate menus and 1 simple menu).
- A ten-course banquet for eight to ten people which can be prepared by one to ten cooks and served course by course or all at once (1 menu).
- "Combined-effort" feasts for six couples or a gourmet club gathering. Everyone helps prepare the food to make the work fun and the party merrier (2 elaborate menus and 1 simpler menu).
- American-style dinner parties for twenty to forty people, with the emphasis on do-ahead, easy-to-cook, large-quantity recipes (3 menus).
- Chinese-style dinner party for twenty to forty people (1 menu).
- Three Chinese picnic menus.

$1/3$ to $1/2$ portion of Pepper Steak
Rice

$1/3$ portion of Chicken with Snow Pea Pods
Rice

$1/3$ lb. Steamed Fish
$1/2$ portion of any cold-mixing vegetable or $1/2$ portion of any stir-fried vegetable
Rice

$1/3$ to $1/2$ portion of fried rice (Additional meat and vegetables may be added to the recipe for a heartier meal.)

$1/3$ portion of Crab Egg Fu Yung
Rice

Wonton Soup
$1/3$ portion of any cold-mixing vegetable

$1/3$ to $1/2$ portion of Stovetop Sweet-Sour Spareribs or Oven-Barbecued Spareribs
Stir-fried vegetable
Rice

---

1 or 2 pieces of Boneless Pork Chop
$1/4$ portion of Vegetarian's Garden
Rice

Cucumber Salad
Pepper Steak
Rice

Chicken with Snow Pea Pods
Ham Fried Rice

Shanghai Red-Cooked Chicken
Broccoli and Cauliflower
Rice

Onion Beef
Sweet-Sour Green Pepper
Rice

Crab Egg Fu Yung
Bean Sprouts and Leek
Rice

Egg Custard
Chicken Kow
Rice

Stovetop Sweet-Sour Spareribs
Tofu with Fresh Mushrooms
Rice

Boneless Pork Chops
Vegetarian's Garden
Rice

Ham and Asparagus Salad
Steamed Fish
Rice

Gong Bao Chicken
Sichuan Cucumbers
Rice

Wonton Soup
Beef Fried Rice
Bean Sprout Salad

Radish Cold-Mixing Salad
Beef with Broccoli and Onion
Rice

Spinach Soup
Beef Chop Suey
Rice

Cold-Mixing Kohlrabi
Hunan Chicken
Rice

Shrimp with Lobster Sauce
Oriental Cauliflower
Rice

Egg Drop Soup
Sichuan Cucumbers
Oven-Barbecued Spareribs

Zucchini Soup
Red-Cooked Shrimp
Sweet-Sour Green Pepper
Rice

Sichuan Pork with Water Chestnuts
Oyster-Flavored Mushrooms
Rice

Broccoli Salad
Chicken Fantastic
Rice

Butterfly Shrimp
Broccoli Salad
Ham Fried Rice

Poached Trout
Vegetarian's Garden
Rice or Chinese Rolls

Stovetop Sweet-Sour Spareribs
Broccoli and Cauliflower
Rice

Red-Cooked Beef
Stir-Fried Asparagus
Rice

Onion Beef Snow Pea Pods with Mushrooms Rice	Poached Eggs Seasoned Turkey Slices Beef Fried Rice
Cucumber Salad Jade Beef Rice	Pepper Chicken Din Asparagus Salad Rice
Cold-Mixing Celery Oyster Beef Rice	Crab Legs Oyster-Flavored Broccoli Rice or Chinese Rolls
Stuffed Mushrooms Watercress Beef Fried Rice	Beef Shao Mai Tofu, Tomato, and Spinach Soup
Asparagus Salad Sweet-Sour Steak Oyster-Flavored Mushrooms Rice	Cold-Style Noodles Spinach Soup
	Wonton Soup Sweet-Sour Green Pepper Ham Fried Rice
Soy-Sauce Cornish Hen Snow Pea Pods with Mushrooms Rice or Chinese Rolls	Sweet-Sour Pork Watercress or Kale Rice
Radish Cold-Mixing Salad Red-Cooked Chicken Wings Spicy Tofu Rice	Scallops Supreme Bean Sprouts and Leek Rice
Oyster Chicken Wings Stir-Fried Asparagus Rice	Moo Goo Gai Pan Scrambled Egg Rice
Red-Cooked Chicken Wings Bean Sprouts in Spicy Vinegar Sauce Oyster-Flavored Fried Rice	Tofu, Tomato, and Spinach Soup Beef Chow Mein

Time-Consuming Dinners

Steamed Meat Rolls
Tasty Chicken Livers
Snow Pea Pods with Mushrooms

Pan-Fried Meat Rolls
Chicken Broth

Boiled Meat Dumplings or Steamed Dumplings
Any cold-mixing salad

Pan-Fried Dumplings
Cucumber Soup

Beer Duck
Bean Sprouts in Spicy Vinegar Sauce
Rice or Chinese Rolls

Egg Drop Soup
Jiffy Egg Rolls or Shanghai-Style Egg Rolls

Cucumber Soup
Mandarin Pancakes
Mu Shu Pork

Egg Custard
Chinese Taco

MENU 1
Egg Custard
Chicken with Snow Pea Pods
Bean Sprouts and Leek
Rice
Tea
Fresh Fruit or Ice Cream

SUGGESTED PROCEDURE

Person A: Boil water to make tea, but pour only one-third of the water over tea in pot. (Add fresh boiling water before serving.)
Person B: Cook rice.
Person A: Slice chicken; prepare green onion, garlic, and ginger; slice leek.
Person B: Beat eggs, add broth, and steam eggs (set timer).
Person A: Get snow peas and other vegetables ready for chicken dish.
Person B: Mix seasonings for chicken dish.
Person A: Stir-fry Bean Sprouts and Leek.
Person B: Stir-fry chicken dish.

MENU 2
Egg Drop Soup
Pepper Steak or any stir-fried beef dish with vegetables
Fried Rice
Tea
Fresh Fruit or Ice Cream

SUGGESTED PROCEDURE

Person A: Make fried rice. (Rice should be cold, preferably cooked the day before and refrigerated.)
Person B: Boil water to make tea as in Menu 1. Prepare ginger and garlic for Pepper Steak.
              Slice beef and marinate; slice vegetables.
Person A: Make Egg Drop Soup.
Person B: Stir-fry Pepper Steak.

MENU 3

Cold-Mixing Cucumbers
Red-Cooked Shrimp in Shells
Stir-Fried Asparagus or Tofu with Fresh Mushrooms
Rice
Tea
Fruit or Ice Cream

SUGGESTED PROCEDURE

Person A: Cook rice.
Person B: Boil water to make tea as in Menu 1.
               Rinse shrimp; devein, pat dry.
Person A: Prepare green onion, ginger, and garlic for shrimp dish. Make cucumber dish.
Person B: Prepare asparagus and stir-fry, or prepare Tofu dish.
Person A: Stir-fry shrimp.

MENU 4

Spinach Soup or Cucumber Soup
Steamed Fish or Poached Trout
Broccoli and Cauliflower
Rice
Tea
Fruit or Ice Cream

SUGGESTED PROCEDURE

Person A: Cook rice.
Person B: Boil water to make tea as in Menu 1. Also bring water to boil for use in cooking.
Person A: Prepare and cook fish.
Person B: Prepare broccoli and cauliflower, and stir-fry.
Person A: Make soup.

MENU 5

Boneless Pork Chops
Vegetarian's Garden
Rice
Tea
Ice Cream

SUGGESTED PROCEDURE

Person A: Cook rice.
Person B: Boil water to make tea as in Menu 1.
Person A: Prepare and cook pork chops.
Person B: Prepare and cook Vegetarian's Garden.

American-Style Dinners for Four

MENU 1

Appetizer: **Butterfly Shrimp** Have everything ready; deep-fry last. Or fry shrimp partially (to a light yellow) and refry to golden brown before serving.
Salad: **Radish Cold-Mixing Salad** Do ahead.
Main Dish: **Soy-Sauce Cornish Hen** Double recipe; serve cold or warm.
Starch: **Ham Fried Rice** Do ahead and leave in wok; warm up.
Vegetable: **Broccoli and Cauliflower** Do ahead, cooking until partially done; finish cooking before serving.
Dessert: **Almond Delight** Do ahead.

MENU 2

Appetizer: **Paper-Wrapped Chicken** Marinate; wrap; deep-fry last.
Salad: **Asparagus Salad** Do ahead.
Main Dish: **Boneless Pork Chops** Double recipe; prepare last.
Starch: **Beef Fried Rice** Do ahead; warm up.
Vegetable: **Bean Sprouts in Spicy Vinegar Sauce** Do ahead; serve at room temperature or cold.
Dessert: **Litchis on Ice** Have everything ready; assemble before serving.

Dinner Parties for Two to Six

MENU 1

Appetizer: **Fried Shrimp Toast** Spread mixture on bread ahead of time. Deep-fry 15 minutes before guests arrive, or cook at last minute.
Soup: **Wonton Soup** Prepare wontons ahead and freeze. Soup may be made ahead and rewarmed.

For 2 people, add Main Dish:	**Beef with Broccoli and Onion** Do preparations ahead of time; stir-fry 10 minutes before eating or right before serving.
For 3 people also add Main Dish:	**Crab Egg Fu Yung** Do ahead and leave in pan to reheat.
For 4 people also add Salad:	**Bean Sprout Salad** Double recipe and do ahead.
For 5 people also add Main Dish:	**Soy-Sauce Cornish Hen** Do ahead.
For 6 people also add Vegetable:	**Oyster-Flavored Mushrooms** Double recipe and do ahead.
Starch:	**Rice**
Dessert:	**Suzhou Cakes** Do ahead and leave in pan at low heat to keep warm before serving, or cover in foil and warm in oven. Cakes may also be served at room temperature.
	Tea

MENU 2

Soup:	**Cucumber Soup** Do ahead and rewarm.
Salad:	**Cold-Mixing Celery** Do ahead.
For 2 people add Main Dish:	**Sweet-Sour Steak** Partially cook and leave in pan; heat up to finish cooking 5 minutes before serving.
For 3 people also add Side Dish:	**Marble Eggs** Do ahead.
For 4 people also add Main Dish:	**Shrimp with Lobster Sauce** Do food ahead and leave covered in wok. Thicken sauce just before serving.
For 5 people also add Main Dish:	**Wine Chicken** Do ahead.
For 6 people also add Vegetable:	**Eight Precious Vegetables** Do ahead and reheat.
Starch:	**Rice**
Dessert:	**Fresh Fruit**
	Tea

MENU 3

Soup:	**Chicken Broth** Do ahead; reheat.
Salad:	**Cold-Mixing Kohlrabi** Do ahead.
For 2 people add Main Dish:	**Red-Cooked Shrimp** Have everything ready and cook last; or do ahead and serve cold.
For 3 people also add Starch:	**Ham Fried Rice** Do ahead and leave in covered wok; reheat.
For 4 people also add Main Dish:	**Oyster Beef** Have everything ready; stir-fry 5 minutes before serving.
For 5 people also add Main Dish:	**Hunan Chicken** Prepare ahead of time; stir-fry 15 minutes before serving.
For 6 people also add Vegetable:	**Vegetarian's Garden** Stir-fry ahead; add broth and cornstarch mixture 10 minutes before serving.
Dessert:	**Almond Delight** Do ahead and refrigerate.
	Tea

MENU 4

Soup:	**Egg Drop Soup** Do ahead and leave in saucepan; reheat.
Main Dish:	**Oven Barbecued Ribs** Do ahead; warm in oven.
For 2 people add Salad:	**Broccoli Salad** Do ahead.
For 3 people also add Main Dish:	**Oyster Chicken Wings** Do ahead and leave in pot; reheat.
For 4 people also add Vegetable:	**Spicy Tofu** Do ahead and leave in wok; reheat.
For 5 people also add Main Dish:	**Butterfly Shrimp** Partially fry ahead of time; deep-fry again just before serving.
For 6 people also add Main Dish:	**Pepper Steak** Have everything ready; cook last.
Starch:	**Rice**
Dessert:	**Ice Cream**
	Tea

MENU 5

Appetizer: **Wonton Chips** and **Shrimp Chips**   Do ahead.
Soup: **Tofu, Tomato, and Spinach Soup**   Do ahead; reheat.
For 2 people
add Main
Dish: **Chicken with Snow Pea Pods**   Have everything ready; cook last.
For 3 people
also add
Salad: **Cucumber Salad**   Do ahead.
For 4 people
also add
Starch: **Oyster-Flavored Fried Rice**   Do ahead; reheat.
For 5 people
also add
Main Dish: **Steamed Fish**   Have everything ready, including boiling water.
Steam 12-15 minutes before serving.

For 6 people
also add
Main Dish: **Jade Beef**   Have everything ready; cook last.
Dessert: **Watermelon Basket**   Do ahead.
Tea

MENU 6

These dishes are to be served all together. Leave the stir-fried dishes to be cooked last. If you object to last-minute cooking, then cook them just before your guests arrive. Leave them in a very low oven, loosely covered with foil to keep meat from drying out. If you have a microwave oven, cook ahead and reheat all but the deep-fried dishes.

Appetizer: **Stuffed Mushrooms**   Cook ahead and leave in pan; reheat.
Soup: **Zucchini Soup**   Do ahead.
For 2 people
add Main
Dish: **Onion Beef**   Have everything ready; cook last.
For 3 people
also add
Salad: **Cold-Mixing Celery**   Do ahead.
For 4 people
also add
Main Dish: **Poached Trout**   Double recipe; cook last.
For 5 people
also add
Main Dish: **Chicken Kow**   Have everything ready; do before Onion Beef.
For 6 people
also add
Main Dish: **Sweet-Sour Pork**   Fry pork once ahead of time; deep-fry again and place on rack over pan in warm oven while making sauce.
Starch: **Rice**
Dessert: **Litchis on Ice**   Do ahead.
Tea

MENU 1

Cold-Mixing Celery
   Double recipe; do ahead.
Eight Precious Vegetables
   Double recipe; do up to a few days ahead; cover and refrigerate.
Soy-Sauce Cornish Hen
   Double recipe; cook 2 days ahead and refrigerate.
Stovetop Sweet-Sour Spareribs
   Make 3 lbs. Do 3 days ahead; defat; warm before serving.
Pepper Steak
   Double recipe; have everything ready; stir-fry 10 minutes before serving.
Oyster-Flavored Fried Rice
   Double recipe; do ahead and leave in wok; warm.
Chinese Taco
   Do ahead and leave in wok; warm.
Crab Legs
   Double recipe; have everything ready; steam 8 minutes before serving.
Egg Drop Soup
   Triple recipe; do ahead and leave in pot; warm.
Fresh Fruit

MENU 2

Marble Eggs
   Do up to 3 days ahead; drain and refrigerate.
Shrimp Chips
   Do ahead.
Bean Sprout Salad
   Do ahead and refrigerate.
Shanghai-Style Red-Cooked Chicken
   Double recipe; do 2 days ahead; warm 20 minutes before serving.
Sweet-Sour Green Peppers
   Double recipe and use both green and sweet red peppers; serve cold.

Beef Fried Rice or Beef Chow Mein
   Double recipe; do ahead; warm.
Beer Duck
   Prepare ahead; roast 2¼ hours before serving.
Pearl Balls
   Have everything ready; steam 10-15 minutes before
   serving.
Scallops Supreme
   Double recipe; have everything ready; stir-fry 10
   minutes before serving.
Sweet Wontons
   Double recipe; do ahead and serve cold. May be
   warmed in oven on a rack over a pan.

MENU 3
Wine Chicken
   Double recipe; do 2 days ahead, marinate overnight.
   Cut and place on plate with garnish ahead of time.
   Cover with plastic wrap and refrigerate.
Oven-Barbecued Spareribs
   Double recipe; bake ahead; glaze last.
Radish Cold-Mixing Salad
   Double recipe; do ahead.
Red-Cooked Shrimp
   Double recipe; do ahead; serve cold or warm.
Bean Sprouts and Leek
   Double recipe; do ahead; serve cold or lukewarm.
Wonton Soup
   Do ahead; warm just before serving.
Mu Xu Pork with Mandarin Pancakes
   Double recipe; have pancakes ready to warm before
   serving; cook pork dish ahead, leave in wok, and warm
   before serving.
Steamed Fish
   Have everything ready on a plate; steam over boiling
   water for 10-15 minutes before serving.
Oyster Beef
   Prepare ahead; stir-fry at last minute, or cook 10
   minutes before guests arrive.
Ice Cream

MENU 4 (Simple Buffet)

Sichuan Cucumbers
  Double recipe; do ahead; warm before serving.
Soy-Sauce Cornish Hen
  Double recipe; do ahead.
Boneless Pork Chops
  Triple recipe; have everything ready; pan-fry 15 minutes
  before serving.
Ham Fried Rice
  Triple recipe; do ahead; warm.
Vegetarian's Garden
  Double recipe; stir-fry ahead; add broth and cornstarch
  mixture before serving.
Wonton Fritters or Fresh Fruit
  Prepare fritters ahead.

Ten-Course Banquet for Eight to Ten

You may serve this banquet course by course (with dishes prepared by one to ten cooks) or all together.

Butterfly Shrimp with Shrimp Chips
> Prepare Shrimp Chips ahead. Butterfly shrimp can be partially fried to light-yellow color. Refry to golden brown before serving.

Egg Drop Soup
> Triple recipe; do ahead; warm before serving, then add garnish.

Ham and Asparagus Salad
> Double recipe; do ahead; serve cold.

Gong Bao Chicken
> Double recipe; have everything ready; stir-fry before serving.

Oyster Beef
> Double recipe; have everything ready; stir-fry before serving.

Ham Fried Rice
> Double recipe; do ahead; warm.

Sweet-Sour Pork
> Have everything ready; fry pork to light brown color. Refry to golden brown before serving; make sweet-sour sauce just before serving.

Beer Duck
> Have garnishes ready. Roast duck 2¼ hours before serving by host.

Vegetarian's Delight
> Double recipe; stir-fry ahead; add broth and cornstarch mixture before serving.

Almond Delight
> Double recipe; do ahead.

There are two ways to serve these feasts. One is to have all the food ready and served at once. The alternative is to start with four appetizer dishes, everyone sitting down to drink and chat. After that, the rest of the food is served course by course, each by a different cook. It eliminates the chaos in the kitchen, and it is fun to take turns being the cook. (In order to have the feast served without interruption, figure out the approximate time required for each cook's dish, and plan the cooking accordingly.)

DINNER PARTY FOR SIX COUPLES

This is the least elaborate of the combined-effort feasts. Here is the menu in serving order:

> Wonton Soup
> Fried Shrimp Toast
> Ham Fried Rice
> Pepper Steak
> Vegetarian's Garden
> Peking Duck with Mandarin Pancakes
> Tea
> Watermelon Basket

Couple 1 makes Fried Shrimp Toast (double recipe).
Couple 2 makes Wonton Soup.
Couple 3 makes Pepper Steak (double recipe).
Couple 4 makes Vegetarian's Garden (double recipe).
Couple 5 makes Ham Fried Rice (triple recipe).
Host couple makes duck and pancakes, watermelon, and tea.

FEAST FOR SIX COUPLES

> Wonton Soup
> Four Cold Dishes
>> Peanuts for Beer Drinking
>> Cold-Mixing Kohlrabi
>> Marble Eggs
>> Fu Yang Salted Chicken
> Oven-Barbecued Spareribs
> Stuffed Mushrooms
> Butterfly Shrimp
> Crisp Wontons
> Sweet-Sour Pork
> Oyster Beef

Steamed Fish
Broccoli and Cauliflower
Rice
Tea
Dessert

If the meal is to be served course by course, the order should be as in the menu above, except that the rice may be served before serving the Sweet-Sour Pork. If everyone is to sit down and enjoy the dinner together, guests should arrive at the host house 30 to 40 minutes before serving time. The four ready-to-serve cold dishes can be set on the table. Deep-fry the shrimp first; then use the oil to fry the egg rolls and the Sweet-Sour Pork.

Couple 1
Stuffed Mushrooms (use Chinese dried mushrooms): Fill mushrooms; cook at host's home.
Broccoli and Cauliflower (double recipe): Have everything ready; cook at host's home.
Couple 2
Oyster Beef: Have everything ready; cook at host's home.
Steamed Fish: Have everything ready; steam at host's home.
(Before doing beef dish, boil water; then put in fish and set timer.)
Couple 3
Sweet-Sour Pork (double recipe): Fry partially at home; fry again at host's home. Make sauce and use as a dip.
Marble Eggs: Do ahead; have ready to serve.
Couple 4
Butterfly Shrimp: Fry partially at home; fry again at host's home.
Cold-Mixing Kohlrabi (double recipe): Do ahead; have ready to serve.
Peanuts for Beer Drinking (double recipe): Do ahead; have ready to serve.
Couple 5
Fu Yang Salted Chicken (double recipe): Do ahead; have ready to serve.
Crisp Wontons: Mix filling ahead; wrap and deep-fry at host's home.
Host Couple
Wonton Soup: Do ahead; warm up before serving.
Oven-Barbecued Spareribs (double recipe): Bake in oven ahead; glaze last.

CHINESE NEW YEAR PARTY FOR SIX COUPLES

Cold-Plate Combination
Wine Chicken
Sichuan Cucumbers
Fried Shrimp Toast
Shanghai-Style Egg Rolls with Dipping Sauce
Onion Beef

Stovetop Sweet-Sour Spareribs
Eight Precious Vegetables
Poached Trout
Vegetarian's Garden
Oyster-Flavored Fried Rice
Beer Duck
Tea
Almond Delight

Couple 1
Shanghai-Style Egg Rolls: Cook filling ahead; wrap and deep-fry at host's home.
Sichuan Cucumbers (double recipe): Do ahead.
Couple 2
Cold-Plate Combination: Do ahead.
Almond Delight (double recipe): Do ahead.
Couple 3
Onion Beef: Have all ingredients ready; stir-fry at host's home.
Eight Precious Vegetables (double recipe): Do ahead.
Couple 4
Fried Shrimp Toast: Have everything ready; deep-fry at host's home.
Oyster-Flavored Fried Rice (double recipe): Do ahead; warm up.
Couple 5
Stovetop Sweet-Sour Spareribs (double recipe): Do ahead; warm up.
Poached Trout (double recipe): Cook at last minute.
Host couple
Wine Chicken: Do ahead.
Vegetarian's Garden (double recipe): Cook up to step 2; finish step 3 at last minute.
Beer Duck
Tea

Plan on a total of ¹/₂ to ³/₄ pound of food per person.

MENU 1

Appetizers: **Stuffed Mushrooms**   Cook ahead; reheat.
Stovetop Sweet-Sour Spareribs   Cook one day ahead; bool and then refrigerate; reheat before serving.

Salad: **Cucumber Salad**   Prepare one day ahead.

Main Dish: **Jiffy Egg Rolls**   Cook filling ahead; wrap and partially fry; refrigerate; deep fry before serving.

Vegetable: **Bean Sprouts and Leek**   Cook ahead.

Starch: **Any recipe for fried rice** or **steamed rolls**   Prepare ahead; reheat before serving.
Dessert
Tea

MENU 2

Appetizers: **Fried Shrimp Toast**   Prepare ahead; deep-fry 30 minutes before serving.
Pearl Balls   Prepare ahead; steam 30 minutes before serving.

Salad: **Cold-Mixing Celery**   Prepare one day ahead.

Main Dish: **Red-Cooked Chicken** or **Red-Cooked Beef**   Cook ahead; refrigerate; reheat.

Vegetable: **Broccoli and Cauliflower**   Do ahead.

Starch: **Any recipe for fried rice** or **steamed rolls**   Prepare ahead; reheat before serving.
Dessert
Tea

MENU 3

Appetizers: **Marble Eggs**   Do ahead.
Wonton Chips   Fry ahead; leave in oven with pilot light on or at lowest temperature to keep warm.

Salad: **Radish Cold-Mixing Salad**   Prepare one day ahead.

Main Dish: **Oven-Barbecued Spareribs**   Cook one day ahead; marinate; roast in oven 45 minutes before serving.

Vegetable: **Snow Pea Pods with Mushrooms**   Do ahead.

Starch: **Rice** or **steamed rolls** or **Cold-Style Noodles** or **Beef Chow Mein**   Make rice or rolls ahead; warm up.
Dessert
Tea

Steamed Meat Rolls
Do weeks ahead and freeze; steam before serving.
Oyster Chicken Wings with Potatoes
Cook a few days ahead; refrigerate; warm before
serving.
Stovetop Sweet-Sour Spareribs
Cook a few days ahead; refrigerate; warm before
serving.
Marble Eggs or Cold-Plate Combination (use eggs only)
Cook a few days ahead; refrigerate; serve cold.
Sichuan Cucumbers
Do one day ahead.
Bean Sprouts in Spicy Vinegar Sauce
Do ahead; serve at room temperature.
Beer Duck
Roast in oven the day of the party.
Shrimp Chips
May be deep-fried ahead; cool; place in airtight cans
or bags.
Crisp Wonton
Wrap ahead; partially deep-fry; cool and refrigerate;
fry again before serving. Or deep-fry until done;
spread apart on rack over foil-covered pan; leave in
oven with pilot light on to keep warm.
Ham Fried Rice
Do as much as one day ahead; refrigerate; steam to
reheat or warm on stovetop.
Tea
Dessert

To plan the amount of food, figure the approximate quantity one person would consume, then multiply by number of guests. For example, each individual plate might contain 1 or 2 rolls, 2 chicken wings, 3-4 spareribs, 1 whole egg, 1 serving of cucumber salad, 1 serving of bean sprouts, 3 pieces of duck, 8-10 shrimp chips, 3-5 wontons, 1/2 cup rice. Or figure on a total of 1/2 to 3/4 pound food per person.

Chinese Picnic Menus

Marble Eggs
Cold-Plate Combination
Cold-Style Noodles

Wonton Chips or Shrimp Chips
Soy-Sauce Cornish Hen
Steamed Meat Rolls or Sweet Bean Rolls

Red-Cooked Chicken Wings
Suzhou Meat Cakes or Green-Onion-Filled Suzhou Cakes
Any Cold-Mixing Vegetable

Tips on Party Planning

- It is wise to plan on using recipes you have cooked at least once before, so that you are familiar with the cooking procedures.
- If you have to prepare a party meal all by yourself, please give yourself ample extra time, as Chinese food is very time-consuming in preparation, and there are lots of details that need tending to. The cutting and slicing alone may take a long time, especially for a beginner.
- Make a shopping list. In one column list ingredients to be prepared ahead of time, then frozen. In another column list dishes to be prepared days in advance. Also categorize your ingredients under the headings of meat, poultry, seafood, canned goods, vegetables, fruits, seasonings, miscellaneous, etc. Shop early for items that need to be cooked ahead of time. Seafood, fresh vegetables, and fruits should be freshly purchased.
- Try to do most of the preparation work ahead of time.

WEEKS AHEAD

1. Plan for party, make guest list, send or phone invitations. Decide on menu and amount of food needed. Shop for food that can be prepared ahead of time and frozen, such as wontons, Suzhou Cakes, Chinese rolls, and Mandarin pancakes.

2. Sweet-sour sauce and apricot sauce can be made a few weeks ahead and stored in a clean, covered glass jar and refrigerated. Hot pepper oil can also be done ahead and stored in the cupboard (see page 30).

3. Cut out decorative characters or symbols for special occasions if desired (see Chapter 6). Fold paper or cloth napkins. Design and visualize the party setting.

TWO TO THREE DAYS AHEAD

1. Red-cooked or Lu food may be prepared ahead of time, then cooled and refrigerated.

2. Egg roll fillings may be cooked, drained, and refrigerated.

3. Make lists of things that need to be done and the food to be served, and post them where you can see them easily. Mark off each item when it is done. Add the things you need to purchase in another column.

4. All the garnishes can be made a few days ahead, placed in a plastic tub, covered, and refrigerated.

ONE DAY AHEAD

1. Defrost frozen duck, chicken, or shrimp.

2. Get cooking utensils out. Gather cooking ingredients (soy sauce, sesame oil, cornstarch, vegetable oil, salt, pepper, etc.). Have measuring cups, spoons, and paper towels ready. Line baking pan with foil if food needs to be warmed on a rack or baked in the oven.

3. Trim, slice, and marinate meat; cover and refrigerate until ready to cook. Defrost meat until 50-75 percent thawed so that it is easy to slice. This saves effort and time. If fresh meat is purchased, put in freezer for 2 hours and then slice.

4. Bone chicken breast, slice, cover, and refrigerate.

5. Devein shrimp.

6. Soak Chinese dried mushrooms, wood ears or cloud ears, and tiger lily buds. After they are softened, clean and snip off the tips of wood ears and cloud ears; remove stems from mushrooms; drain off water; cut tiger lily buds. Cover and refrigerate for next day's use.

7. Wash and cut vegetables. For large colume, place in plastic bag, seal tight, and refrigerate for next day's use. For small portion, place on a plate and cover with plastic wrap. Mincing of vegetables can be done ahead (with a food processor, if you have one).

8. Cut all the required green onions, slice ginger roots, crush garlic; cover and refrigerate for next day's use.

9. Cook red-cooked dishes ahead of time and refrigerate.

10. Make dessert and refrigerate.

11. Make soup and refrigerate.

12. Make additional ice cubes.

THE DAY OF THE PARTY

1. Set out platters, serving pieces, glasses, tablecloth, napkins, silverware, and plates.

2. Set table.

3. Chill wine, beer, etc.

4. Place tea leaves in teapot. Have sugar and cream ready if coffee is also being served.

5. Open all cans; drain, defat, or slice canned food.

6. Defat soup or precooked food.

7. Cook rice. If rice cooker is used, it will keep rice warm.

8. Mix sauces for various dishes, label each with tape to avoid mixup.

9. If noodles are to be served, cook, drain, and add oil.

10. Go over the list for each recipe. Group vegetables, green onion, ginger root, and garlic in different areas of a plate. Place dish of sauce next to plate. Leave only meat in the refrigerator.

11. Arrange dishes in the sequence they are to be cooked (the closest to the stove to be cooked first).

12. Visualize the whole dinner plan and the order of cooking and serving.

13. Put all sauces and dips on the table (with covers on).

14. Chop chicken or duck into pieces. Put garnishes into place.

15. Do the first-time, partial deep-fry.

16. Place cold appetizer dishes with their garnishes on table about 15 minutes before guests arrive.

17. Warm up precooked food.

18. Wash and rinse dishes as you go along. (If you have a double sink, fill one sink with soapy water.)

19. Cook stir-fried dishes.

20. Cook deep-fried dishes.

5

Casual Entertaining

Wonton Luncheons

ALL ABOUT WONTONS

Wonton is a savory mixture sealed in a noodle-type wrapper and often served in a soup. The name is translated as "cloud swallowing" in colloquial Cantonese. Since authentic wonton skins are very thin, they are silky and transparent when boiled. A spoonful of the morsel along with the soup is so soothing to the palate it is like swallowing a light cloud. In Sichuan, wontons are tossed in a spicy red sauce made with dashes of soy sauce, sesame oil, hot pepper oil, and minced preserved kohlrabi. Thus, wonton is also called "tossing hand." Wonton soups served in Chinese restaurants in the United States are mostly noodles with very little filling. Wonton appetizers are also mostly pasta when deep-fried.

Wontons can be served in many forms. In China, they are often a meal by themselves, or a snack or a soup course. The fillings may be made of ground meat, meat with shrimp or crab, or meat with a vegetable. Since vegetables are often added to wonton soup, it makes a well-balanced meal. Cooked noodles may also be included to make the soup heartier.

Irregularly cut or torn and deep-fried wonton wrappers make crunchy chips. Cut in half and fried, they make wonton fritters. These fried wontons are an ideal finger food or appetizer to serve with cocktails. Filled with a sweet mixture and deep-fried, wontons make a good dessert.

Wontons can be wrapped ahead of time; or even cooked ahead of time and then warmed up. Fried wontons can be kept warm on a rack in the oven before serving, or left in an unheated oven with the pilot light on.

Wontons may be cooked in chicken broth, drained, and served with soy sauce and vinegar dip. Garnish with chopped green onions.

Wonton wrappers can be made at home, but it is hardly worth the effort, as they are available in Chinese grocery stores and at many supermarkets. They are inexpensive and can be frozen for up to six months. The unused portion can be rewrapped and frozen again, or it can be used for wonton chips, noodles, or fritters. If your supermarket stores them in the produce section, be sure they are fresh. Some packages are date-stamped. If there is no date stamp, find out from the produce manager when they were delivered. Don't buy wonton wrappers that look grayish. Because the wrappers are made of flour, eggs, and water, they have a tendency to mold from the inside out if not properly refrigerated. Check the wrappers before you start your cooking project. If wonton wrappers stick to each other, they are no longer fresh.

To avoid drying out and hardening of wonton wrappers, take only a few pieces out at a time, leaving the rest in the plastic bag. Or cover them with a moistened cloth or plain white paper towel. (Colored paper towels tend to stain the wrappers.)

Wrapping wontons can be family fun. If you do it alone, save time and effort by laying five or six pieces on the table at one time. Spoon the filling in the middle of each piece and then wrap.

Wrapped wontons can be frozen for future use.

SIMPLE LUNCH MENUS

Making wontons by yourself is a chore; making them with a friend is fun. Invite a friend and visit or have coffee while you fold the wontons. Cook a batch for lunch, and deep-fry some for appetizers. Then you can keep some and your friend can take some home for dinner, or freeze for future use.

LUNCH FOR TWO
Crisp Wontons with Dipping Sauce
Any cold-mixing salad
Wonton Soup

LUNCH FOR FOUR
Crisp Wontons with Dipping Sauce
Wonton Soup
   Do ahead.
Cucumber Salad
   Do ahead.
Chinese Tacos
   Have lettuce ready and do all preparations ahead;
   stir-fry meat 10 minutes before guests arrive.
Dessert

LUNCH FOR SIX
Any cold-mixing salad
   Double recipe; do ahead.
Wonton Soup or boiled and drained or fried wontons
Crab Egg Fu Yung
Ham-Fried Rice
   Do ahead.
Dessert

WONTON SOUP

FILLING
12 water chestnuts
2 green onions
2-3 slices (½ tsp. minced) ginger root
½ lb. lean ground pork or beef

SEASONINGS
1 tsp. salt
1 tsp. sherry
1 egg
1 tsp. soy sauce
¼ tsp. pepper
¼ cup water
1 lb. wonton wrappers

SOUP
5 cups Chicken Broth (see page 49)
1 4-oz. jar of button mushrooms, drained
1 cup torn raw spinach or watercress, rinsed

GARNISHES FOR SOUP
2 whole green onions, chopped
1 egg crepe, shredded (see page 70)
dash of white pepper (optional)
sesame oil

Preparation

1. Mince water chestnuts, green onions, and ginger root.
2. Mix ground meat with minced water chestnuts, green onions, and ginger. Add seasonings and mix well, being sure to stir always in the same direction.
3. Lay one wonton wrapper flat on a clean surface. Place 1 tsp. of meat mixture in the center.
4. With a finger dipped in water, moisten the top edges of the wrapper and fold downward in half, sealing edges and enclosing meat.
5. With sealed edges toward you, fold up in two so that sealed edges are now toward the top (away from you).
6. With a wet finger, moisten the back of the right-hand top corner. Bring both top corners toward each other, and pinch them together firmly. Wonton now looks like a nurse's cap.

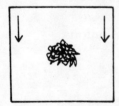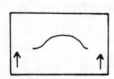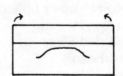

7. As each wonton is finished, place it on a floured platter and cover with foil, white paper towel or clean cloth towel.

Cooking

1. Bring 2 quarts of water to a boil. Drop in wontons one by one. Stir lightly to prevent sticking. Return to boil. Add 1 cup cold water and bring to boil once again. Turn off heat.

2. At the same time, in another pot, bring chicken broth to a boil. Add button mushrooms, then add spinach or watercress, then immediately turn off heat.

3. Into a large serving bowl or into each individual soup bowl, put some chopped green onion, egg crepe shreds, and dash of white pepper. Ladle in drained wontons, then add hot chicken broth with spinach and mushrooms. Finally add a little sesame oil (1-2 drops per soup bowl); stir slightly and serve.

Hints

- If recipe is doubled, use 1 egg. If tripled, use 2 eggs.
- To freeze uncooked, filled wontons for future use, lay them, side by side, flat on a floured plate or cookie sheet. Place in a large plastic bag or cover with foil paper, and leave in the freezer for a few hours. When wontons are hardened, lift out plate and leave (or put) wontons in plastic bag to freeze. Do not thaw wontons before cooking.

CRISP WONTONS

Filling and seasonings are the same as for Wonton Soup.

Preparation

1. Mix meat with minced water chestnuts, green onions, and ginger root. Add seasonings. Mix well in one direction, either clockwise or counterclockwise.

2. Fill and fold wontons as described below. Then put wontons on a lightly floured plate.

Folding

Use any one of the following methods.

Simple Folding: Lay one wonton wrapper flat on work surface. Place 1-1½ tsp. meat mixture in center. Moisten edges with water and fold in half; seal edges, enclosing meat.

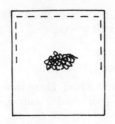 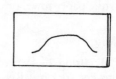

Nurse's Cap: See page 162, steps 3-6.

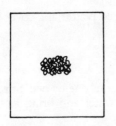 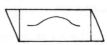

Candy Roll: Place 1 tsp. filling in the center of the lower half of skin. Roll it up from bottom to top and seal the top edge with water; now it is an open-ended cylinder. Wet the tip of your index finger and use it to moisten the inside of both ends. Twist both ends of the wonton wrappers to form a candy roll.

 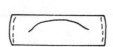 

Parallelogram: Place 1 tsp. filling in the center of the lower half of the skin. Flip it up from the lower edge, make three turns, and seal top edge with water; now it is an open-ended cylinder. Seal inside of two ends with moistened fingertip and press. Wet and lift the lower left-hand corner to form a triangle aligned with the top. Then wet the upper right-hand corner and fold downward even with the bottom.

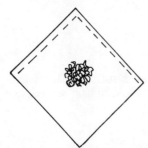 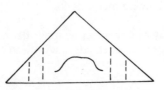 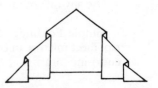

Butterfly: Place wonton wrapper in a diamond position. Place 1 tsp. filling in the center. Moisten the two top sides with water. Lift the bottom point to the top and fold into a triangle shape, with meat concealed in the center. Wet two vertical lines on each side of the surface away from the meat portion. Make two pleats with the same facing meat on each side.

Cooking

Heat oil to high (test with an old wooden chopstick; it is hot enough to deep-fry if bubbles appear around the chopstick). Then turn heat to medium-high and drop in wontons 4-5 at a time. For pork filling, fry for 3-4 minutes, then turn to other side for another 1-2 minutes; for beef filling, fry until both sides are brown. Remove, drain, and serve. Wontons may be deep-fried a few hours ahead, placed on a rack over a foil-covered pan, and kept warm in oven.

Hints

- If wonton wrappers are not available, use egg roll wrappers cut into quarters.
- Sweet-sour sauce, bottled plum sauce, and mustard sauce can all be served as dipping sauces for Crisp Wontons. See the recipes on page 170.

Egg Roll Party

ALL ABOUT EGG ROLLS

The name "egg roll" would puzzle someone newly arrived in the United States from China. Translated directly from the Chinese, this tasty dish is really called "spring roll." Originally it was prepared specially for the Chinese New Year, so the meaning is "Spring will roll in."

The authentic Chinese spring roll skin or wrapper is very thin, made of an eggless dough on a thick piece of steel plate over heat. It is freshly made daily in the market. When the skin or wrapper is fresh and warm, people sometimes choose just to add the filling, wrap, and eat without deep-frying. But most people prefer spring rolls deep-fried, with the paper-thin wrapper very crisp. In the United States, authentic egg roll skins can be obtained from the freezer case in Chinese groceries. They come in either square or round shapes under different names, such as "spring roll skin," "egg roll wrappers," or "lumpia wrappers" (the Filipino term).

Peeling the thin wrappers apart after defrosting is tricky and time-consuming. The easiest way is to divide them in the center to form two piles. Put one pile back in the plastic bag or cover with a moistened towel to prevent drying out. Separate the other pile again in the center, then gently peel the skins apart piece by piece. They are somewhat pliable, but easy to break.

Egg rolls taste best when freshly fried. If the filling is moist, it may dampen the wrapper and cause the surface of the egg rolls to break.

American-made egg roll skins are thicker and much easier to handle. The skins are made of flour, water, and eggs. Ideally, they should be stored in the freezer or refrigerator to retain freshness. If stored unfrozen where you buy them, make sure the skins are fresh. If they show a grayish color, they are not fresh. Like wonton wrappers sealed in a plastic bag, if they start to mold because of improper refrigeration, the mold most usually starts from the center and is not visible.

PLANNING A PARTY

Make egg rolls with friends and then enjoy the result in an informal lunch. Make the following preparations for the party:

- Have egg roll wrappers (either Chinese or American—or both if possible—defrosted; or make sure the wrappers are fresh.
- Have sauces made ahead of time and refrigerated.
- Have ingredients and utensils ready.
- Figure out the available time. Cutting and shredding the ingredients is time-consuming. Cooked filling must be cooled and drained before it can be wrapped and the egg rolls deep-fried.

A soup dish such as a Cucumber Soup, Egg Drop Soup, Egg Custard, or Chicken Broth, which the hostess can prepare ahead of time, goes well with egg rolls.

SHANGHAI-STYLE EGG ROLLS

An all-time favorite.

1 lb. lean pork or chicken fillet

MARINADE FOR MEAT
2 tsp. sherry
2 tbsp. soy sauce
1 1/2 tsp. cornstarch

1 lb. fresh or cooked shrimp

MARINADE FOR SHRIMP
1 tsp. sherry
1/4 tsp. cornstarch
1/2 tsp. sesame oil

2 lbs. napa cabbage or white cabbage
3 oz. (1/2 cup) bamboo shoots
1 leek or 5 green onions
2 tbsp. cornstarch dissolved in 1/2 cup water
2 tbsp. flour dissolved in 2 tbsp. water (for paste to seal wrappers)
3 tbsp. oil for stir-frying vegetables
6 tbsp. oil for stir-frying meat
1 tbsp. soy sauce
2 tsp. salt
2 lbs. egg roll wrappers
oil for deep-frying

Preparation

1. Shred meat. Combine marinade ingredients and mix with meat.
2. Clean and devein shrimp, slice large shrimp in half lengthwise, and marinate.
3. Slice cabbage in half lengthwise, then cross-cut into 1/8-inch shreds.
4. Shred bamboo shoots and leek (or green onions).
5. Dissolve cornstarch in water. Dissolve flour in water for paste.

Cooking Filling

1. Heat 3 tbsp. oil and stir-fry cabbage until it wilts (approximately 6-8 minutes for napa cabbage, 3-4 minutes for white cabbage). Drain cooked cabbage in a colander. Rinse wok and wipe dry.

2. Heat wok, then add 6 tbsp. oil. Divide pork into 3 batches and stir-fry each batch about 1 minute. Drain and remove; leave oil in wok.

3. Reheat oil to stir-fry shrimp. Remove when shrimp turn pink.

4. Reheat oil (add 1 tsp. oil if necessary) and stir-fry bamboo shoots and leek (or green onions) for 30 seconds. Add pork, shrimp, and cabbage. Add soy sauce and salt; mix well.

5. Push the mixtures to the sides, leaving a hole in the center. Remove all but 3 tbsp. liquid. When liquid in center boils, add cornstarch mixture. Stir well until it starts to thicken, then stir in the food from the sides, mixing well. Now the mixture will be coated with a light glaze.

6. Drain, then cool the entire mixture to room temperature before wrapping.

Wrapping

1. Place egg roll wrapper in diamond position. Put 2 tbsp. cooled filling in center of lower part. Lift the lower triangular flap over the filling and tuck point under filling.

2. Fold left side toward center; fold right side toward center. (Make sure the folding line is straight for a neat shape.)

3. Roll in a tight roll. Seal top triangle with flour paste. Place egg roll seam side down on a plate to keep it sealed and retain shape.

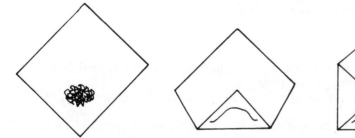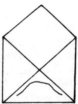

Deep-Frying

Heat oil to 375°F and deep-fry egg rolls 4 at a time, turning them over and over until golden brown (about 3-4 minutes). Drain egg rolls, and deep-fry the next batch. Serve immediately with one of the dipping sauces on page 170. (See hints following Jiffy Egg Rolls recipe.)

12 oz. ground pork or beef

MARINADE FOR MEAT
1 tsp. sherry
4 tsp. soy sauce
1 tsp. cornstarch
1 tsp. oil

6 oz. cooked shrimp

MARINADE FOR SHRIMP
1 tsp. sherry
1/2 tsp. cornstarch
1/2 tsp. sesame oil

6 tbsp. vegetable oil
1 lb. cabbage, shredded
1 lb. fresh bean sprouts
2 tsp. salt
1/4 tsp. sugar
1/4 tsp. pepper
1/8 tsp. five-spice powder (optional)
4 tsp. peanut butter
1 lb. egg roll wrappers
oil for deep-frying

Preparation

1. Marinate meat for 10 minutes.
2. Rinse shrimp and pat dry. Marinate shrimp.

Cooking Filling

1. Heat 2 tbsp. oil in wok or frying pan on high heat. Stir-fry ground meat. Remove meat when it changes color. Drain oil.
2. Add 4 tbsp. oil to wok on high heat. Stir-fry shrimp for 15 seconds and remove. Leave oil in wok.
3. Stir-fry cabbage and bean sprouts. Add salt, sugar, and pepper, and cook until cabbage softens (about 3-4 minutes). Add cooked meat and shrimp, five-spice powder, and peanut butter. Mix well. Turn off heat.
4. Transfer food to a colander and drain thoroughly. Use the back of a spoon to press out excess liquid. Cool filling completely.

Wrapping

1. Place an egg roll skin in a diamond position. (See illustration for Shanghai-Style Egg Rolls.) Put 1/4 cup filling on lower center. Fold lower triangular flap over filling; tuck point under filling.

2. Fold left side toward center; fold right side toward center. (Make sure the folding line is straight for a neat shape.)

3. Roll in a tight roll. Moisten top triangle to seal. Place palm on top of egg roll, and roll back and forth once or twice.

Deep-Frying

1. Heat oil to 375°F and deep-fry 4-5 egg rolls at a time. Turn them over and over until brown (about 3-4 minutes).

2. Drain egg rolls in vertical position so that oil concealed in seam drips through. Serve immediately with or without dipping sauce.

Hints

- To make hard, crispy egg rolls, the filling must be cooled and excess liquid pressed out before wrapping. Otherwise the moistened filling may make the wrappers soggy.
- Rolling back and forth ensures a rounder, fuller shape and seals the egg roll well.
- The best-tasting egg rolls are freshly filled and fried and served immediately.
- The fillings can be made days ahead, drained, and refrigerated.
- Egg rolls may be partially deep-fried for 2 minutes, removed, and cooled, then frozen or refrigerated. Before serving, heat oil and return to deep-fry until crispy. If frozen, do not thaw.
- Partially deep-fried egg rolls may also be warmed in oven at 425°F for 15-20 minutes. Turn over once. To ensure crispness, place egg rolls on a rack over a foil-lined pan that will catch oil drippings.
- Freshly fried egg rolls may be placed on a rack over a foil-lined pan to keep warm in oven before serving.
- Slicing takes time, and this jiffy recipe requires no slicing. If you wish to add celery, onion, water chestnuts, bamboo shoots, green onion, and/or leeks, slice to matchstick size and add to recipe.

All of the following sauces may be made ahead of time, cooled, and refrigerated.

SWEET-SOUR DIPPING SAUCE

2 tsp. cornstarch
1/2 cup cold water
1/4 cup ketchup
3 tbsp. sugar
2 tbsp. pineapple juice
1 tbsp. cider vinegar

Preparation

Blend cornstarch with water: Use 2 tbsp. water to mix with cornstarch first, then add rest of water and blend. Stir in remaining ingredients.

Cooking

Heat to a boil, stirring occasionally; boil until contents become transparent (about 2 minutes).

TANGY APRICOT DIPPING SAUCE

1/2 cup apricot preserves
1 tbsp. water
1 1/2 tsp. cider vinegar
1/2 tsp. ketchup

Combine ingredients and mix well.

MUSTARD DIPPING SAUCE

1 tbsp. mustard powder
1 tbsp. water
1 tsp. oil
1/4 tsp. cider vinegar
1/8 tsp. sugar

Combine ingredients and mix well. Let stand 10-15 minutes before serving.

AUTHENTIC EGG ROLL DIPPING SAUCE

1 tbsp. soy sauce
2 tbsp. vinegar

Combine and mix well.

Mandarin Pancake Party

Mandarin pancakes, a northern Chinese specialty, are fun to make from scratch. You simply mix the hot water with the flour, cover, and let it stand for at least 30 minutes or up to a few hours. Then you divide the dough into equal pieces and roll them out into thin circles. (Roll them two at a time, with sesame oil brushed in between to prevent them from sticking together.) Cook in an unoiled frying pan. Food is placed in the center of a pancake and folded to eat.

Mu Xu (Mu Shu) Pork is the traditional filling for the Mandarin pancake. Pork, wood ears or cloud ears, and eggs are the essential ingredients. *Mu xu* is the Chinese name for cassina flower; the eggs in this dish have a similar color.

If you invite friends to help prepare the meal, you may ask them to bring an apron, rolling pin, chopping board, cleaver or knife, or frying pan. Assign the following tasks:

- Mix dough: It is easier to knead dough in a small quantity (a large piece is difficult to handle). Follow the Mandarin Pancake recipe, and make several batches of dough.
- Slice meat: For easier slicing, defrost meat about 75 percent (until a knife can cut through it easily).
- Peel and shred carrots. Shred green onions.
- Soak wood ears and snip off ends (may be done ahead).
- Make egg crepes (may be done ahead) and shred. (See page 70.)
- Soak bean threads and tiger lily buds (may be done ahead) and cut into sections.

Mandarin pancakes have to be cooked individually; cover the cooked ones on a heatproof plate and keep them warm in the oven. Or you can buy ready-made Mandarin pancakes at an Oriental grocery. Egg roll wrappers, flour tortillas, or crepes may be used as substitutes.

Stir-frying Mu Xu Pork does not take long, but it may be cooked ahead of time and warmed up. Besides the traditional Mu Xu filling, you may wish to prepare ahead of time a variety of cold fillings—shredded cooked meat and raw vegetables. Place them in a sectional server or pile them up in sections on a large platter. Guests help themselves to the fillings of shredded egg crepes, ham, beef, roast pork (or any kind of cooked meat), lettuce, carrots, green onions, and celery. Crisp bacon bits or deep-fried almond chips (see page 94) may be added for crunchiness.

MANDARIN PANCAKES

The Chinese name for these pancakes is *bo-bing* or *dan-bing*, meaning "thin crepes."

2 cups all-purpose flour
7/8 cup boiling water
1 tbsp. sesame oil or vegetable oil

Preparation

1. Add boiling water to flour and use wooden chopsticks or a wooden spoon to mix well. Then use hands to form a soft dough and knead for 5 minutes. Cover with a lid or a large plate, and let stand at least 30 minutes or up to several hours.
2. Knead dough thoroughly on a lightly floured surface until smooth and elastic.
3. Cut dough into 16 equal parts: Either divide it in half, cut each half into another half, and repeat until you have 16 equal pieces, or roll dough into an 8-inch cylinder and cut off 1/2-inch slices. Arrange dough pieces in two rows. With palm of hand, flatten each piece into a circle.
4. Pour oil into a saucer or dish. Lightly brush 8 circles with oil. Place an unoiled circle on top of each oiled circle. You now have eight "sandwiches" of dough with oil in between. Cover with a dry towel to prevent drying out.
5. With a rolling pin, roll out each "sandwich" into a 6- to 8-inch circle. Cover with a dry towel or cook right away.

Cooking

1. In an unoiled skillet heated to medium heat, cook pancakes one sandwiched pair at a time. Cook each pair until bubbles rise (about 1-1½ minutes). Turn and cook until lightly speckled with brown. Remove to a heatproof plate and cover with a lid. Plate may be placed in a warm oven if it is to be served right after cooking. Or you may stack pancakes on a plate and cover with a dry towel. When pancakes are all done, steam them warm in a steamer or over a rack in a dutch oven before serving.
2. Continue to cook remaining pancakes. If necessary, adjust heat; different stoves and different utensils require different heating time.

Hints

- Pancakes may be served with Peking Duck, chicken slices, roast pork, or stir-fried shredded pork.
- Pancakes can be made in advance, stacked, and covered. When cooled, wrap in foil paper and refrigerate or freeze. When ready to use, uncover pancakes and steam for 5 minutes, or wrap in foil and warm in oven preheated to 350°F for 10 minutes.
- Some guests can roll pancakes while others cook, thus saving time.

MU XU PORK

12 oz. lean boneless pork

MARINADE
 1 tbsp. sherry
 1½ tbsp. soy sauce
 1½ tsp. cornstarch
 1½ tsp. sugar
 1½ tsp. oil

20 tiger lily buds
20 wood ears or 10 cloud ears
2 oz. bean threads (optional)
4 green onions
1 carrot (optional)
2 eggs
½ tsp. sherry
1 tsp. oil (for egg crepes) or 2 tbsp. oil (for scrambled eggs)
5 tbsp. oil for stir-frying
1½ tsp. salt
1½ tsp. soy sauce
½ tsp. sesame oil

Preparation

1. Slice pork into thin pieces, then stack several pieces and cut into shreds 2 inches by ⅛ inch.
2. Combine marinade ingredients and marinate pork for 15 minutes; mix thoroughly.
3. Soak tiger lily buds and wood ears or cloud ears in warm water for 20 minutes or in hot water for 5 minutes. Snap off and discard hard ends. Wash tiger lily buds well and cut across in half. Wash cloud ears and cut into 2-3 pieces.
4. If bean threads are used, soak them in warm water for 5-10 minutes and cut into 2-inch pieces.
5. Shred green onions. Peel carrot and shred into matchstick-sized pieces.
6. Beat eggs to lemon-yellow color; add sherry.

Cooking

1. Heat 1 tsp. oil in wok or pan. Add eggs and make a round, thin crepe. When cool, shred into thin, matchstick-sized pieces. (Or add 2 tbsp. oil to scrambled eggs, and cut into small pieces while cooking.)
2. Heat 5 tbsp. oil in wok or pan. Stir-fry pork until it changes color (approximately 2-3 minutes). Add tiger lily buds, wood ears, bean threads, green onions, and carrot, and stir-fry for 30 seconds. Add salt and soy sauce; mix well and stir in egg shreds. Stir-fry for another minute. Add sesame oil and remove. Serve with warm Mandarin pancakes or serve with rice as an entrée.

Hints

- Snipping off the hard ends of wood ears can be time-consuming. They may be prepared ahead of time and kept covered in the refrigerator.
- Bean threads and carrots add color as well as texture to this dish.

Chinese Dumpling Party

Jaoi-zi, or Chinese dumplings, are the specialty and favorite of northern China. The dough is formed by mixing flour with cold water for boiled dumplings, with warm water for pan-fried dumplings, or with hot water for steamed dumplings. After being kneaded and "resting" (the Chinese call it "waking up"), the dough is divided into small pieces. Each piece is rolled out to a 2½- to 3-inch thin circle and filled with seasoned meat or a meat-and-vegetable filling, which is then enclosed with pleats. Since the shape after folding resembles an ingot (old-fashioned monetary form), dumplings become a "must" food for the Chinese New Year and special holidays.

To roll and to fold each individual dumpling is a rather time-consuming project, as each person eats ten to twenty during a meal. Dumpling making is usually done by family members or a group of friends in an informal gathering. It is also a good way to pass time on a nothing-to-do, dull rainy afternoon. An old hand at rolling dough usually can continuously supply rolled-out dumplings for several people. Wrapped dumplings are placed on floured trays (to avoid sticking), and cooking can start as soon as the tray is full. Uncooked dumplings may be frozen for future use. Leftover cooked dumplings may be warmed in a little oil in a shallow pan the next day for lunch.

All three kinds of dumplings—pan-fried, boiled, and steamed—can be either served alone or combined with other dishes. Pan-fried dumplings are usually served as an appetizer.

In China, the water used to boil dumplings is often served as a soup after the dumplings are eaten. It is believed that this cooking water aids in the digestion of the dumplings.

2 1/2-3 cups flour
1 cup cold water
10 Chinese dried shrimp (optional) or 1/2 lb. fresh or frozen raw shrimp
  (optional)

MARINADE FOR RAW SHRIMP (OPTIONAL)
  1 tsp. sherry
  1 tsp. cornstarch
  1/4 tsp. salt
  1/2 tsp. sesame oil

2 green onions
2 slices ginger root
1/2 package frozen chopped spinach, thawed
1/2 lb. ground pork or beef

SEASONINGS
  2 tbsp. sherry
  1 tbsp. soy sauce
  1 tsp. salt
  1 tbsp. sesame oil
  1/2 cup water

1 tbsp. oil

DIPPING SAUCE (OPTIONAL)
  soy sauce
  vinegar (plain or with crushed garlic added)
  sesame oil
  mustard sauce
  minced garlic in soy sauce
  hot pepper oil

Preparation

1. Mix 2 1/2 cups flour with cold water to form a dough. Knead until smooth. Add more flour if necessary. Put in a bowl or pot. Cover with a lid or a clean wet cloth or a moist white paper towel. Let dough stand for at least 30 minutes or up to several hours.

2. Soak dried shrimp in warm water for 15 minutes. Chop fine. If fresh shrimp are used, wash, pat dry, and marinate for 15 minutes.

3. Chop green onions and ginger fine.

4. Squeeze water out of chopped spinach.

5. Mix pork (or beef) with seasonings and stir thoroughly in one direction until it becomes very smooth and sticky. Add green onions, ginger, dried shrimp, chopped spinach, and 1 tbsp. oil. Continue to stir in same direction.

6. On a lightly floured board or counter top, knead dough until smooth. Divide into 6 equal parts. Take 1 part out and put the other 5 parts back into the bowl and cover to prevent drying out.

7. Divide the one part into 10 small equal pieces. Flatten each piece with your palm and use rolling pin to roll into 2½ to 3-inch thin circles with thinner edges. (This is done by first rolling dough into a round, thin piece, then holding it in your left hand and rolling with your right palm in a swift back-and-forth motion. Keep turning the dough on your left hand in a counterclockwise direction as your right palm continues to roll over the edges.)

8. Place ½ tbsp. filling in the center of a circle. If fresh shrimp are to be used, place one shrimp on top of the filling. Fold over, press, and seal the middle point. On each side, make 2 pleats on the outside piece, and seal to the inner piece (the one closer to you) by pinching together. Then pinch both ends so that the filling is concealed.

Cooking

1. Fill a dutch oven or deep pot half full of water and bring to a boil. Drop dumplings from the edge one by one (25-30 dumplings may be cooked in one pot). Use a large spoon to stir gently to prevent sticking to the bottom.

2. Return water to boil. Add 1 cup cold water and bring to another boil.

3. Again add a cup of cold water and bring to a boil a third time. Dumplings are now fully cooked. Use a slotted spoon to drain and remove them to a serving plate. Serve hot with various dipping sauces. Each guest mixes her or his own sauce (soy sauce, vinegar, sesame oil, hot pepper oil) in individual saucers or bowls.

PAN-FRIED DUMPLINGS
MEAL-BY-ITSELF/APPETIZER   PAN-FRYING   YIELDS 60

These dumplings are known as *guo-tie*, or "pan stickers."

> **DOUGH**
> 2½-3 cups flour
> 1 cup warm water (⅔ cup boiling water plus ⅓ cup cold water)
>
> Meat filling and seasonings: same as for Boiled Meat Dumplings (page 175)
> ½ cup water
> ½ tsp. vinegar
> ½ tsp. sesame oil
>
> **DIPPING SAUCE (OPTIONAL)**
> 1 tsp. sliced or grated fresh ginger root
> 1 tbsp. vinegar
> soy sauce
> 2 tbsp. oil

Preparation

1. Add warm water to flour in a mixing bowl. Mix well with wooden chopstick or wooden spoon. Knead until smooth. Cover with a wet cloth or paper towel. Let stand for at least 30 minutes or up to several hours.
2. Mix the filling as for Boiled Meat Dumplings, except wash and pat dry fresh shrimp and mince fine. Then mix with the meat filling. You may omit spinach if you wish.
3. Wrap dumplings individually as for Boiled Meat Dumplings.
4. Mix water with vinegar and sesame oil.
5. Combine dipping sauce ingredients, adding soy sauce to taste, if you wish.

Cooking

1. Heat frying pan or skillet. Add 2 tbsp. oil and swirl around. Add dumplings one at a time. Turn heat to medium; cover for 2 minutes. Pour mixture of water, vinegar, and sesame oil into pan. Turn to medium-high heat, cover, and cook for 2-3 minutes. Shake pan to make sure dumplings are loose and done. (When water is fully absorbed, the bottoms of the dumplings form a crust. When shaken, they become loose.) Remove from heat.
2. Remove dumplings to a serving plate. (Or cover them with a plate; tilt pan a little to pour out remaining oil; then invert pan to transfer dumplings to plate.)

Hint

Pan-Fried Dumplings can be served with or without dipping sauce. They may also be deep-fried in hot oil until golden brown.

STEAMED DUMPLINGS　　　　　*MEAL-BY-ITSELF/APPETIZER　STEAMING　YIELDS 60*

Preparation

Follow directions for Pan-Fried Dumplings (above), but use 1 cup *boiling* water instead of warm water to mix the dough.

Cooking

1. Arrange uncooked dumplings in a steamer. Line with a piece of cheesecloth or with lettuce or cabbage leaves.
2. Bring water to a boil in a wok. Place steamer on wok and cover. Steam over highest heat for 10 minutes.
3. Serve on a plate, or bring the steamer to the table if it is attractive or a conversation piece.
4. Dipping sauce is optional. See Pan-Fried Dumplings.

Hint

Steamed Dumplings can be prepared ahead of time and frozen. Do not thaw before cooking.

Chinese Fondue (Hot Pot) Party

This is a party for four to twenty people. Each of you will cook at the table for yourself in boiling broth. All the preparation may be done ahead of time. It is a particularly welcome meal in winter, as cooking together adds warmth and fun. The preparations are quick and cleanup is simple. You can choose different combinations of ingredients.

PREPARATION

1. Count number of guests, and shop for food. Figure that each guest will eat about ¾ pound of meat, as people tend to eat more when in a relaxed mood, and there is no way of telling how much food will be consumed before guests are full.

2. Make a sweet dessert. Suzhou Cakes with sweet filling is a good choice and can be made ahead and frozen. Any Western-style dessert, cake, cheesecake, or pie would go nicely, too.

3. Slice meat while it's still quite frozen—just thawed enough so that the knife can cut through. If you buy fresh meat, put it in the freezer for 2-3 hours before slicing. It is easiest to shave meat paper-thin if it's frozen.

4. Table settings: Seat 4-6 people at a round table, or 4 at a card table. Place an electric skillet, an electric fondue pot, or an electric wok in the center. Make sure the cord is long enough to reach the electrical outlet. If not, use a heavy-duty extension cord; and be careful of the cord, as the hot broth used in cooking could be dangerous if spilled. Set 2 tables for 8 people, or a ping-pong table or any large, long table covered with a tablecloth for a larger group. Plan on one skillet for every 4-6 persons, and place it within everyone's reach.

5. Set out plates, bowls (or deeper dishes), wire baskets, fondue forks (or regular forks), spoons, and wineglasses. Have sauces and drinks ready. Put dipping sauces on the table.

6. If you wish, serve one or two appetizer dishes with drinks, such as Fried Shrimp Toast, Butterfly Shrimp, Chicken Fantastic, Stuffed Mushrooms, and Marble Eggs.

7. Add broth to the skillet, wok, or fondue pot. Turn on heat and bring to a boil.

8. Ways to arrange ready-to-cook foods:

- Ready-to-cook raw foods may be placed on the table around the cooking utensils if there is enough room for all the plates.
- If not, when guests are seated, pass around the food to be cooked (with forks on serving plates). Each guest takes some and puts it on his or her own plate, then starts to cook. Supply more food as needed.
- Set a larger table next to card tables (away from the electrical cords), and place ready-to-cook food in different plates. Each guest helps himself. Hostess refills meat plates with sliced meat kept covered in the refrigerator. (Do not leave raw meats out in the air for very long.)

In China, a brass chafing dish or "fire pot" is used for this dish. Hot charcoal briquettes are placed under the pot. However, you can use an electric skillet or fondue set. Everyone uses wooden chopsticks, fondue forks, or wire spoons to cook one or several kinds of meat or vegetables to individual taste, then dips food in sauce and eats.

MEATS AND SEAFOOD
    1/2 lb. top sirloin, London broil, rump roast, or tip of round
    1/2 lb. leg of lamb
    1/2 lb. lean boneless pork
    1/2 lb. raw shrimp
    1/2 lb. frozen fillet of sole, pike, or Greenland turbot
    2 filleted chicken breast halves (3/4-1 lb.)
    Optional: oyster, squid, pork kidney, liver (pork, calf, or chicken), chicken
        gizzard, canned boneless fish balls, Japanese fish cakes

VEGETABLES
    2 medium tomatoes
    1 lb. fresh mushrooms
    1 lb. napa cabbage
    1/2 lb. fresh spinach
    2 cakes of tofu
    2 oz. bean threads
    Optional: lettuce, bok choy, bamboo shoots, snow pea pods, turnip greens,
        mustard greens

1 bunch green onions
1 bunch Chinese parsley (optional)
noodles or vermicelli
1 tsp. sesame oil

DIPPING SAUCES
    1 egg per person
    oyster sauce
    sesame oil
    lemon wedges
    Tabasco sauce or Chinese hot pepper oil
    sherry
    soy sauce
    vinegar
    mustard
    sha-cha sauce
    Optional: peanut butter, sesame butter, or fermented red bean curd

8 cups soup stock or chicken broth
1 tsp. salt

Preparation

1. Slightly thaw frozen meat. (Fresh meat may be kept in freezer for a few hours to firm it for easy slicing.) Using a sharp knife, cleaver, or serrated frozen-food knife, shave or cut the meat into the thinnest possible slices. Place them in overlapping layers on individual plates or in separate sections on two large plates.

2. Cut shrimp lengthwise and devein. Cross-cut slightly thawed fish into 1/2-inch slices.

3. Cut chicken breast into thin slices.

4. Slice tomatoes; rinse mushrooms. Rinse napa cabbage thoroughly; cut into 3-inch pieces and put on a separate plate. Rinse spinach.

5. Cut tofu into 1/2-inch cubes.

6. Soak bean threads in warm water for 10 minutes, then cut into pieces about 2 inches long.

7. Chop green onions and Chinese parsley, and place on a plate.

8. Cook noodles or vermicelli until done; rinse in cold water; add 1 tsp. sesame oil. Mix well, place on plate.

9. You may want to mix a basic sauce for everyone, and each person can add additional items. If so, mix soy sauce, sherry, and sesame oil.

Cooking

1. Each person first mixes dipping sauce in his or her own bowl. The amount and variety varies according to taste. For example:

- 1 tsp. sha-cha sauce plus 2 tbsp. soy sauce and 1/2 tsp. vinegar plus chopped green onion and 1 tsp. sesame oil.
- Soy sauce and raw egg. Stir well.
- Soy sauce plus Tabasco sauce plus sherry.

The traditional sauce for the famous "rinse lamb fire pot" consists of soy sauce, sesame butter, fermented red bean curd, wine, shrimp sauce, and Chinese parsley.

2. When the broth in the skillet starts to boil, add 1 tsp. salt. Each person dips meat slices in boiling broth. In seconds, the meat is done. Dip in your own sauce bowl and eat. Replenish broth when necessary.

3. After the meat, fish, or seafood is consumed, it is customary to cook vegetables and ladle the broth into the bowl and drink it as soup. Be sure to remove any scum from the broth first. You may add precooked noodles to it.

4. Hot steamed rolls can be served if guests are still hungry.

Summer Barbecue Party

A barbecue party is very informal. Choose two or three kinds of meat and marinate ahead of time. Count on ½ pound of meat per person. All vegetable, noodle, or fried rice recipes serve four, so double or triple them as needed, or serve two kinds of vegetables. To make the party fancier, one or two appetizer dishes may be served before the meal.

MENU 1 (Serves 4-6)

Fried Shrimp Toast
Marble Eggs
Sichuan Cucumbers
Cold-Style Noodles
Barbecued Pork Slices or Chops
Sha-cha Beef
Watermelon Basket
Beer
Tea/Iced Tea

MENU 2 (Serves 4-6)

Crisp Wontons
Cold-Mixing Celery or Radish Cold-Mixing Salad
Fried Rice
Chicken Barbecue or Barbecued Ribs
"Six Happiness" Beef Kabobs
Almond Delight
Beer
Tea/Iced Tea

"SIX HAPPINESS" BEEF KABOBS

1½-2 lbs. flank steak, top round, round, sirloin tip, or beef fondue meat

MARINADE
- 4 tbsp. soy sauce
- 2 tbsp. sherry
- ¼ cup oil
- 2 tbsp. honey
- 1 tsp. five-spice powder
- 1 tsp. curry powder
- 4 cloves garlic

fresh mushrooms
green peppers or sweet red peppers
cherry tomatoes
water chestnuts
pineapple chunks

Preparation

1. Cut meat into 1-inch cubes. Marinate for several hours or overnight.
2. Rinse and cube green peppers; rinse mushrooms. Dip both in hot water for 1 minute to avoid splitting when placed on skewer.
3. Rinse cherry tomatoes; drain water chestnuts and pineapple.
4. Fill skewers with meat, vegetables, and pineapple. Broil over hot coals 3 minutes on each side or to desired doneness.

SHA-CHA BEEF

You may vary this dish by using pork or lamb instead of beef.

1½ lbs. beef (flank, sirloin, round, or breakfast steak, etc.) or pork loin or leg of lamb

MARINADE
- ¼ cup soy sauce
- 2 tbsp. oil
- 1 tbsp. sherry
- 2 tbsp. sugar
- ½ tsp. pepper

½ lb. chicken livers or fresh mushrooms or smoked oysters
1 bunch green onions
4 tbsp. sha-cha sauce
8 oz. water chestnuts

Preparation

1. Remove any fat and membrane from meat. Cut into thin slices 3 by 1½ inches. Marinate meat for 30 minutes.
2. Cook chicken livers in boiling water for 1 minute, then rinse under cold water.
3. Slice green onions into thin strips.
4. Brush sha-cha sauce on meat. Place chicken livers (or mushrooms or smoked oysters) and water chestnut in center of meat. Roll up meat and pierce with skewer.
5. Place green onions on grill, and place meat above the green onion. When onions have softened, push to side and broil meat until brown.

BARBECUED PORK SLICES

MAIN DISH   BARBECUING   SERVES 4

1½ lbs. boneless pork loin or pork chops (½-¾ inch thick)

MARINADE
1½ tsp. creamy peanut butter or sesame butter dissolved in 5 tbsp. sesame
  oil
6 tbsp. soy sauce
¼ cup sherry
3 tbsp. sugar
½ cup apple juice
1½ tsp. oyster sauce
1 tbsp. hoisin sauce or sweet bean sauce
5 cloves garlic, crushed
3 slices ginger root

Preparation for Pork Loin

1. Slice pork loin very thin, about ¼ inch thick. (Half-thawed frozen meat is easy to slice.)
2. Combine marinade ingredients, add meat, and marinate, covered, in refrigerator six hours or overnight.
3. Lace slices on skewers if you wish. Grill or broil slices 3-4 inches from heat until pork is golden-brown, about two minutes, turning once. Serve immediately.

Preparation for Pork Chops

1. Rinse chops and pat dry.
2. Pound with a mallet or the blunt edge of a cleaver to tenderize and loosen the texture until meat is much thinner—about ¼ inch.
3. Marinate for several hours.
4. Grill or broil as directed for pork loin. Turn and baste with marinade occasionally. (Increase cooking time slightly if thicker pieces of meat are used.)

CHICKEN BARBECUE

2½-3 lbs. chicken parts

MARINADE

¼ cup hoisin sauce	1 tbsp. sugar
¼ cup soy sauce	4 cloves garlic
¼ cup sherry	4 slices ginger root
2 tbsp. oyster sauce	3 green onions, tied in knots

Preparation

1. Rinse chicken pieces and pat dry.

2. Combine marinade ingredients and marinate chicken several hours or overnight.

3. Broil over medium-hot coals until done, turning and basting with marinade occasionally.

BARBECUED RIBS

2½-3 lbs. spareribs or country ribs or back ribs
1 tbsp. sherry
2 green onions, tied in knots
2 slices ginger root

MARINADE

¼ cup hoisin sauce	1 tbsp. sugar
¼ cup soy sauce	1 tbsp. oil
¼ cup sherry	4 cloves garlic
2 tbsp. oyster sauce	4 slices ginger root

Preparation

1. Put ribs in pan and add water to cover. Add sherry, green onions, and ginger slices.

2. Bring to a boil, then turn down heat to simmer for ½ hour.

3. Remove scum and fat from liquid. Cool and drain.

4. Combine marinade ingredients, and marinate ribs.

5. Broil over hot coals until done, turning and basting with marinade occasionally.

6

Beautifying Your Table

Garnishing

Garnishing is decorating and beautifying a dish with ornamental or symbolic foods (or flowers and the like). Garnishes add color and interest to food to make it more appetizing.

This section deals only with simple, easy-to-make items. They can be prepared two days ahead and then refrigerated in a covered plastic container, or placed flat in a sealed plastic bag after the garnishes have become full-bloomed in ice water. Or they can be prepared minutes before serving.

You will need a small, thin-bladed paring knife, a serrated knife, and a small pair of scissors. Other essential items are round toothpicks, string, food coloring or beet juice or grape juice, and ice water.

Ingredients may be chosen from any of the following fruits and vegetables, classified by color.

FRUITS
Green: lime, kiwi, seedless grapes, double gimlet cherries
Indigo: grapes, blueberries
Yellow: grapefruit, lemon, pineapple
Orange: oranges
Red: maraschino cherries, bing cherries, strawberries

VEGETABLES
Green: asparagus, broccoli, chili peppers, coriander (Chinese parsley), cucumber, escarole, green onion, green bean, green pepper, leek, lettuce, parsley, snow pea pods, watercress, zucchini
Orange: carrots, yams
Purple: eggplant, purple onion, red cabbage
Red: beet, cherry tomato, chili peppers, radish, sweet red pepper, tomato
White or cream color: Belgian endive, cauliflower, green onion (white bulb), lobak (Chinese radish, daikon), parsnip, turnip, white radish, yellow onion
Yellow: yellow chili peppers

The basic principle of color coordination is to choose one of the following:
1. Garnishes whose colors contrast with the food, obtaining a combination such as:

orange and white
orange and green
orange and purple
red, yellow, and white (cream)
yellow and purple
white (cream) and purple

2. A harmonious color scheme such as:

pink and red
white and pink
green and yellow
yellow and orange

3. A complementary color scheme such as:

red and green
blue and orange
yellow and purple

SIMPLE GARNISHES

- Place eight to twelve coriander sprigs or pieces of parsley on top of a stir-fried dish.
- Place a bunch of coriander or parsley at each end of the plate, and put two to four cherry tomatoes or maraschino cherries on top of the bunches.
- Arrange four to six parsley pieces in groups around a large platter, and put two half-slices or wedges of tomato between the parsley pieces.
- Shred two or three green onions diagonally into thin slices, or chop onions or chives, and place in the center of the food. (May be prepared ahead of time, placed in plastic sandwich bags, and refrigerated.)
- Use lettuce or escarole leaves as a bed. Arrange shredded lettuce on top of the food, and put a cherry tomato or fresh cherries in the middle.
- Place a bunch of escarole in the center of the plate, then surround or cover it with tomato and orange wedges.
- Place uniform-sized tomato slices or lemon wedges around the plate.
- Place eight thin, uniform-sized half-slices of cucumber or zucchini on two sides of plates. (Use the tines of a fork to score the cucumber lengthwise before slicing.) Arrange each slice so that it overlaps the next one a little. Or, on each end of the plate, arrange four slices facing each other in a flower shape, and put a cherry in center.
- To make a lemon or orange twist, cut a thin slice from the rind. Make a slit from the center of the slice to the edge. Grasp the edges of the cut gently, and twist them open in opposite directions. Place a cherry, olive, or grape in each curve.
- To make a pineapple twist, follow the directions for making an orange twist, using one slice of pineapple. Place a maraschino cherry or cherry tomato on each curve.

FRUITS

Lemon or Lime Petals
1. Slice a thin (⅛ inch) cross-section from the widest portion and cut it in half.
2. Slice another thin cross-section from the smaller end portion, and cut it in half.
3. Place large half-slices at a sixty-degree angle, facing each other.
4. Place small halves in the same way, but overlap the large slice a little. Place a cherry in between.

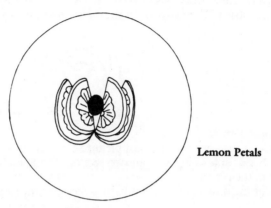

Lemon Petals

Orange Cups
1. Cut orange in half and scoop out fruit, leaving rind.
2. Serrate the edges. Use as containers for dipping sauce.

Grapefruit or Orange Basket
1. Cut a small piece from one end of the fruit to form a flat base.
2. Find the center point on top of the grapefruit or orange. A half-inch away from the center on each side, make a vertical cut, but stopping halfway down on the grapefruit or orange. This forms the handle.
3. Slice the fruit in half horizontally; make sure you stop cutting at the handle base.
4. Remove the upper portions around the handle.
5. Scoop out the fruit pulp and fill the basket with a dip or with parsley, olives, cherry tomatoes, or vegetable flowers.

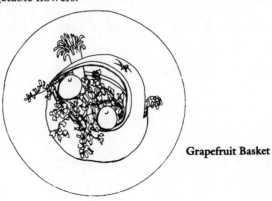

Grapefruit Basket

Lemon, Lime, or Orange Rose

1. If the base of the orange, lemon, or lime is not flat, peel off a piece first, so that it can stand.

2. Holding the fruit sideways, start to cut a thin slice of peel from near one end, but leave 1/2 inch not cut through as the base for rose. Start above the base line to cut a spiral peel continuously to the end (as you would peel an apple).

3. Starting at the end that was cut last, tightly curl the long peel toward the base, then let loose, letting the "rose" rest on its base.

A navel orange could make two small roses. Peel orange halfway and cut off. Curl tight and loosen. Then start from the other end of the orange to start another rose.

Lemon Rose

Pineapple Petals

1. Cut a slice of canned pineapple into four sections.

2. On one side of a plate, put two sections facing each other. Place a maraschino cherry in the center.

3. Put the other two sections with a cherry at the opposite side of the plate.

Pineapple Petals

Pineapple Butterfly

1. Cut a slice of canned pineapple into three equal sections.

2. Layer-cut one section into two thin pieces.

3. Place the two equal sections so that they face each other, overlapped by thin pieces facing each other.

4. Put a maraschino cherry in the center.

5. Cut 2 1/2-inch sections from the base (white end) of a green onion, and slice off two 1/8-inch slivers. Roll each sliver around a toothpick into a coil, then release to form a curled shape like a pair of antennae. Place them back to back above cherry.

Pineapple Butterfly

Pineapple Rose with Stand
1. Layer-cut a slice of canned pineapple into two thin pieces.
2. Slit one piece from the outer edge to the center hole, and roll it into a rose.
3. Place the curled rose in the center hole of the other piece, forming a flower.

VEGETABLES

Beet Flower
1. Cut a raw beet into very thin ($1/8$-$1/16$-inch), pliable slices. Coil one small piece as the center.
2. Place two pieces around the center as the second layer.
3. Add more pieces to the spaces between the petals.
4. Use a toothpick and string to fasten; cut off the exposed portion of the toothpick.
5. Surround flower with vegetable greenery.

Carrot Shapes
Peel carrots diagonally, and slice into $1/8$- to $1/16$-inch pieces. Use very small cookie cutters to cut into various shapes.

Cherry Tomato Flower
1. Use the tip of a knife to make five skin-deep cuts halfway down a cherry tomato.
2. Drop tomato into boiling water for 1 minute, then rinse under cold water.
3. Peel back the sections of skin plus a little flesh between cuts to form flower petals.
4. Sprinkle minced chives or sieved hard-cooked egg yolk onto the flower, or place a parsley sprig in the center of it.

Cucumber Flower
1. Cut cucumber into nine identical paper-thin slices, and place them in a circle, with each piece overlapping the next one, to form petals.
2. Place a maraschino cherry in the center. (The cherry may also be placed on top of a pineapple slice in the center.)

French or Belgian Endive
1. Unfold leaves one by one, ever so gently.
2. Bloom in ice water.

Green Onion Brush
See page 115.

Leek Sparkler
Follow directions for Green Onion Brush.

Lobak or Turnip Daisy
1. Slice radish or turnip into thin horizontal pieces.
2. Use a daisy-shaped cutter to make daisies.
3. Cut a slice of carrot for the center of the daisy. Or cut a thin, round piece from a lobak or turnip, dip in yellow food coloring, and use as the center.

Lobak Rose

Lobak or Turnip Rose

1. Peel lobak or turnip, and cut it into six to twelve paper-thin slices.
2. Curl up the smallest piece as the center. Place two large pieces around the center; then place the third piece in between the first two petals. (Use a toothpick to skew; snip off ends of toothpick.)
3. Continue to add larger pieces in alternative positions around the already formed petals. Fasten with string or with toothpicks, snipping off ends.
4. Use a toothpick to skew or string to secure the lower part of the petals.
5. Dip rose in food coloring. The longer it is left in the food coloring, the darker the color will be. For a pink rose, dilute red food coloring with water and dip for a short time. If only tinted edges are desired, stain edges with a brush or a cotton swab stick dipped in food coloring or beet juice or grape juice, etc.

Lobak or Turnip Lily

1. Peel lobak or turnip, and cut a paper-thin slice from the widest part.
2. Use pickled young corn, canned baby corn, or even the tip of an asparagus as the stamen.
3. Fold the petal into a conelike shape, enclosing the stamen in the center.
4. Use a toothpick to pierce the overlapped folds and stamen.
5. Place in ice water to bloom.

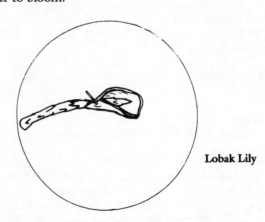

Lobak Lily

Onion Chrysanthemum

1. Peel a yellow or purple onion.
2. Cut the onion from top to bottom into four sections, stopping ½ inch from the root end of onion. Continue cutting each quarter in half, making eighths, then each eighth in half, making sixteenths. Continue to make partial cuts as long as there is room.
3. Place in ice water to bloom.
4. Dye the onion with yellow, blue, or rust food coloring—or color only the tips.

Red Chili Pepper Flower

1. Use small scissors to cut five to seven strips to within 1 inch from bottom. (Wear rubber gloves to protect hands from this irritating spice.)
2. Bloom in ice water.

Pepper Flowers

Yellow Hot Pepper Flower I

1. Use scissors to cut eight to nine strips, leaving 1½ inches at the bottom.
2. Trim the straight strips at an angle to form pointed tips.
3. Place in ice water to bloom.

Yellow Hot Pepper Flower II

1. Cross-cut pepper at the center. Use only the lower portion.
2. Use scissors to cut many thin identical lines, leaving 1 inch at the bottom.
3. Trim the strips at an angle to form pointed tips.
4. Place in ice water to bloom.

Sweet Red Pepper Flower

1. Use scissors to cut ½-inch-wide strips starting at the narrow end of t pepper. Leave 1½ inches uncut at the bottom.
2. At the tip of each strip, make cuts at an angle to form points.
3. Bloom in ice water.

Radish Ball

Radish Ball
1. Cut both ends flat.
2. Make eight even vertical slits around the radish. Cut out an 1/8-inch-wide section at each slit.
3. Cut another radish into eight thin slices, each slice 1/8 inch thick.
4. Insert the thin slices into slits of the first radish.

Radish Accordion

Radish Accordion
1. Trim both ends.
2. Make parallel vertical cuts, leaving 1/4 inch at the bottom.
3. Place in ice water to bloom.

Tomato Rose
1. Using a serrated knife, carefully peel a continuous circular strip of tomato skin plus a small width of the flesh.
2. Coil peels very tightly and let loose.
3. Arrange sprigs of parsley or coriander (Chinese parsley) or watercress around rose.

Tomato Basket
1. Cut base flat.
2. Follow directions for Orange Cups.

Tomato Flower
1. Make six even cuts vertically on a tomato to form petals.
2. Push down the petals.
3. Trim the petals into a rounded shape.

Bean Threads
Cut into 2-inch sections and deep-fry; they are ready in seconds. Use as a bed for other foods.

Egg Shreds
Make a thin egg crepe (see page 70). Cut into thin shreds.

Egg White Shreds
Beat egg white. Pan-fry over low heat to make a thin crepe. Remove and cool. Cut into thin strips.

Rice Sticks
Break rice sticks into 2-inch sections. Deep-fry. They are ready in seconds. Use as a bed for other foods.

Shrimp Chips
See page 61. Use fried Shrimp Chips as an edible accompaniment for dishes such as Butterfly Shrimp.

Wonton Chips
See page 61. Wonton Chips may be used as a border for a dish containing no sauce, such as Soy-Sauce Cornish Hen.

Oriental Decor

A creative way to give an Oriental atmosphere to a dinner party is to make decorations using the appropriate Chinese characters or symbols for the occasion.

The Chinese language is vastly different from any other language. Written Chinese has no alphabet but consists of characters, which were originally derived from pictograms. Each character is unique and has its own one word, one sound and one tone, and denotes one or several meanings, depending on the combination of words. For example, *shang ma* means "getting on a horse." If the word order is reversed to *ma shang,* the meaning becomes "at once" or "immediately"—or "on horse."

Spoken Chinese is complicated by the use of different intonations, or tones. The same sound spoken with different tones has entirely different meanings. For example, *ma* said with the level tone means "Mom"; said with the second (rising) tone, *ma* means "linen" or "numb"; with the third (curving) tone, *ma* means "horse"; and with the fourth (falling) tone, *ma* means "scold." Historically, the written form of Chinese was the same all over China. However, the People's Republic of China has adopted the simplified form for some characters, and Chinese who do not live on the mainland need to consult a dictionary for these words. The dialects of China are countless and complex. If it were not for the establishment of an official language, Mandarin, the Chinese would have had a very difficult, if not impossible, time communicating orally with each other. When people speak two different dialects, they must rely on written Chinese to communicate.

Despite the complexity of the language, the most commonly used characters and symbols for various occasions are universal in China. *Xi (hsi)* applies to a wedding or wedding anniversary and means "double happiness." *Shou* refers to longevity and is used at birthday parties for the elderly. The symbols of longevity could be either of the two characters on pages 195 and 196. *Chun* means "spring" and refers to the Chinese New Year festival.

Paper cutouts traditionally are done on red paper, or on gold-colored paper against a red background. Red and gold are rich-looking, auspicious, happy colors.

For *xi,* use a piece of paper 3½ by 3¾ inches. Fold it in half, then in half again to obtain a long rectangular shape. Trace the quarter section as shown below, with the folded part to your left. Then cut the pattern out, making sure not to cut through the left-hand fold. For either longevity symbol, use paper 4½ by 4½ inches. Fold in half, then in half again to obtain a square shape. Trace the pattern for *shou* as shown on pages 195 and 196, cut out, and unfold.

Use double-sided cellophane tape to stick four identical red-paper characters on top of the tablecloth at the four corners. (The tops of the characters should point inward toward the center of the table.) If you use a red tablecloth, cut the characters out of gold paper. (Gift wrap is good for this.)

These cutouts may also be pasted onto a gift box or placed on top of the gifts in a box, or even used to make a birthday or anniversary card.

To make a place mat, paste a red cutout character in the center of a piece of thick white paper. Cut two pieces of laminating paper 1 inch wider than the white paper. Then sandwich the white paper in between and seal the edges.

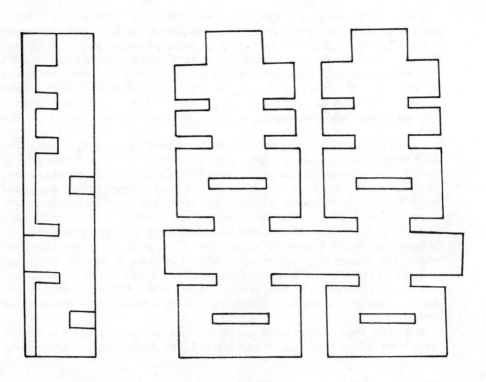

Xi (Double Happiness)

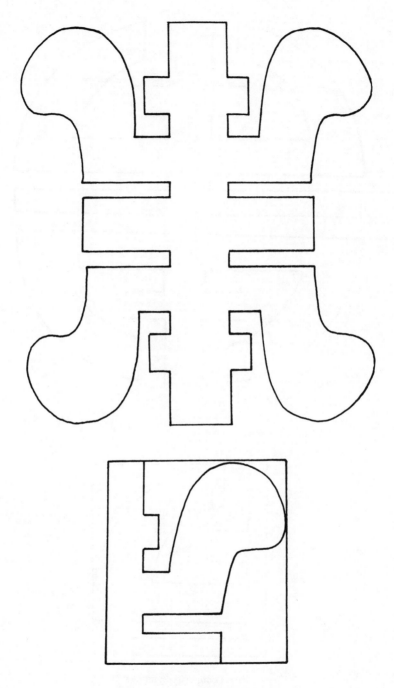

Shou (Longevity Symbol #1)

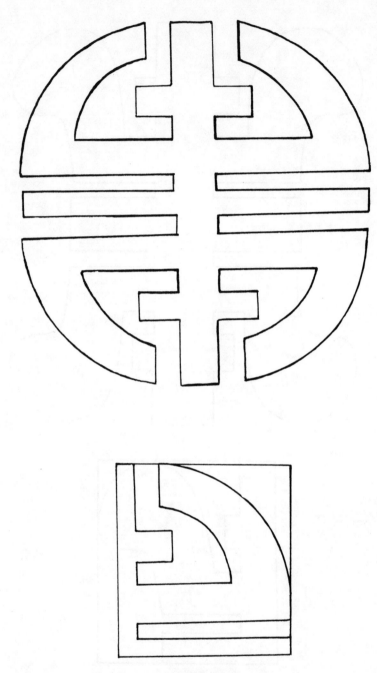

Shou (Longevity Symbol #2)

Chun (Spring)

A square cloth or paper napkin folded into a Chinese pagoda or a fan will add interest to your table. The folding can be done well ahead of party time, and children eight years old or older can help. Use paper clips to keep the folds in place if folding is done ahead of time.

HOW TO FOLD A PAGODA

1. Fold a square paper or cloth napkin in half (so that the opening is at the bottom).
2. Fold sideways toward right in half again (now the openings are at the right and the bottom).
3. Use right hand to hold down the bottom three sheets. Use left hand to lift the lower right-hand corner of the top sheet (B) and bring it far to the left, pushing down to form a triangle (ABC). Turn napkin over and do the same on the reverse side.
4. Bring corner B up to meet the tip of the triangle (A). In other words, bring BX in line with AX. Thus a small triangle (BYX) is formed, with its opening at the right.
5. Holding down the inner sheet, bring tip B down to meet X, forming a square. Bring point B up to corner Y to form a small triangle.
6. Flip the folded piece over to the right, then fold it backward in half. Then flip the piece back to the left again.
7. Repeat steps 4-6 for the right side. Then flip entire napkin over and repeat for the remaining two sides.
8. Push point D at the bottom center up to EF, and press the paper flat to form the rim of the pagoda. Repeat on the reverse side. A two-sided pagoda is now formed. It can be laid flat on the table, or it can be stood up if the napkin is starched and stiff.
9. If you wish, the pagoda can be made to stand up by folding the two bases up and outward in line with the rim of the pagoda. To be sure the pagoda will stand firmly, gently pull folded bases on both sides outward.

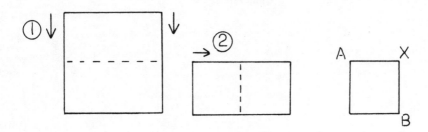

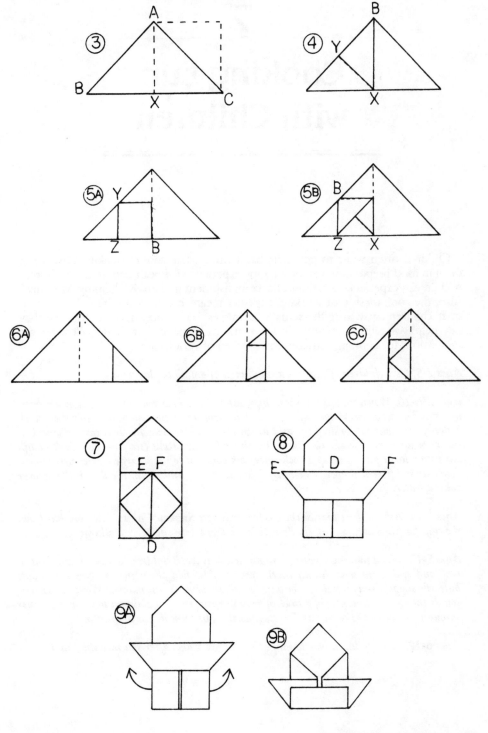

7

Cooking Fun with Children

Children often want to get their hands into what you are making. Involving them in food preparation can be a happy experience for both parents and children. A child can experience a feeling of accomplishment and enjoy "helping Mommy." Also, the comradeship of working together means much to children. Try to keep small children away from the actual cooking, especially deep-frying, although they can help you with the preparatory work to some extent. The following are suggestions for cooking activities for children of various ages.

Ages 2-5. Give children of this age a small piece of dough to play with.

Ages 2¹/₂-10. When making wonton chips, ask them to help you to tear wonton wrappers into small pieces of any shape and size and put them into a mixing bowl. After their work is done, it is your job to deep-fry and drain them. These crunchy chips can be served as snacks or appetizers. Make the Basic Dough for Chinese Rolls (see page 63). Roll dough out into a large piece about ¹/₂ inch thick; ask children to use a large cookie cutter to cut dough into different shapes or designs. Allow it to rise, and steam the dough shapes over boiling water.

Ages 4-12. Ask children to stick the sesame seeds onto Suzhou Cakes. After you hard-boil the eggs for Marble Eggs, ask children to crack them with the back of a large spoon.

Ages 5-12. When making Crispy Wontons, you may teach children to fold wonton skins in half and seal them with filling in the center. Also fold them into nurse's cap shape, butterfly shape, candy roll shape, or parallelogram form. When making Wonton Fritters, you do the cutting in center of a stack of wonton wrappers. Ask children to turn one corner through the slit in the center and stretch gently. Then you do the deep-frying.

Ages 6-12. Show children how to make the Suzhou Cakes after you mix the dough.

Ages 8-12
   Wrap egg rolls.
   Spread filling on Shrimp Toast.
   Fill Stuffed Mushrooms.
   *Mandarin Pancakes: knead dough, brush sesame oil on dough, and pair them together
      and roll out.*
   Knead dumpling dough and wrap dumplings.
   Paper-Wrapped Chicken: cut parchment paper into squares and wrap food inside.
   Wrap Shao Mai Beef dumplings.
   Peel broccoli stems, carrots, cucumbers, and zucchini.
   Break broccoli and cauliflower into individual florets.
   Slice onions and tomatoes.
   Remove strings from snow pea pods.
   Beat eggs.
   Peel and devein shrimp.
   Dissolve cornstarch in water.
   Mix sauces.
   Fold napkins.
   Set table.

Sprouting Beans

Sprouting beans is an easy and rewarding experience. It takes only a few days, and children enjoy seeing—and eating—the result.

MATERIALS
   A colander, or a steamer rack with lid, or any utensil with flat bottom with
      drainage holes and a cover, or a brown-colored sprouting jar with mesh
      cover and lid
   A pan or pot
   2 pieces of white cheesecloth double-layered or white paper towels
   1 piece of dark cloth or foil paper
   ½ cup mung beans or soybeans (to make 3 cups sprouts)
   water

1. Measure and wash mung beans or soybeans; pour 1 cup boiling water over; swish beans in water and drain. Soak overnight in cold water.
2. Drain water.
3. Dampen two pieces of clean double-layered cheesecloth (or white paper towel). Place one piece on the bottom of the colander.
4. Spread beans on top of cheesecloth, and place another piece of cheesecloth over the beans. Sprinkle ½ cup of warm water over the top cheesecloth, and let it drain through.

5. Cover the colander with a lid, place it on top of a pan to catch the water drippings, then drape it with a dark cloth or foil paper. Place it in a dark, warm place (an oven or a cabinet is a good spot).

6. Rinse at least 3-4 times a day with ½ cup of lukewarm water. Or place the cheesecloth-covered colander in water for 10 minutes, then drain and return to dark place.

7. In 4-5 days, bean sprouts will be ready. Remove dark cloth and cheesecloth. Pour bean sprouts in a pot of cold water. Let them sit in water for several hours. Rinse, and remove the bitter green hulls of mung beans. Drain and prepare for eating, or store in refrigerator.

Hint

The sprouts will be more plump if a heavy object is placed on top of the covered beans while they are sprouting.

Growing Garlic Greens

Garlic is an indoor as well as an outdoor plant with edible greens. The scallionlike green is fragrant and adds flavoring when stir-fried with a meat dish. Your children will enjoy watching the garlic sprout as they water it each day.

Indoors: Peel the skin off each garlic clove. Use a 6-inch bamboo skewer to skew 5-6 garlic cloves together sideways, with the pointed ends upward. Put the skewer in a plastic strawberry container, with its ends held in place within the openings in the side of the container. Set the container in a shallow dish. Add cold water to cover the bottom, round parts of the garlic (where the roots are), and let stand on a kitchen counter. In a week to ten days you will notice green shoots starting to sprout. Change water daily, making sure it covers the bottom root part only. (Prolonged soaking will make the garlic rot.) When garlic greens reach a height of 6-8 inches, cut them off and slice into 2-inch sections. Use as a stir-fried condiment. Discard rotting cloves. (Cloves in good condition will sprout again after you cut off the greens.)

Outdoors: Peel the skin off each garlic clove. Plant cloves in your vegetable garden with the soil covering the round bottom part.

Peeled garlic cloves can also be planted indoors or outdoors in a shallow dish or flower pot with soil covering the bottom root part. Be sure to place them in a sunny location. Add water when soil is dry.

Planting Green Onions

Instead of discarding the root part of the green onions, plant them in your vegetable garden. Your children will enjoy watching the new shoots grow.

8

Chinese Festivals and Celebrations

Festivals and celebrations are deeply ingrained in the Chinese way of life, and food and feasting play an integral part of each celebration. Each festival has its special foods, and each food has its own symbolic meaning. The main festivals are the Chinese New Year (Spring Festival), Lantern Festival, Dragon Boat Festival, and Mid-Autumn Festival (Moon Festival). The main celebrations are births, birthdays, and wedding.

Chinese New Year

When is the Chinese New Year? The dates of all Chinese festivals are determined by the lunar or farmer's calendar, which is based on the waxing and waning of the moon. The Chinese New Year—the first day of the first new moon each year—falls on a different day each year between January 20 and February 20. For example, February 5 of 1981, January 25 of 1982, and February 13 of 1983 were Chinese New Years. The lunar calendar divides the year into twelve months, but each month has twenty-nine or thirty days and begins with the appearance of the new moon. Therefore, there are only 354 days in a lunar year, whereas the solar calendar has 365 days in a year. On the average, every two to three years an extra month is included to bring the lunar year back in sequence with the solar year. For example, in 1979 the lunar month of June and in 1982 the lunar month of April were repeated before the next month started.

Each year is represented by its own animal, one of the twelve Chinese zodiac symbols:

Rat	1972	1984
Ox	1973	1985
Tiger	1974	1986
Hare	1975	1987
Dragon	1976	1988

Serpent (Snake)	1977	1989
Horse	1978	1990
Ram	1979	1991
Monkey	1980	1992
Rooster (Cock)	1981	1993
Dog	1982	1994
Boar (Pig)	1983	1995

A baby born in 1983 (to be exact, on or after February 13, since February 12, 1983, was the last day in the year of the Dog) will be a "Boar" according to his natal year. Twelve years later, his natal year will come around again. People who are older than this baby by twelve, twenty-four, thirty-six, forty-eight, or sixty years will share the same animal symbol with him. Thus, it is common for Chinese people to give their ages away by mentioning the zodiac animal of the year of their birth. Old-fashioned Chinese count a person's age not by the actual number of anniversaries since his birth, but rather by how many new years he has lived through. Everyone grows one year older when the new year arrives. A baby is considered a year old at birth, as life is considered to start at conception.

The New Year is supposed to be a felicitous time for a marriage. But many people prefer to be married in the old year in order to have a happier new year, with the new spouse at his or her side.

Chinese New Year is the most colorful, exciting, and important festival of the year. It is also called Spring Festival, as spring usually starts then or soon after (according to the lunar calendar).

In a rural, agricultural society, seasons are closely associated with work in the fields. At the end of a year of toil, farmers offer thanks to heaven, earth, and the gods for the harvest. At the same time they celebrate and relax with family and friends. In the cities, businesses close for three days. All schools take a winter recess. Everyone heads for home, and families are all reunited for the holidays.

The celebration starts with lengthy preparations in advance. The New Year is ushered in with the ear-shattering sounds of firecrackers and the colorful sight of the "lion dances." Families and friends enjoy lavish feasting. The celebration ends with new expectations and hopes for the coming year. My feeling is that the Chinese New Year combines the festive elements of the American Easter (spring cleaning, new outfits), Halloween (ringing of doorbells and giving of candy), Thanksgiving (offering thanks and feasting), Christmas (family reunions, feasting, exchanging gifts), and New Year (new aspirations, a new start with new hopes).

PREPARING FOR THE HOLIDAY

Preparations for the New Year start early in the last month of the old year. Since markets usually close for three to five days at the New Year, much shopping must be done ahead to be sure there is plenty to serve. Large cuts of pork, chickens, ducks, and fish are bought and salted (cured) to be ready for the New Year. Traditional dishes are prepared.

Candy boxes and New Year items are taken from storage. Silver is polished. Repairs, painting, and a thorough housecleaning are all carried out. The living room is decorated with the best pictures and new tablecloths and chair coverings. Debts are paid to ensure a clean slate. Business accounts are cleared, and bonuses are distributed.

As a token of appreciation, families exchange gifts such as a whole cured ham or a live fowl, baskets of fruit, delicacies, fine liquors or wines, cigarettes, tea, or material for clothing. New clothes are bought or made to order; new shoes, new hats, and new accessories are all in order. Men and children have their hair cut; women get permanents or have their hair set in a fancy style. Tips to the barbers and hairdressers are generously given at the year's end.

Firecrackers, a new picture of the "kitchen god," red good-luck hangings for doors or walls, incense, candles, and imitation paper money or silver paper (to fold into ingots for ancestral worship) are all purchased.

Front doors display propitious Chinese characters such as *fu* (which means "many blessings" and is an all-encompassing word for all good things) or the word for spring (which means both "spring" and "new year"). The characters are written on squares of red paper before being affixed to the door. (Red is the color for all happy occasions. It is the emblem of joy, righteousness, and truth.) Red scrolls inscribed with messages of happiness, prosperity, and longevity are pasted on walls.

In the old days, homes had an indentation built into the wall especially for the kitchen god. A portrait of the god in a shrine was placed in this niche. Above it appeared the words "The palace of blessings and longevity." On the sides of the niche hung red scrolls; the right side read, "To heaven, he reports only the merits"; the left side read, "On earth, he blesses the family with peace and tranquillity."

Nowadays, for those who still follow the tradition, a picture of the kitchen god is pasted on the wall in the kitchen, usually above the stove. On the twenty-fourth night (in some places, the twenty-third) of the twelfth moon, a ceremony of sending the kitchen god to heaven is performed in each household. He is first honored with food and wine. Candles are lit and incense is burned before his picture. Everyone in the family comes to wish him a good trip to heaven. In order to encourage him to report only the merits of the family to heaven, the people rub his lips with honey or malt candy. Then they take his picture down and burn it together with imitation money purchased for the occasion or with silver paper ingots, which are supposed to assure him a comfortable journey. Fodder is even burned for his horse. According to legend, he rides his horse to heaven. On New Year's Eve he returns to the spotless house. A new picture of him is pasted in the same spot in the kitchen. A rich feast greets him, and everyone welcomes his return.

NEW YEAR'S EVE

In the last hours of the old year, family members gather at the home of the eldest family member. Adults and children all sit around a table full of delicious dishes. Wines or liquor are served to adults, soft drinks to children. Toasts are offered to those present, usually in the order of seniority. A husband and wife offer and receive toasts together, as a unit. The drinking game of *gan-bei* ("bottoms up"), which challenges the guests to empty their cups in a single gulp, is played while toasting to make the occasion merrier. Cheers are given to the one who first turns his cup upside-down to prove he finished first. (The ladies do not drink as much as the gentlemen on these occasions.) Out of politeness, the person proposing the toast may finish up his own drink but asks the person who is toasted to drink only as much as he or she pleases.

A popular amusement for two male guests as they drink is a finger game somewhat similar to the "scissors, paper, rock" game played by American children. Each player calls out a number between zero and ten. Simultaneously, each flings out his right hand displaying any number of fingers or just his fist. If the combined total of outstretched fingers of both players matches the number called by one of the players, he is the winner, and the loser must down a drink. The game gets faster and faster, the calling of the numbers get louder and louder, and the spectators laugh and cheer.

The feasting can go on for hours. Toward the end, a complete fish dish is traditionally served because the Chinese word for fish *(yu)* sounds like the word that suggests "having plenty left for the coming year" or "always having plenty in reserve."

After the feast, it is time for playing games or for singing, dancing, and performances. To have fun together is the aim, and these are all suitable forms of entertainment. In my childhood years, this was the time when gifts were given. My grandmother, as head of the family (my grandfather had passed away long before), received gifts from her children—a stack of new bills in a red envelope. My uncle, my father, and my aunts each presented such gifts to her, one after another, along with an expression of good wishes. Then came the moment we children had long been waiting for—*our* turn to get red envelopes with money tucked inside. First Grandmother gave to her own children and their spouses according to age (eldest first). Then she gave to all her grandchildren, either grouped by families (still according to ages) or by the ages of all children. In my family there were more than twenty grandchildren born to my grandmother's four children.

We children loved to line up as if forming a long dragon. Each child went forward to get a red envelope as his or her name was called, and then sat down. I recall how much fun we had peeking inside the envelopes! After Grandmother finished giving gifts to her children, grandchildren, and servants, then it was my uncle's (Grandmother's eldest son's) turn to give to everyone, followed by my father (second eldest) and my aunts' husbands (third and fourth in rank). People who are unmarried are considered to be "youngsters" whatever their age, and they are not expected to hand out the red-envelope money. Children place their red-envelope money under their pillows and sleep on it.

The very young go to bed. Adults and older children stay up till midnight. (Some adults stay up all night.) At the stroke of twelve, the old year is sent off in a burst of firecrackers, and the New Year is ushered in. Cries of *Gong-xi! Gong-xi!*—Happy New Year! Happy New Year!—ring out everywhere. As a gesture of respect and friendliness, one cups the hands and moves them up and down while saying this. *Gong-xi* literally means "Congratulations" in Mandarin. In Cantonese the greeting is pronounced *kung hee*. In Honolulu and San Francisco, where the first groups of Cantonese immigrants settled, *Kung hee fat choy!* ("May you be prosperous!") is the most common greeting for the New Year.

NEW YEAR'S DAY

Firecrackers usually wake everyone early in the morning. The loud noise is supposed to chase evil spirits away, and is also a sign of celebration and happiness. Children eagerly put on their clothes—everything brand-new from head to toe. Adults put on either new clothing or fresh-looking holiday attire. In our family, we woke on New Year's Day to find a plateful of candy, sweets, candied fruits, peanuts, walnuts, oranges, and the like, which my mother had prepared after we children had gone to bed the night before. It was a joy to be greeted in the morning with such colorful, delightful goodies, which symbolize "sweetness throughout the year." The traditional New Year's breakfast is New Year's cake, in either steamed, boiled, or pan-fried form, a broth of lotus seeds and longan, and tea eggs (marble eggs).

Later on, friends come to call on the family. Elderly people are much respected in China, so they are always the first to be greeted and visited. Guests are warmly entertained and served with tea, a sweet broth, tea eggs, New Year's cakes, and treats from the candy box, including almonds, crystallized ginger root, candies, dried litchis, longan fruit, kumquats, honeyed dates, peanuts, walnuts, and watermelon seeds.

SYMBOLISM OF THE CHINESE NEW YEAR

The Chinese New Year is full of symbolism. Every animal, every food, every sound, every shape, every plant has its own special meaning. Often the symbolism is based on a homonym, as in the previously mentioned example of fish, since the Chinese word for fish sounds like the word meaning "plenty" or "more than enough." Here are some other examples of food symbolism:

- The word for "chicken" (*ji*) has the same sound as the word for "fortunate."
- Pork, being fat, represents abundance.
- The spring roll (called "egg roll" in the U.S.) represents the rolling in of spring.
- Chinese dumplings (*jiao-zi*) are auspicious because *zi* means "sons," and having sons means good fortune. Also, the shape of dumplings resembles the old-fashioned currency of China (gold and silver ingots).
- Egg dumplings signify golden ingots.
- Spinach or another green leafy vegetable connotes health and liveliness.
- The Chinese name for hairlike seaweed is a homonym for "getting rich."
- "Eight precious vegetables" is a dish that symbolizes perfection.
- Tea eggs (marble eggs) represent ingots.
- The round shape of meat balls denotes completeness and family togetherness.
- The Chinese name of New Year's cake (glutinous rice cake) sounds like the words meaning "going higher and higher," thus suggesting promotions, increasing health, wealth, happiness, and wisdom. For children, it means being healthier, stronger, taller, and smarter.
- Red dates (jujubes) are auspicious because of the color red and because their name, *zao-zi*, has the same sound as the words for "to have sons early."
- The word for "seed" in Chinese is *zi*, which sounds like the word that means "sons," so foods such as lotus seeds and melon seeds are considered to have a favorable symbolism.

- Walnuts represent harmony and kindness.
- Candied kumquats represent gold, as kumquats are called "golden oranges" in Chinese.
- Peanuts in the shell are called a "longevity fruit."
- Oranges represent the wish for abundant happiness and prosperity.
- The word for "apple" sounds the same as the words for "peace" and "fruitful."

The special symbolic flowers of the Chinese New Year are narcissus and peony. The narcissus is called "water fairy" in Chinese. It is grown in porcelain bowls filled with pretty pebbles and clear spring water. The flowers are forced to bloom exactly at New Year's time. They are believed to bring good luck and fortune for the coming year. Blooming is a symbol of prosperity. The peony is called "the flower of high esteem." It is not only a symbol of beauty but also a sign of spring. A blooming peony with green leaves is considered the perfect expression of good fortune.

As a tradition, there are many do's and don'ts for the Chinese New Year.

- Do honor your ancestors on happy occasions, and remember your origin.
- Do respect your elders.
- Do be kind, good-tempered, and cheerful. Do not quarrel, curse, or spank children.
- Do watch your language, and do not say any word that sounds the same as the words for "death," "empty," or "finish."
- Do enjoy yourself. New Year is the time to relax and have fun.
- Do not sweep the floor on New Year's Day—the accumulation of "wealth" should stay.
- Do not use knives or scissors, so as not to cut the continuity of luck for the year to come.
- Do not sew or paste, to avoid piercing or patching good luck.

In short, the theme of the Chinese New Year is family togetherness and all good things such as happiness, peace, health, prosperity, fortune, good luck—and many children and grandchildren.

Lantern Festival

Officially, the Chinese New Year merriment ends after fifteen days, on the fifteenth day of the first moon, which is called Yuan Xiao ("First Bright Moon") Festival. The exhibition of various beautiful hand-made lanterns in the evening is the highlight of the annual celebration. Thus, this occasion is also called Lantern Festival.

The traditional food eaten on this holiday is also called *yuan xiao*. It is a white ball of glutinous rice flour mixed with water, containing either a sweet or a salty filling. The balls are cooked in plain water and served warm. The spherical shape symbolizes completeness and fullness. This not only refers to the full moon in the sky, but also reflects the togetherness of the family on earth.

Dragon Boat Festival

The Dragon Boat Festival is held on the fifth day of the fifth moon, generally between May 28 and June 28. It is the biggest event of the summer, highlighted with rowboat races. Each rowboat is decorated with a dragon's head on the bow, the dragon being the traditional symbol of royalty.

It is popularly believed that this yearly boat race is a commemoration of the attempt to rescue a great statesman named Qu Yuan. Qu was an honest and upright official, but was sent into exile by the government. Thus, leading the life of a hermit, he wrote many poems to express his sorrow and to protest the corruption of the ruling party. In desperation, he finally drowned himself in the Milo River in Hunan on the fifth day of the fifth moon in 295 B.C. People loved him for his virtue and fidelity, and rushed to rescue him, but it was too late. They then threw a special food wrapped in leaves into the river to comfort his spirit.

That was the origin of the custom of eating this special food, *zong-zi*, on this holiday. *Zong-zi* comes in either a triangular or oblong shape. Presoaked raw glutinous rice is wrapped in bamboo leaves, stuffed with sweet bean paste, red beans, shelled peanuts, or seasoned meats. Strings are used to bind the leaves so that the rice grains do not drop out. String is also used to connect *zong-zi* together when they are cooked in water for two to three hours before serving.

Mid-Autumn Festival (Moon Festival)

Mid-autumn's colorful festival falls on the fifteenth day of the eighth moon. It is uniformly believed by the Chinese that the moon appears its fullest and brightest at that time of the year. Moon-viewing parties are held outdoors everywhere. Poets gather to sip wine and compose verses in honor of the moon. Famous lines by ancient poets, revering the moon, are recited and savored anew.

The special food for this holiday is moon cake. The perfect round shape of the cake recalls the fullness of the moon. Its brown crust is a dough made with flour and egg. The filling varies and can be sweet red bean paste, sweet date paste, egg yolk, or miscellaneous nuts or seeds. The dough is first put into a special mold with designs carved into the bottom. The filling is added, and the dough is sealed. The moon cake is then removed from the mold, having been imprinted with a design. It is finally brushed with an egg yolk mixture and baked in the oven.

Moon cakes are popular gift items during this festival. Legend has it that during the Yuan dynasty (A.D. 1279-1368), when China was under Mongolian rule, Chinese patriots plotting to overthrow the Mongols concealed secret messages inside moon cakes and exchanged them as gifts. Thus it became a tradition to eat and to give moon cakes.

Birth

In China the birth of a baby has always been considered one of life's happiest events. The expression for "getting pregnant" is *you xi*, meaning "having good news."

A newborn baby receives gifts from relatives and friends. The most common gift is the ever-popular red envelope containing money. Chinese characters expressing best wishes for long life and prosperity are often written on the top of the red envelope, or else these sentiments are spoken to the baby at the time of presenting the gift. Another typical gift to a baby is a thin gold locket with the words for longevity and prosperity engraved on one side, and peonies and designs on the other. Some people give a tiny golden charm bracelet that contains bells which tinkle when the baby moves its hands. These gold mementos are always kept in the family as keepsakes.

The proud parents distribute red eggs (hard-boiled eggs dyed with red food coloring) to relatives and friends to announce the birth.

A banquet or a family get-together is always held when the baby is one month old. It is a very important occasion for the family and the baby. Now the baby is considered to be beyond the newborn stage, and the mother has completed her month-long recuperation and is able to assume her regular activities.

Birthday

Instead of a birthday cake with candles, noodles are a must for a Chinese birthday celebration. A long strand of smooth noodle symbolizes the continuity of a long, smooth life. Noodles are served in a flavored broth, topped with meat and vegetables. Noodles can be served as a meal by themselves for lunch, but to make the birthday celebration fancier, other dishes are added to the meal.

Children are considered "little people," too young to have a celebration among friends. A special family meal of noodles is the usual way of celebrating a small child's birthday at home. Adults are "big people." To celebrate or not is up to the individual. Some people prefer to have a quiet birthday retreat with the immediate family, not wishing friends and relatives to do anything special for them. However, considerate relatives and close friends still send a gift to the house. Some people may have a well-planned birthday party for guests, possibly at a restaurant.

In China, birthdays celebrating the decades forty, sixty, seventy, eighty, ninety, and one hundred are called "big birthdays." Usually large, formal parties are held. Other birthdays are considered "little birthdays," and these celebrations are rather simple.

Elaborate parties are held for elders who reach sixty, seventy, eighty, or ninety. The Chinese respect elders for their age, wisdom, and experience. It is a great joy for older Chinese to have their children, grandchildren, and great-grandchildren all gathered together to celebrate the happy occasion. Family members plan and send out the invitations well ahead of time, inviting all the relatives, friends, and associates to join the feast. The feast is usually held at a big restaurant or rented hall. The place is beautifully decorated with fresh flowers and wall hangings displaying gold characters on red material. The character *shou*, meaning "longevity," is placed in the center of the hall, and red candles are lit on the table. Dried noodles and peach-shaped rolls, which legend associates with the god of longevity, are placed on trays on the red-cloth-covered table.

The beaming guest of honor and his or her spouse sit in the center hall to receive guests. (On happy occasions, husband and wife, even the whole family, share the pleasure and happiness and are honored as one.) Guests offer their greetings and gifts, and wish him or her a long life full of blessings.

At large parties, gifts are received at the entrance, where guests sign their names on a piece of red silk or in a red souvenir book. (It is considered inappropriate and impolite to open a gift in front of the guests, so the recipient waits until after the guests have left.) Photographs are taken to commemorate the event. Sometimes entertainment is provided before or after the feast. When the party is over, some families present each guest with a souvenir rice bowl engraved with all the children's names and the date of the celebration.

In Chinese culture the ultimate good life contains blessings, prosperity, longevity, happiness, comfort, and peace. A person is considered to be the most fully blessed if he has all of the following ten perfect happinesses:

1. Enjoys good health and good spirits, and has a long life
2. Has healthy, loving parents and parents-in-law
3. Has a healthy, loving, good spouse
4. Has a successful or satisfying career
5. Leads a financially comfortable life
6. Is well respected by the community and friends
7. Has children, including sons as well as daughters
8. Has lots of grandchildren of both sexes
9. Has good friends
10. Has children and grandchildren who are loving, caring, respectful, supporting, and still obedient to their parents

Wedding

The Chinese character symbolizing "wedding" *(xi)* combines two characters for "happiness," thus forming a "double happiness." (See page 194 for a sample cutout of this character.) It appears on wedding invitations and on wall hangings in the ceremonial hall.

Red invitations are sent to relatives and friends from the parents of both the bride and groom, with their names imprinted as hosts of the wedding, cordially inviting the entire family to attend the wedding ceremony and the banquet afterward. Parents also place an announcement of this happy event in the newspaper, printed in red and edged with double-happiness symbols.

The wedding itself can vary from a single private ceremony for a single couple to a mass wedding, and may take place in a house of worship or in court, presided over by a judge. The most popular style of civil ceremony is usually held in a rented hall or a restaurant. No matter which ceremony the family chooses to have, a wedding banquet, which Chinese call a "happy wine feast," is always held after the ceremony. There may be only a small group of people at one table, including the wedding party, parents, and witnesses, or a hundred or more guests at many tables. Each round table usually seats twelve to fourteen persons.

Here is a description of a typical ceremony from my own recollection:

The hall is cheerfully decorated with fresh flowers and red wall hangings inscribed with sayings in gold, expressing sentiments and wishes such as "This Match Was Made in Heaven," "Perfect Harmony," "To Bathe in the River of Love

Forever," "To Keep Each Other Company Till White-Haired Days," and "Double Happiness." A neon light in the shape of the double-happiness character is lit in the center stage and is usually flanked by a dragon and a phoenix on each side, symbolizing the union of male and female. Red candles are lit for good fortune.

Guests start to arrive about a half-hour before the ceremony and present their gifts at a table which has been set up by both families at the entrance. They are asked to sign their names on a red satin cloth as a souvenir for the newlyweds. The guests proceed to mill about, congratulating the parents, chatting with old friends, and meeting new friends. They can sit at any of the round tables flanking the center aisle, which is covered with a red carpet and decorated with fresh flowers.

A burst of fireworks can be heard when the bridal party arrives at the hall, usually after having had their pictures taken at a photo studio, with the bride in a white gown and veil and the groom in a suit—the only concession to Western influence seen in the Chinese wedding.

The master of ceremonies calls for the attention of the noisily chatting guests and introduces the ceremonial witnesses, including the person who will perform the marriage—usually a high-ranking government official or some other person of prestige. Also introduced are two men, one to represent each family, who supposedly are the "matchmakers" of this wedding, and the groom's father (considered the sponsor of the wedding). These people all gather at the center stage, and a space is reserved for the bride's father. At this time the hall is very quiet, as everyone is waiting to see the bridal party. Wedding music is played. The best man is the first one to walk down the aisle, followed by the groom; then come the flower girl and ring bearer, if any, the bridesmaid, and finally the bride on her father's arm. A printed certificate of marriage is read by the officiating person, and personal seals of bride, groom and the ceremonial witnesses are all placed on the certificate to make the document official. Then the officiating person gives a speech to congratulate the newlyweds. Other speeches are followed by the two "matchmakers," and finally the master of ceremonies asks attending guests to make speeches; these are often filled with humor and cause much laughter. After the ceremony, on their way out, the bride and groom are showered with confetti.

The banquet starts about six P.M., right after the ceremony. Guests are all seated, and wine or liquor is served with the four appetizer plates, which have already been placed on the table, followed by four hot stir-fried and deep-fried dishes, one sweet soup, four more main dishes, and one dim sum. The total banquet is served course by course, and the feast usually lasts two to three hours. The newlyweds are introduced again when the bride has changed into her Chinese attire, called *chi-pao* (*cheongsam* in Cantonese). Then, after several courses of food, the bridal party will go to each table to offer drinks to the guests. This is the time when the merriment reaches its climax. More food is served as guests toast each other and play finger games. Rice is usually served last, along with four big dishes such as fish and chicken soup. By this time the guests can hardly eat another bite!

At the end of the banquet, the bride changes into a third outfit and stands with the bridal party and parents at the exit to bid farewell to the guests and thank them for coming. After that, the closest friends go to the bridal chamber and subject the bashful newlyweds to some good-natured teasing until midnight.

Index

Crab Legs, 120
Fried Shrimp Toast, 56-57
Poached Trout, 116-17
Red-Cooked Shrimp in the Shell, 118
Scallops Supreme, 121
Shrimp with Lobster Sauce, 119
Steamed Fish, 117
see also Seafood
Five-spice powder, 29
Flavor, 136
Floral tea (*hua cha*), 32
Flowers, symbolic, 208
Flower type, of vegetables, 20
Folding, of wontons, 163-64
Food preparation, 40-48
  boning chicken breast, 47
  chopping up whole fowl, 48
  cutting methods, 42-46
  shapes of ingredients, 46-47
  tips for healthful cooking, 41-42
French or Belgian Endive, 189
Fresh-flavored ingredients, 18-19
Freshness, of ingredients, 32-33
Fresh noodles (*lo mein*), 27
Fried Shrimp Toast, 56-57
Fruits, 25, 42, 135
  garnishing with, 185, 187-89
Fruit type, of vegetables, 20
Frying, *see* Deep-frying; Pan-frying; Stir-frying
Fungi, Chinese edible, 22
Fu Yang Salted Chicken, 110

G

Garlic, 19, 22
Garlic greens, growing, 202
Garnishing, 185-93
  and colors, 186
  with fruits, 185, 187-89
  simple, 186
  with vegetables, 185, 189-92
Gifts, 194, 206
  at birthday parties, 211
  exchange of, 205
  to newborn baby, 210
Ginger root, 19, 22-23
Glutinous (sticky) rice, 26
Glutinous rice cake, *see* New Year's cake
Gold, as color, 194
Gold mementos, 210
Gong Bao Chicken, 103-4
gong-xi, 206

Gourmet Delight (company), 31
Grapefruit Basket, 187
"Green bean sprouts," 86
Green onion, 19, 23
  Green-Onion-Filled Suzhou Cakes, 66
  planting, 202
Green Onion Brush, 115, 189
Green-Onion-Filled Suzhou Cakes, 66
Green pepper
  Pepper Steak, 87-88
  Sweet-Sour Green Peppers, 81
Green tea (*lu cha* or *ching cha*), 32
Guangdong, *see* Canton
Guangzhou (Canton Province), 15

H

Ham
  Ham and Asparagus Salad, 73-74
  Ham Fried Rice, 122
  see also Jin-hua ham
Ham and Asparagus Salad, 73-74
Ham Fried Rice, 122
Hangzhou (Hangchow), 15
Hangzhou's Dragon Well, 32
Healthful cooking, tips for, 41-42
Hoisin sauce, 30
Home-style dinners, 136, 139-40
Hot bean sauce, 30-31
Hot pepper oil, 30
hsi, see xi
Hunan Chicken, 105-6
Hunan cuisine, 14, 17

I

Indoors, growing garlic greens, 202
Ing, Lillian, 27
Ingredients, 18-33
  categories of, 18-19
  freshness of, 32-33
  main food types, 19-27
  shape and size of, 46-47, 136
  see also Oil; Seasonings; Spices; Tea
Instant noodles, 27

J

Jade Beef, 90-91
Jiffy dinners for two cooks, 136-37, 142-44
Jiffy Egg Rolls, 168-69

Red Chili Pepper Flower, 191
Red-Cooked Beef, 94-95
Red-Cooked Chicken Wings, 107
Red-Cooked Shrimp in the Shell, 118
Red-cooking, 41
    Red-Cooked Beef, 94-95
    Red-Cooked Chicken Wings, 107
    Red-Cooked Shrimp in the Shell, 118
    Shanghai-Style Red-Cooked Chicken, 106-7
    Soy-Sauce Cornish Hen, 109
    Stovetop Sweet-Sour Spareribs, 96-97
Red dates (jujubes) *(zao-zi),* 207
Red eggs, 210
Red-envelope money, 206, 210
"Red tea" *(hong cha),* 32
Red vinegar, 30
Regional cuisines, 14-17
    Cantonese, 14, 15
    Hunan, 14, 17
    Mandarin, 14-15
    Peking, 14-15
    Shanghai, 14, 15
    Sichuan, 14, 17
Rice, 25-27, 135
    Beef Fried Rice, 124
    cooking, 26-27
    Ham Fried Rice, 122
    Oyster-Flavored Fried Rice, 123
    see also New Year's cake
Rice noodles (or rice sticks), 27
Rice Sticks, 193
Roll cut, 44
Rolling pin, *see* Chinese rolling pin
Root type, of vegetables, 20

S

Salads, 70-75
    Asparagus Salad, 74
    Bean Sprout Salad, 72-73
    Broccoli Salad, 75
    Cold-Mixing Celery, 71-72
    Cold-Mixing Kohlrabi, 72
    Cucumber Salad, 70
    Ham and Asparagus Salad, 73-74
    Radish Cold-Mixing Salad, 71
Salt, 28
Saté paste, *see* Sha-cha sauce
Sauce
    bean, 30-31
    hoisin, 30
    oyster, 30
    plum, 30

sha-cha, 31
soy, 28
sweet bean, 31
see also Dipping sauce
Sausage, Chinese, 19
Sawing-motion cut (shaving), 43
Scallion, *see* Green onion
Scallops Supreme, 121
Scrambled Eggs, 67
Seafood, 20
    Chinese Fondue, 179-80
    see also Fish
Seasoned Turkey Slices, 60
Seasonings, 19, 28-31
    Boiled Meat Dumplings, 175
Seaweeds, 20, 207
Seeds *(zi),* 207
    sesame, 29
Sesame butter, 29
Sesame oil, 29
Sesame seeds, 29
Sha-Cha Beef, 182-83
Sha-cha sauce (saté paste), 31
Shandong cabbage, *see* Napa cabbage
Shandong (Shantung) cuisine, 14, 15
Shanghai cuisine, 14, 15
Shanghai-Style Egg Rolls, 166-67
Shanghai-Style Red-Cooked Chicken, 106-7
shang ma, meaning of, 193
Shapes, of ingredients, 46-47, 136
Sherry, 23, 30
Short-grain rice, 26
shou (longevity symbol), 194, 195, 196, 210
Shrimp, 33
    Butterfly Shrimp, 57-58
    Fried Shrimp Toast, 56-57
    marinade for raw, 175
    Red-Cooked Shrimp in the Shell, 118
    Shrimp Chips, 31, 61, 193
    Shrimp with Lobster Sauce, 119
Shrimp Chips, 31, 61, 193
Shrimp with Lobster Sauce, 119
Sichuan Cucumbers, 76
Sichuan (Szechuan) cuisine, 14, 17, 160
Sichuan (Szechuan) peppercorns, 29
Sichuan Pork with Water Chestnuts, 98-99
Side dish
    Basic Dough for Chinese Rolls, 63
    Egg Custard, 68-69
    Marble Eggs (Tea Eggs), 69
    Poached Egg, 67-68
    Seasoned Turkey Slices, 60
    see also Jiffy side dish

ABOUT THE AUTHOR

Pat Hsu Tung was born in Shanghai, a Chinese city famed for its fine cuisine. She came to the U.S. in 1961 to study at the University of Hawaii. A teacher of Chinese cooking in the midwest for many years, Pat has often appeared on television and been featured in newspapers, and she now markets her own product, Super Batter Mix, under the trade name Pat Tung's Gourmet Delight. Pat Tung lives in Rocky River, Ohio, with her husband and their two children.